Summer of Palms

The story of John Wall Hendry and
Fort Myers' first professional baseball club

Ken Breen

"Fort Myers owes a debt of gratitude to John W. Hendry for taking time by the forelock in his application for franchise. His early action assured the city a place in the league and all the benefits that go with it—entertainment, advertising, prestige."[1]

John Wall Hendry rests in Saluda, North Carolina. "Tip of the Cap" photo by Ken Breen (2023). Fort Myers Miracle and Fort Myers Mighty Mussels logos used with the permission of the Fort Myers Mighty Mussels baseball club.

Contents

Preface i

Foreword v

Introduction vii

History of Professional Minor League Baseball in Fort Myers 1

Major League Spring Training in Fort Myers 1914 – 1925 3

John Wall Hendry – The Early Years 7

1925 Real Estate Market in Fort Myers 13

1925 Baseball in Fort Myers 23

1926 31

Play Ball! 51

The Race for the Second-half Pennant! 101

The Great Miami Hurricane of 1926 139

1927 141

John Wall Hendry – The Later Years 151

Curtain Call 161

1926 Fort Myers Palms Statistics 189

Special Thanks 199

Endnotes 201

Preface

My interest in the 1926 Fort Myers Palms began while working on a proposal for the Fort Myers Mighty Mussels baseball club. A website entry suggested the franchise had begun in 1926 as the Fort Myers Palms, but "citation needed" appeared in brackets immediately following that comment.[2] My interest piqued, I set out on a small research effort to prove that was true.

A quick internet search brought me to a 2006 *Fort Myers News-Press* story by Glenn Miller. He explained he was researching local history stories when he stumbled across a team photo of the 1926 Fort Myers Palms. He assumed they were a local amateur team until *News-Press* copy editor Steve Bloch noticed in the Florida State League Media Guide year-by-year standings that Fort Myers was listed for 1926.[3] That caused Miller to dig deeper, and he shared his findings in the article.

Miller was genuinely excited about this discovery. It is hard to believe that 80 years after a professional baseball team represented Fort Myers, no one seemed to know they existed. That is consistent with an exchange I had with Ken Picking. Mr. Picking was a sportswriter for the *News-Press* in 1978. You'll read excerpts from his articles in the Introduction. I asked Mr. Picking if referring to the 1978 Fort Myers Royals as Fort Myers "first ever" professional baseball team was a conscious promotion, or was the 1926 team simply not something anyone knew of? "I would have likely gotten that from the late baseball historian Chuck Ross," Picking explained. He said he knew nothing about the 1926 team.[4] In Mr. Miller's article, he noted a history book published in 1949 and republished in 1982, *The Story of Fort Myers,* did not include one mention of the 1926 Fort Myers Palms in any of its 348 pages.[5]

Mr. Miller's article shared some learnings and posed some questions. "Who was Buck Conroy? How did he become the manager? What became of him? Who were Davenport and Domingo? And Williams, Grandio, Hernandez, and others?...The Palms' president was John W. Hendry, a well-known Southwest Florida name." Fort Myers Attorney Hank Hendry had never heard of the Palms, but suggested the team's president would have been John Wall Hendry, who was born in 1895 and died in North Carolina in 1979. Miller noted that low attendance doomed the Palms but wondered how low the attendance was since newspapers did not report attendance figures.[6]

With Glenn Miller's good questions in hand, I started reading every article I could find about the 1926 Fort Myers Palms. I shared the research I'd been doing with Jim Gates, Librarian Emeritus for the National Baseball Hall of Fame and Museum. Jim responded, "Wow!!! It looks like you have been conducting some amazing research. Congrats on everything you have put together. You may have enough for a nice local history book when this is all through."[7] That note got me thinking…the story of the Fort Myers Palms is a gap in Fort Myers history…why not take the time to thoroughly research and share the story of the team with the community? That's how this all started.

One glorious summer a century ago, the City of Fort Myers, Florida welcomed its first professional baseball franchise – the Fort Myers Palms. The mid-1920s were an exciting time in Fort Myers. Connie Mack's Philadelphia Athletics moved their spring training to Terry Park in March of 1925. In July, John Wall Hendry, a young, energetic real estate dealer who was intensely passionate about baseball announced he had purchased a professional minor league franchise for the City of Fort Myers. What followed was a series of emotional highs and lows, both on and off the field.

After spending months researching and writing, I have thoughts, ideas, and feelings about what went on in Fort Myers from April 1925 to April 1927, but that's not the purpose of this book. The goal of this work is to share a dispassionate summary of the record. While reading the story, you'll learn the names of the players and staff, and you'll be introduced to a few other interesting characters and events of the day.

As you read, be sure to keep inflation in mind. One dollar in 1926 is the equivalent of more than $17 in 2023.[8] Said differently, if someone paid $6,000 for something in 1926, that would be the same as paying more than $103,000 in 2023. During the mid-1920s, average income was about $2,200 a year,[9] and the minimum wage in states that participated was 16 cents an hour[10] ($2.76 per hour in 2023 dollars). Gas was 25 cents a gallon at the new Tamiami Filling Station and Auto Laundry at Victoria Street and Grand Avenue in Fort Myers,[11] [12] or 19 cents a gallon at the Palm Filling Station at the corner of Lee and Anderson, opposite the fire station.[13] After filling up, you could stop by the Piggly-Wiggly grocery store and pick up a dozen eggs for 38 cents, a package of Jell-O for 9 cents, and quarter pound of butter for 54 cents.[14] Gentlemen could purchase a new Palm Beach suit for $9.95 and a straw hat for $1.00 at Heitman Clothing Company.[15] Ladies silk dresses were $4.95 at W. H. Swan and Company.[16]

Summer of Palms cites primary sources whenever possible. Trusted secondary sources are used as needed. For each part of the story, and each game of the 1926 season, multiple news stories were read and synthesized into a simple recap. Every reference is cited. There is no insertion by the author that attempts to change the editorial integrity of the account of the day. There were times when new players arrived where their names were reported incorrectly or misspelled. Once I realized, for example, that Masi and Massey were early references to Vincent Macey, I corrected his name to Macey each time it appeared. From time to time, a small number of words are inserted in square box brackets to provide clarification or context.

After completing the book, you may have questions. "Why did…?," or "What ever happened to…?" I promise you, if your question is something I also wondered about, I probably passed out from exhaustion trying to find the answer. There are some things we are left to speculate about, and there may be some things that through the course of future research someone may determine the answer.

For now, grab yourself a bottle of NuGrape, find a comfortable seat in the shade, and get ready to read the story of John Wall Hendry and the 1926 Fort Myers Baseball Club.

Foreword

I met Ken Breen in 2007, when he made several visits to the National Baseball Hall of Fame and Museum in Cooperstown, New York as part of an effort to convince his company to digitize the Hall of Fame archives. As part of this endeavor, I was a guest of Ken at his company headquarters in Michigan for a customer focus group that same year.

Ken was very passionate about the historic baseball artifacts in the archives. He read through a tiny book called *The Crank*, that taught 19th century fans the terminology of baseball. He was in awe of boxes of baseballs autographed by Hall of Famers. In *Summer of Palms,* Ken manages to include a story about Fort Myers most famous "Crank," Thomas Edison, and he recently shared a story about the day in 1925 when 36 Babe Ruth autographed baseballs were handed out in Fort Myers.

In recent years, Ken has researched and published a paper on *Fort Myers First Spring Training,* the 1914 Louisville Colonels. In *Necessarily Incomplete,* Ken built on the 2003 work of Gabriel Schechter, a researcher at the Hall's library, who compiled a list of the Hall of Fame inductees who were at historic Terry Park in Fort Myers.

During my 25 years of service as Librarian at the National Baseball Hall of Fame, I read hundreds of papers and books about baseball players and teams of the past. Among my favorites, were those which portrayed the history of baseball on a local level. *Summer of Palms* is the result of a very thorough research project that tells the story of the Fort Myers Palms minor league baseball club. He also tells the story of John Wall Hendry, the businessman and passionate baseball fan who brought Florida State League baseball to Fort Myers in 1926. Anyone who enjoys reading about baseball or local history will take pleasure in this story.

I congratulate Ken on the completion of *Summer of Palms* and look forward to his future projects.

James L. Gates Jr., Librarian Emeritus
National Baseball Hall of Fame and Museum

Jim Gates served as Library Director at the National Baseball Hall of Fame from 1995 until he retired in 2020. During these 25 years, he was responsible for the management of more than 3 million documents related to our great national pastime. Jim and his staff worked with museum curators, the media, publishers, educators, researchers, fans, and anyone who is interested in conducting baseball research. He previously served in academic libraries for fifteen years. He holds degrees from Belmont Abbey College, the University of Notre Dame, and Indiana University. During his career, Jim authored multiple articles, delivered lectures around the country, and has served in an editorial capacity on multiple book, magazine, documentary, and museum projects. He also served as host for the Annual Cooperstown Symposium on Baseball and American Culture. He is an ardent Baltimore Orioles fan and has enjoyed scorekeeping for more than forty years.

Introduction

On Tuesday evening, April 11, 1978, in front of 557 fans at Terry Park in Fort Myers, Florida, left-handed pitcher, Mike Morley, of the Fort Myers Royals, took the mound and delivered the first pitch of the first game of the Florida State League season. The pressure on Mr. Morley must have been fantastic because at least four times in the previous month, local newspaper articles helped get the community of Fort Myers excited about "Fort Myers first-ever professional baseball team, the Royals."[17]

An article about a pre-season exhibition game with their major league affiliate, the Kansas City Royals, who were completing their spring training workouts read, "The Fort Myers Royals are no longer myth. If you don't believe it, you can go see for yourself today when Fort Myers' first-ever professional baseball team makes its debut at Terry Park."[18] Followed by a recap of the game that reported, "A crowd estimated at 550 came out to Terry Park…to welcome Fort Myers' first-ever professional baseball team…"[19]

Four days later was opening day. The lead article on the sports page of the Fort Myers newspaper read: "A Royal birth will take place tonight at Terry Park, beginning at 7:30. At that time, the Fort Myers Royals will begin for real in the Florida State League, challenging the West Palm Beach Expos at Terry Park. 'This spring training stuff was getting old,' said Fort Myers Manager Gene Lamont. 'We're ready to go for real. The players are excited about being a first-of-a-kind. The whole prospect of playing in Fort Myers has everybody up. I just hope we can give the area a team they can be proud of.'"[20]

A newspaper article the last week of June announced, "the first 2,000 fans…to pass through the gates for tonight's game will receive a color photograph of Fort Myers' first-ever professional baseball team."[21]

The Fort Myers Royals did bring professional baseball to Fort Myers in 1978, but Fort Myers' first professional baseball team opened their Florida State League season on that same diamond at Terry Park in 1926, more than a half-century earlier. That team was known as the Fort Myers Palms. This is their story.

History of Professional Minor League baseball in Fort Myers

"A ball club in a professional league is a great advertising asset for any city because of the great amount of publicity obtained through accounts of games played by the team and because the name of that city is constantly before the world."[22]

If you drive past beautiful Hammond Stadium on Six Mile Cypress Parkway in Fort Myers, Florida, you'll likely notice a bright sign with an electronic billboard advertising the next professional baseball game featuring the Fort Myers Mighty Mussels. The Mighty Mussels are affiliated with Major League Baseball's Minnesota Twins, and they spend the summer months battling teams from other Florida cities that comprise Minor League Baseball's Florida State League. Residents of Southwest Florida have an amazing opportunity each April to September to watch professional baseball players on the first step of their journey toward the major leagues.

The Mighty Mussels (formerly the Fort Myers Miracle) have played in this town since relocating from Pompano Beach, Florida, in 1992. Prior to the Miracle, the Fort Myers Royals (who were affiliated with the Kansas City Royals) played their Florida State League games at historic Terry Park in Fort Myers from 1978 to 1987. For 51 summers prior to that, there was no professional minor league baseball team in Fort Myers.[23]

Major League Spring Training in Fort Myers
1914 – 1925

Professional baseball has been played in Fort Myers since March of 1914, when the Double-A Louisville Colonels trained at Terry Park for three weeks. The major league Philadelphia Athletics and St. Louis Browns sent representatives to Fort Myers to play spring training exhibition games against the Colonels.[24] Shortstop and future Hall of Famer Bobby Wallace appeared in the Browns lineup on March 12, 1914.[25]

Connie Mack was so impressed with Fort Myers that in March of 1925 he brought his Philadelphia Athletics to Terry Park for spring training, a ritual that would continue through the spring of 1936.[26]

Anticipation of the Philadelphia Athletics training in Fort Myers began on Christmas Eve, 1923, when R.Q. Richards, president of the Kiwanis Club of Fort Myers, shared a letter he received from Connie Mack. Mack told Richards the Athletics had arranged to train in Montgomery, Alabama, in the Spring of 1924, but he would be coming to Florida in January of 1924 to look at several towns interested in having the Athletics train there in 1925, including Fort Myers.[27]

The County Commissioners agreed they were prepared to start constructing a grandstand at the Lee County Fairgrounds that would meet the Kiwanis' and Mack's specifications immediately following the Lee County Fair in February of 1924.[28]

On January 23, 1924, after being a guest of the Kiwanis and Fort Myers for three days, Mr. Mack agreed to terms, and it was announced that the Philadelphia Athletics would conduct spring training in Fort Myers in March of 1925.[29]

On July 10, 1924, Dick Richards reported the new baseball diamond at the fairgrounds had been completed to Connie Mack's specifications. "The diamond between the plates has been laid with clay and then covered with siftings from the stone crusher. Mr. Richards says he was out there after a heavy rain and there was no water on the diamond. The outfield has been leveled and planted with grass.... The new diamond, which has been made for the use of [the Philadelphia Athletics], is one of the best in the state, Mr. Richards says, and was made from plans and specifications furnished by the famous Philadelphia manager."[30]

On December 16, 1924, the contract for the new grandstand was awarded to Edward V. Goodman & Son, a Fort Myers contractor and builder. The project was to be completed in plenty of time for the Lee County Fair that would take place February 24 to 28, 1925. "The grandstand is to be 90 feet long and large enough to seat 1,500 people. The seats are to be arranged in tiers and the grandstand will face the racetrack and ball diamond. It will be under roof and protected from rain and sun."[31] The roof was described as "a six-ply built-up roof of Barrett specifications and is a ten-year roof."[32] [Barrett specifications were an industry standard for a pitched roof covered with layers of felt paper and gravel. The specifications were created by the Barrett Manufacturing Company. A responsible contractor was required to do the roof work and a Barrett-provided inspector would approve each part of the project. A roof built to Barrett specifications was insured against roof trouble and upkeep expense for 10 or 20 years by a Surety Bond of The U. S. Fidelity and Guarantee Company of Baltimore.][33]

On January 5, 1925, Connie Mack inspected the ballpark and was pleased with what had been accomplished.[34] On February 5, 1925, the new 24-foot by 40-foot club house was completed.[35] The "locker and bath house included hot and cold water, individual showers, lockers, a rubbing table, lounging benches, and several other things to add to their comfort while training here."[36]

In February and March of 1925, the Philadelphia Athletics were the toast of the town as they completed their daily workouts and exhibition games. On March 12, 1925, 3,000 citizens witnessed the Philadelphia Phillies defeat the Athletics 6 to 3 in the first game of the spring.[37] Perhaps the most anticipated game that spring took place on March 25, 1925, when 5,000 people crowded the field at Terry Park to see Babe Ruth in an Athletics uniform.[38]

On March 21, 1925, Connie Mack signed a contract committing the Philadelphia Athletics to train in Fort Myers for the next ten years. The contract specified several improvements be made to the ball field:

- The infield was to be torn up to the depth of three inches and resurfaced with a mixture of clay and black loam.
- Right field was to be leveled and Bermuda grass planted throughout.
- The cluster of palmettos in left field was to be removed.
- The entire field was to be fenced in.
- The clubhouse was to be rearranged so each player would have their own locker.
- The grandstand was to be remodeled to allow more space for the newspaper men.
- Members of the press would have a spacious chamber of their own screened off and equipped with shower under the grandstand.[39]

The Philadelphia Athletics played their final exhibition game of the season at Terry Park on March 27, 1925. They easily defeated a semi-pro team from Wauchula, Florida, 14 to 1. After the game, a clubhouse ceremony followed during which "each player cut his initials in the wood, threw water over his left shoulder for good luck, and slammed the door twice on his way out." The team attended a farewell banquet at the Royal Palm Hotel that evening.

The players, staff, and traveling news reporters left Fort Myers by bus on March 28, 1925, hoping to return to Fort Myers the following February as reigning World Series champions.[40]

Stan Baumgartner, a pitcher for the Athletics and a reporter for *The Philadelphia Inquirer,* shared some observations about Florida with readers back in Pennsylvania. Mr. Baumgartner explained that Florida was experiencing a real estate boom. Land that sold for $50 an acre eighteen months earlier was now selling for $500. People with capital and the foresight to turn over land quickly were making money in tremendous quantities.

Several Philadelphia Athletics were getting into the real estate game in Fort Myers. Mr. Baumgartner noticed that during the final week of their training, pre-game conversations that would normally be about the day's game had changed to discussions about property the players had invested in. From "What are they charging us to clear that group of palmettoes from that tract?" and "How much do we have to make on the first payment?", to "What is the lowest we will take for it?" They discussed how Grover Hartley, catcher for the New York Giants, made more last winter in real estate than he made playing baseball in all of 1921. And how Bill Doak, pitcher for the Dodgers, had retired to devote his energies to his real estate transactions.[41]

John Wall Hendry – the Early Years

John Wall Hendry was born in Fort Myers, Florida on December 23,[42] 1895.[43] He was the grandson of one of the early settlers of Fort Myers, Captain Francis Asbury Hendry,[44] who Hendry County, Florida, is named for.[45] His father, Louis Asbury Hendry, was a prominent attorney who served as mayor of Fort Myers three times and served in the Florida State legislature three times.[46] His mother, Ella (Frierson) Hendry, passed away in August 1904,[47] just days before young John was to begin the third grade.

The Hendrys were considered a very wealthy family.[48] Louis and Ella Hendry raised their children to always be polite and to conduct themselves in a proper manner.[49]

John Wall Hendry always needed to be busy doing something. At all times, he had an activity or project he was working on. One of the stories Hendry shared occurred when he was 10 or 11 years old, he would pick up work in Fort Myers cleaning inventor Thomas A. Edison's boats. Mr. Edison paid him each day he worked. Hendry recalled witnessing some meetings Edison had in the backyard of his Seminole Lodge estate – meetings with his next-door neighbor and friend Henry Ford among others.[50]

In the fall of 1913, Hendry attended Gwynn High School where he served as junior class president[51] and was a member of the Gwynn Debate Club.[52] The following school year, now a senior, Hendry served as Athletic Editor on the yearbook staff.[53] His senior class photo and write-up (facsimile on page 9) notes that he was vice president of the Hyacinthian Literary Society. At 5 feet 11 inches tall and weighing 157 pounds, he was the manager of the boys' basketball team. It is noted that he was cunning and willing to debate the side of an issue that no one else wanted.[54]

John Wall Hendry authored the "Athletic Editorial" page of the yearbook. Mr. Hendry, who played guard for the boys' basketball team[55] wrote that he was proud of how the team performed and suggested the girls' team would have done better if they had shown up to practices. The teams played a short season because they had trouble finding schools that could afford to travel to Fort Myers and vice versa. Gwynne High School invited Tampa and Miami to play against them, but both played their games on indoor courts [Gwynne High School only had an outdoor basketball court].[56]

In preparation for the State High School track meet held at the University of Florida in Gainesville in April 1915, Gwynne High School held its annual Field Day at the Country Club. Hendry's competitive spirit was on full display on March 20, 1915, when he placed in five different contests including third place in the 70-yard dash, second place in the running high jump and running broad jump, first place in the 1/4-mile relay, and he threw a 12-pound shot put 31 feet 1 inch.[57]

Hendry's hobby that year was listed as "Quebec," his favorite pastime was discussing the war [presumably what we now refer to as World War 1], his gift was "bluffing," his characteristic expression was "Let me prevaricate on it some," and his aspiration was to become a lawyer.[58]

On September 13, 1915, Hendry departed Fort Myers to begin classes at the University of Florida.[59] His photo appeared in the 1916 University of Florida yearbook.[60] He was a member of The John Marshall Debating Society.[61]

The 1918 University of Florida yearbook lists John W. Hendry among the 354 University of Florida men serving in association with the war. The preamble notes that men frequently change rank, branch, or location.[62] He appears in a photo of 49 Florida Men at Officers Training Camp in Fort McPherson, Georgia in 1917.[63]

After completing his service, which included time in an administrative role for the U.S. Navy, Hendry lived in Macclenny, Florida, and worked as a traveling salesman. He would sell by day and earn money in the evening as a journeyman ballplayer, helping local semi-pro baseball teams who needed to fill a position on a short-term basis. He might pitch two nights in a row on one team and the third night be on the other team – it was a function of who needed a player and how much they were willing to pay for his services. He loved baseball and was still very athletic – he was an excellent ballplayer.[64]

JOHN WALL HENDRY
"Soap"

"He draweth out the thread of his verbosity, finer than the staple of his argument."

Height 5 ft. 11 in.; weight 157 lbs.; Hyacinthian Literary Society; Scientific Course; Vice-President Hyacinthian Literary Society; President Junior Class; Athletic editor Caloosahatchian; Manager Boys' Basketball team '15.

Here we have a born debater who always takes for his side the one which no one else would choose. He is not a peculiar kind of fellow, but he likes to look at all subjects different from everybody else. He always loses his point on account of a majority being on the opposite side. When he sees he is defeated he turns and joins the victorious side and then claims the victory for himself.

On account of his cunning ways with people he has won the name of 'soap'; he is slick enough to have such a name! He has many nicknames such as, "Prig", "Quebec John", and "Peddler", which go to show that he is a "jolly good fellow"

Facsimile of *The Caloosahatchian* (Fort Myers, FL: 1915), page 88.

On February 16, 1921, John Wall Hendry and Gladys Roper Needham of Leesburg, Florida, were married.[65] On January 2, 1922, Mrs. Hendry gave birth to the first of three children, a boy they named John Wall Hendry Jr.[66] They nicknamed him Jack, and that is how he would be addressed by his friends and family.[67] In 1923, daughter Elizabeth Parker Hendry was born. She would be known as Betty to her friends, and her parents called her "Bette."[68]

They moved from Macclenny to Fort Myers and were staying with Hendry's father Louis Asbury Hendry and his wife Mary (Apthorp). With a third child on the way, John and Gladys decided it was time to move the growing family (Jack, age 3, and Elizabeth, age 1) into their own house. The family was doing very well financially.[69]

Mr. Hendry was active in Fort Myers business circles and community causes. From attending a lunch with businessmen to learn about plans for a professional quality golf course to be established at the Palm City Golf and Country Club,[70] to participating on a citizens committee to bring the Seaboard Air Line Railroad to Fort Myers.[71]

On July 21, 1925, John W. Hendry purchased the residence of J. C. Nowling.[72] The home was at 1015 Providence Street. The house was built by Lucius C. Curtright, president of Fort Myers Real Estate, sometime between August, 1922, and January, 1924. Mr. Curtright sold the house to J. C. Nowling. After purchasing the property in 1925, Hendry purchased the lot next door, combining the lots to make a "double lot."[73]

On November 25, 1925, Gladys Hendry gave birth to their third and final child, a boy named Robert Needham Hendry.[74]

The John Wall Hendry family residence in Fort Myers from 1925 – 1928.
Photo by Ken Breen (2023).

1925 Real Estate Market in Fort Myers

In 1925, John Wall Hendry was "living the millionaire lifestyle."[75]

Words of Caution in the Public Forum

In April of 1925, "He sat in the lobby of one of the leading hotels and talk came gradually around to real estate as any conversation is likely to do in these days of activity among the real estate men in Fort Myers. He was a stranger to all of us....

'Yes sir, I remember a town that started to grow just like Fort Myers has started. Everybody was making money and real estate values were reaching towards the zenith. People quit their regular avocations to go into the real estate game and Fords became scarce as it was a sign of lack of prosperity to drive a flivver.

'Hudsons, Chalmers, Paiges, Cadillacs, Dodges, Lincolns, Willis-St Claires, and Wyllis Nights were the cheapest cars in daily use and many of the richer real estate men imported cars from France and Germany.

'People were sure that the boom would last and lived and acted accordingly. Half the dry goods dealers sold their places of business; the doctors quit practicing, and if you got sick, you could either die or get well without medical attention. When it came to a death in the city, undertakers had to be called from other cities for the only undertaker there, would likely be out of the city showing acreage to a prospect. People had so much money....

'Business continued good for a few months and lo, there was a lull. New people failed to come in, and the old ones had nobody to sell real estate or anything else to.

'Soon lots, lands, and business places were a drug on the market and the town was as dead as a doornail. Of course, Fort Myers is growing, and everybody is prosperous, but I wonder..."[76]

The Florida Boom

In 1920, the City of Fort Myers had a population of 3,678, and all of Lee County numbered 9,540.[77] By the mid-1920s, the Florida economy was booming, and if you had a job, it was easy to borrow money to buy land.

In December, 1924, Bardin's Grocery was located on the first floor of the Heitman Building at the corner of First Street and Jackson Street in downtown Fort Myers. The southwest corner of the store was partitioned off and would be used by Gus Hendry (brother of John Wall Hendry) to establish his real estate office.[78] Hendry Brothers Real Estate would eventually occupy the entire corner of the first floor.[79]

In 1925, Hendry Brothers Realty flourished. An advertisement appeared in the newspaper nearly every day promoting the company or properties they were representing.

Facsimile of Hendry Brothers ad in *The Fort Myers Press* – USA TODAY NETWORK, August 10, 1925.[80]

Hendry Brothers managed a broad book of business, from residential to office and commercial real estate transactions. They collaborated as sales agents in other realty company's subdivision projects,[81] and they purchased 10 acres adjacent to the river in East Fort Myers for $160,000, to develop a new subdivision of "modern houses" to be sold for $10,000 each, including the lot.[82]

By late 1925, Hendry Brothers expanded into the cement works business with a factory in East Fort Myers.[83]

BUILD FIRE SAFE

With

INTERLOCKING CEMENT TILE

Then you will have a home that will eliminate all worries because durability and pleasing appearance are also outstanding features of our product. The home is cooler and the cost is less, than if the home had been built with lumber.

SAND **CEMENT** **BASES**

UPRIGHT AND SEPTIC TANKS

HENDRY BROS. CEMENT WORKS

OFFICE: 1st Floor Heitman Bldg.

FACTORY: East Fort Myers

"Born and Raised in Fort Myers"

Facsimile of Hendry Brothers Cement Works ad in *The Fort Myers Press* – USA TODAY NETWORK, November 5, 1925.[84]

Hotel Casa Ybel on Sanibel Island

Built in 1895, Hotel Casa Ybel was a landmark in Southwest Florida. Its guest log included the most famous names of the day. In 1925, it had the distinction of being the only hotel on Sanibel Island with baths and running water.[85]

On Monday, February 16, 1925, "Mr. and Mrs. Thomas A. Edison, Mr. and Mrs. Henry Ford, and a party of four visited and had dinner at Hotel Casa Ybel…. They gathered a quantity of shells on Sanibel Beach, among which were several very rare ones."[86]

On Sunday, March 15, 1925, Connie Mack and his Philadelphia Athletics, presidents and secretaries of the Fort Myers Kiwanis and Rotary clubs, chamber of commerce officials, and representatives of the press had dinner at the Casa Ybel.[87]

On April 28, 1925, it was reported that Casa Ybel, and 360 acres of land surrounding it had been sold by Mr. and Mrs. C. J. Knapp to Hendry Brothers Realty Company for an undisclosed sum. The announcement stated the Hendrys would take possession in 30 days and planned "to erect between ten and twenty cottages near the waterfront in a short time."[88]

On May 5, 1925, a half-page ad in *The Fort Myers Press* advertised properties available from Hendry Bros. Realty. It prominently featured a description of the Casa Ybel Hotel Property along with 30-, 50-, 85-, and 172-acre properties in other parts of town.[89]

On June 19, 1925, Knapp, and Hendry completed the transaction of Casa Ybel for $87,500.[90]

On June 22, 1925, it was announced that Hendry had sold the Casa Ybel Hotel and surrounding land on Sanibel Island for $100,000, to developers from Miami, Florida, and Columbus, Ohio, who would be developing the property into a high-class subdivision.[91]

[For purpose of illustration, Hendry made an agreement to purchase Casa Ybel on April 28, for $87,500 and "closed" on the purchase on June 19 with a 2% binder. That means he paid $1,750 on June 19. He then sold the property for $100,000 on June 22 (or shortly thereafter) before the balance of the $87,500 was due. Hendry invested $1,750 and made a $10,750 profit in three days ($100,000 - $87,500 note - $1,750 initial Binder = $10,750 profit). That is the equivalent of $182,750 profit in 2023. This scenario happened several hundred times a month in 1925, and enormous wealth was accumulated by those in Fort Myers who understood the game and were able to execute.]

The Binder Boys

By the middle of 1925, a group of Binder Boys had settled in Fort Myers and began to type contracts for property as fast as they could. They worked day and night transacting property. A "binder" was a non-refundable deposit and commitment to purchase land. An offer typically required 2% down (the "binder"), and the balance was due in full in 30 days. Real estate agents would buy property for the cost of the binder and work to sell it for a profit before the balance was due.

Land speculators purchased large properties at cheap prices and sold it for profits without seeing the property and without any intention of ever developing the land. Local businessmen and elected officials were resigning from their jobs and securing their real estate licenses to try to get in on the commissions associated with property sales.[92]

Land was selling and reselling for as much as 100 times what was paid for it. "L. C. Curtright recalls selling 80 acres north of the river for $60,000, $160,000 and finally $425,000."

People owning acreage could either sell it all at once or subdivide it into lots from 5 acres all the way down to 10-foot lots (the idea being the purchaser could buy as many lots as they wanted to achieve the configuration they desired).[93]

The *Fort Myers Tropical News* included a "Realty Barometer" in the bottom corner of the front page itemizing the previous day and month-to-date number of real estate transfers and the total value.[94]

On July 21, 1925, Hendry announced the sale of 43 acres of property located a half mile south of the Naples pier to Boiling Brothers of Kentucky for more than $150,000[95] [$2.55 million in 2023 dollars].

On August 11, 1925, H.B. Mayer and Logan I. Evans announced they had left Hendry Brothers Realty and formed their own company. Mayer and Logan were operating from Rooms 1 and 2 in the Heitman Building (the same building Hendry Brothers occupied). They advertised 130 acres in Naples for sale at good terms.[96]

"H. B. Mayer, 'the man who knows where money grows,' didn't seem to know where to find land. 'Made $350,000 in sales and could only deliver $80,000', he announced, 'so H. B. Mayer goes back to Hendry Bros.'"[97]

Hendry Brothers took out a quarter-page ad in *The Fort Myers Press* on August 22, 1925, that read, "We take pleasure in announcing that we have with us as assistant manager, Mr. H. B. Mayer. Mr. Mayer will be glad to serve his friends and wide acquaintances at his new connection. He knows values."[98]

On August 21, 1925, John W. Hendry purchased 5,000 acres of land one mile from Estero for $500,000, from John Dee of St. Petersburg.[99]

"A striking thing about the boom never registered with the speculators. A riverfront lot could sell for $19,000, but a lot and a nine-room house brought only $10,500. New cottages on paved streets sold for $2,500, but empty lots on sand ruts were offered for $5,000. Valencia Terrace lots skyrocketed to $20,000 at the same time as a house and a lot there went for $17,500."[100]

Recognizing the unsustainable phenomena of properties being bought and sold for a profit multiple times a day without any payments being made, the real estate board increased the binders from 2% to 5% in mid-August of 1925. This was to eliminate the buying and selling in which properties were transacted from owner-to-owner a half dozen times before any payment was made. "'This will bring a deflation in values and improve the market,' they declared, but few listened."[101]

Interviewed in 1950, Harry J. Wood, who was Chairman of the Fort Myers Real Estate Board in 1925, was reflecting on the carnival-like atmosphere in real estate at the time said, "The 'Boom' was breaking right then, in September, 1925, but we didn't know it."[102]

"The point that seemed to strike everyone almost at the same time was that lots could never be worth what they were bringing. The result was a gradual dying away of the boom. In Fort Myers, many agree the turning point came at the end of September, 1925…. The boom dragged on in name only until September, 1926…."[103]

An article in *The Fort Myers Press,* October 14, 1925, discussed that work on the new offices of Hendry Brothers Realty Company would be completed before their new sales force arrives on October 20. John Wall Hendry proclaimed it would "be the largest and most complete office of its kind in Fort Myers." Hendry Brothers Realty had purchased Bardin's Grocery store and were expanding their real estate office to occupy the entire corner at First and Jackson streets. Hendry explained the office would not be fancy—there would be a general office and reception room, with five private offices. Their information bureau would be available to anyone in the city, and they would sell railroad tickets to any part of the country.[104]

Hendry Brothers Realty Co. occupied the first floor of the Heitman Building at the corner of First Street and Jackson Street, Fort Myers, Florida. Photo by Ken Breen (2023).

Hendry Brothers Realty Company ran a full-page ad in *The Fort Myers Press* in October of 1925 itemizing properties for which they could guarantee delivery, properties they believed they could deliver, and 1,280 acres within a mile of Fort Myers that could be developed into a subdivision, "Part of it platted and staked."

We Can Guarantee Delivery of The Following:

14 Acres-Naples-Lot 6, Sec. 27, Twp. 49
80 Acres-Naples-E1-2 of NE 1-4 Sec. Range 25, Township 49
35 Acres-Across River-Sec. 2, range 24, Twp. 44
10 Acres-Across River-NE 1-4 of NW 1-4 of SW 1-4, Sec. 4 Twp. 44, R. 24
5 Acres-Across River-Back of Filling Station, SE 1-4 of SE 1-4 Section 35, T 43, R 24
2 Large Lots, Next to Edison Residence, Lots 2 and 3, King's Place.
37 Water front Lots, ten Minutes from Bank of Fort Myers
Dean Park, well built House, Large Lot, Beautiful Surroundings, $30,000.

We Believe We Can Deliver The Following:

2 Water front Lots-Estero Island- facing Gulf of Mexico.
5 Acres-near Whiskey Creek-W 1-2 of SE 1-4, NW 1-4 of SW -4 Sec. 5, Twp 45, Range 24
10 Acres-Pine Island-NE 1-4 of SW 1-4 of SW 1-4, Sec 4, t 44, R 24
35 Acres-Buckingham on Boulevard
80 Acres on McGregor Boulevard, opposite Twin Palm Grove
150 Acres on Road No. 2, NW 1-4 Sec. 1, Range 25 Township 42
250 Acres, six miles N. LaBelle, Sec. 1 T 42, R 29 (Bargain)
590 Acres-Charlotte County, near Tamiami Trail
640 Acres-Section 36, T44, R25, Lee County
4290 Acres-Manatee County, between Sarasota and Tampa
1000 Acres-near Fort Myers-worth investigating

Superb Subdivision proposition

1280 Acres, within one mile of Fort Myers. Good Terms. Part of it platted and staked
1 Lot, Allen Court
2 Lots, Riverside
10 Lots, Rosenfield Sub, East Fort Myers
1 Lot-water front-Valencia Terrace
1 Exceptional Corner Location, 45x290. Beach frontage, Estero
3 Lots in one block, back from beach, Estero Island

If You Want to Buy or Sell, See

Hendry Bros. Realty Company, Inc.

John W. Hendry, President   Gus Hendry, Vice-President

"Born and Raised in Fort Myers"

Facsimile of Hendry Brothers ad in *The Fort Myers Press* –
USA TODAY NETWORK, October 15, 1925.[105]

On October 12, 1925, "Stanley 'Lefty' Baumgartner, popular pitcher of the Philadelphia Athletics arrived in Fort Myers…ready to sell real estate for Cavalli, Matthews, and Lester until the arrival of his teammates for spring training. 'Lefty' has a great many friends in Fort Myers and with the close of the Athletics season, accepted the offer of Mr. Cavalli and joined their ranks of Fort Myers realtors. He is accompanied by Mrs. Baumgartner."[106]

Charles Ponzi's Florida Pyramid Scheme

All kinds of people attempted to profit from buying and selling land during the Florida Boom, including disgraced Boston "financial wizard" Charles Ponzi. In February of 1926, Ponzi was arrested in Jacksonville, Florida, on federal charges of using the mail to defraud in connection with his Florida real estate activity. Operating a company under the name Charpon Land Syndicate, Ponzi was arrested for the sale of units of indebtedness in connection with the sale of lots of the Rosa Maria tract in Columbia County, south of Lake City, Florida.[107] Ponzi stood to make $5.3 million in two years by selling lots for $10 each if his pyramid scheme had been allowed to continue. Photos of the Charpon Land syndicate showed several of the lots were literally "under water."[108]

1925 Baseball in Fort Myers

Philadelphia Athletics First Spring Training in the City of Palms

Aerial photo of Lee County Fairgrounds with grandstand, circa 1925.
Photo courtesy of *The Sporting News.*

The spring of 1925 was a proud one for residents of Fort Myers, Florida. Connie Mack and his Philadelphia Athletics completed a series of workouts and spring training exhibition games at the Terry Park fairgrounds baseball field in East Fort Myers. The city had welcomed Major League Baseball teams for individual games in springtimes past, but 1925 was the first year a major league team adopted Fort Myers as its spring headquarters. The Athletics were an excellent team, but to add to the excitement in Fort Myers, Connie Mack orchestrated a deal with the New York Yankees, and the legendary Babe Ruth played a game in an Athletics uniform at Terry Park.[109]

Before departing for Philadelphia in March 1925, Connie Mack signed a deal committing the Athletics to training in Fort Myers each spring for the next decade. Terms of the deal included some improvements to field and facilities at the Fairgrounds.[110]

The Fort Myers "Regulars" and Royal Palms
Semi-pro baseball teams

"'Fort Myers must have a good ball team this season is the opinion of Bert Graughon, manager of last year's ball games. Now that the boys have an opportunity to learn what real baseball looks like, there is much enthusiasm among them, and it is hoped that it will be possible to organize a real team. With a professional diamond to play on and the example of Connie Mack's players to emulate, there should be some real good ball played in Fort Myers this season, say local fans."[111]

Two semi-pro baseball teams were assembled to represent Fort Myers in summer baseball games. One team, managed by Robert Heath, was referred to as the "Regulars" and the other was the "Royal Palms." The teams played in different leagues, each playing teams from Lee and neighboring counties.

On April 12, 1925, the semi-pro season opened on Sanibel Island. At one o'clock in the afternoon, Kent R. Smith, manager of the Royal Palms, and his ballplayers boarded a bus at Terry Park and made the 18-mile journey to Punta Rassa, where they boarded a boat for Sanibel Island. That afternoon, 75 fans watched as Fort Myers won the season opener 22 to 4 over Sanibel.[112]

By early July, the Royal Palms had a record of 7 wins, 3 losses, and 2 ties. They had played teams from Sanibel, Punta Gorda, Sarasota, Bradenton, and Bowling Green. The Regulars had a similar record and had played teams from Punta Gorda and Wauchula.

On July 7, 1925, it was announced the Royal Palms and the Regulars would play each other in a three-game winner-take-all Fort Myers Championship. The games would be played at the fairgrounds for three consecutive Thursdays beginning at 3:30 p.m.

The Regulars roster would include Bryant, Lightsey, Blankenbaker, Chambless, Thompson, Scotty, Draughn, Swan, Dehon, Hawkins, and Roush. The Royal Palms included S. H. Ellison, J. L. Gross, R. M. McConnell, H. M. Hope, Bill Moger, Pape, George Fox, Ihrig, Warren Bylaska, Paul Bracewell, H. E. Bowman, and Alderman. Stanley and Bryant would be two of the four umpires, and Sherouse would be the scorekeeper.[113; 114]

The Fort Myers City Championship began. This was an important series not only because there was money involved, but "because of the intense rivalry which exists between the two clubs. To ensure non-interference on the part of partisan rooters, the police have agreed to be present in force and to keep the crowd in the grandstand."[115]

Game 1 – July 9, 1925: A rain shower before the start of the game made for a wet field and a small crowd. The Regulars defeated the Royal Palms 3 to 1.[116]

Game 2 – July 16, 1925: 200 fans witnessed a game that featured 22 combined strikeouts—pitchers Bryant of the Regulars getting 12, and Gross of the Royal Palms mowing down 10. The Regulars beat the Royal Palms 2 to 1.[117]

Game 3 – July 23, 1925: Pitcher Bryant of the Regulars threw another 12-strikeout game and was backed up by a long running catch by centerfielder Swan in the sixth inning. The Regulars scored the lone run of the game in the top of the tenth inning to defeat the Palms 1 to 0 and sweep the Fort Myers City Championship.[118]

John W. Hendry Purchases a Professional Baseball Team for Fort Myers!

On July 10, 1925, in all capital, two-inch tall letters, the front-page headline of the *Fort Myers Tropical News* read "LEAGUE CLUB FOR FORT MYERS." The article shared the exciting news that John W. Hendry had purchased the Florida State League's Sanford Celeryfeds players and franchise. Hendry planned to bring the team to Fort Myers as early as the following week. He envisioned a new name for the team that would properly represent Fort Myers such as the Royal Palms, but he would consider input from local fans. [The Celeryfeds nickname was likely chosen in honor of the dominant crop grown in the Sanford area in the early 1900s—celery. Sanford was known as "Celery City," and the high school team's nickname was the "Celery Feds."[119]]

Terms of the deal were not disclosed, but it was noted the Sanford owners had asked $5,000 for their players and transfer of franchise. Hendry had been working on the deal for several days, and prior to reaching final agreement, he asked Don M. Wilkie, the Secretary of the Fort Myers Chamber of Commerce, to wire Connie Mack of the Philadelphia Athletics to ask if the use of the ballpark by a Fort Myers league team would interfere with the Athletics spring training. Mack sent a congratulatory telegram indicating he fully supported Fort Myers having a team in the Florida State League, and that he would do anything in his power to help ensure the team's success.

Hendry's attorney, S. Watt Lawler, was working with the county fair commissioner to secure use of Terry Park for the team. The Celeryfeds finished last in the first-half of the season, and the club's second-half record was 4 wins and 17 losses. Hendry planned to make an immediate investment in the team to begin building talent for the 1926 campaign, and he hoped that Connie Mack might leave a few players in Fort Myers for additional training the following spring.[120]

On July 11, 1925, the front page of the *Fort Myers Tropical News* included a story announcing the Fort Myers baseball team had lost two more games, referring to the Celeryfeds dropping a double-header to the Tampa Smokers.[121]   [The Smokers nickname was chosen by team directors during a meeting at Tampa City Hall on June 26, 1919.[122] No specific reason was given but it was likely in recognition of Tampa's flourishing cigar industry.]

Hendry was expecting C. L. Britt, the Sanford owner, to come to Fort Myers that afternoon as promised. Instead, Britt sent a telegram indicating he had new backers that agreed to put up the money needed to keep the Celeryfeds in Sanford. He went on to suggest Hendry could purchase additional real estate with the money he would not have to spend to purchase the ball club.

Hendry was extremely upset that Britt had reneged on the verbal deal to sell the Sanford club. Mr. Hendry considered legal action,[123] but instead sent a telegram to Florida State League President Al Lang's office requesting a hearing on the matter. Hendry took this course of action after being advised by legal counsel that Sanford could delay trial until after the conclusion of the season.[124]

"Though disappointed in their hopes for a team this year, local fans are trusting that John W. Hendry and S. Watt Lawler will continue their efforts toward having this city represented in organized baseball not later than 1926."[125]

On July 22, 1925, Hendry offered to purchase the Lakeland franchise of the Florida State League. Charlie Henley, president of the Lakeland Baseball Club, notified the civic clubs of Lakeland that if funds that had been promised were not received by August 1, he would sell the franchise and it would be moved to Fort Myers. Connie Mack weighed in that he supported Fort Myers having a team in the Florida State League.[126]

On July 23, Hendry received a wire from Sanford that if he was still interested, he could purchase the franchise. It was suspected that Sanford was having difficulty collecting the money citizens had pledged. Feeling he had been fooled once, Hendry chose not to respond.[127] John Wall Hendry was a 3 strikes you're out (or one big strike) kind of personality.[128] He was still willing to discuss the purchase of the Lakeland franchise if they were unable to collect the funds needed to keep the team, but Hendry suspected they would be successful. Hendry was contemplating the formation of a winter league to include teams from Fort Myers, Bartow, Sarasota, and Lakeland.[129]

On July 31, Hendry offered the owners of the Lakeland Highlanders $7,000, which was equal to the amount of debt the team was carrying. The Lakeland owners told him they would accept the offer if Lakeland businessmen did not contribute that amount. On August 1, Lakeland President Clare Henley wired a counter proposal. Hendry said he would not likely accept the offer because he told the team previously the proposal would be the "first, last, and only one they would get from him."[130] Hendry did not embrace his Scottish heritage, but he was thrifty. He was willing to spend a dollar if it was worth it, but he did not want to unnecessarily overpay for anything.[131]

In August, the Fort Myers Royal Palm Baseball Club signed several players of the Fort Myers Regulars after their season ended. Newly signed Palms included Bryant, who was considered one of the best pitchers in South Florida, along with Davis, and Swan.[132] On August 14, "the reorganized Fort Myers Palms played their first game…defeating Wauchula 4 to 3"[133] at Terry Park. Sentiment among baseball fans in Fort Myers was there should be only one baseball club in Fort Myers in 1926 so the best talent is all on one team, rather than being divided between two teams.[134]

In the Florida State League, the final weeks of the second half of the season saw three teams in contention – St. Petersburg, Lakeland, and Tampa. Kent R. Smith, manager of the semi-pro Fort Myers Royal Palms, in collaboration with John Wall Hendry, proposed a three-game series with the eventual league champion, to take place in Fort Myers immediately following the end of the season. When Tampa won the second half over Lakeland, discussions continued with St. Petersburg and Tampa. Upon learning the Tampa Smokers had won the Florida State League pennant, Smith contacted Smokers Manager Jimmie Snead to confirm they would come to Fort Myers to play three games at the fairgrounds. The games would be sponsored by Hendry Brothers Realty Company who guaranteed the Smokers $2,700 purse to make the trip.[135]

Hendry and Smith announced the Tampa Smokers, champions of the Florida State League, had accepted the challenge, and a three-game series would take place September 17-19 at Terry Park.[136] *The Fort Myers Press* made sure residents knew that local businessmen would be evaluating attendance and gate receipts to make sure there was enough support in the community to support continued efforts to acquire a franchise in the Florida State League.[137]

The umpire for the series was expected to be E. N. Stanley.[138] The box score for the first game indicated there were two umpires, Stanley and Conroy.[139] The second[140] and third games had only one umpire, Conroy. When the series concluded, the sentiment from the Fort Myers players was that Umpire Conroy had called the games very professionally and accurately. It is likely Umpire Conroy was Buck Conroy, who had many years of experience as a baseball umpire.[141] Conroy had moved to Tampa recently and had been put to work right away as an umpire.[142] Fort Myers would learn more about Buck Conroy in the months ahead.

The Smokers shutout the Palms in the first game, but fan turnout was strong and "every available seat in the bleachers was taken."[143] The Palms won the second and third games. The third game was delayed for more than fifteen minutes while rain poured down soaking players and fans. "As a result of the Palms' two wins over the Tampa nine, it is expected that men of the character of John W. Hendry will find sufficient co-operation to secure the entry of the local team into State League Ball and bring baseball to this city."[144]

Hendry Brothers Realty Company, located at First Street and Jackson Street, announced the play-by-play results of all seven games of the World Series between the Washington Senators and the Pittsburgh Pirates. Everyone was invited to be present to hear the call and celebrate the series.[145]

In November of 1925, Dr. H. E. Opre, president of the Tampa Smokers Baseball Club, passed through Fort Myers on the way to Sanibel Island. Dr. Opre expressed his optimism that Fort Myers would have a team in the Florida State League in 1926. Opre speculated there would be an eight-team circuit with Lakeland, Tampa, St. Petersburg, and Fort Myers in the West; and Miami, Palm Beach, Daytona, and Jacksonville on the East Coast.[146]

1926

About Fort Myers in 1926

The mid-1920s were a time of rapid population and building growth in Fort Myers. New house permits doubled from March 1925 to March 1926.[147]

In August of 1925, representatives from the Polk City Directory were canvassing the 18-square mile area that would form Polk's 1926 edition. Polk representatives were usually trusted in declaring the population of a city between each town's official U.S. Census. Mrs. F. B. Langley, supervisor of the Polk canvassers, declared the population of Fort Myers is now 15,000.[148] The number of telephones in Fort Myers doubled from 600 to 1,200 between 1925 and 1926. Smith and Jones were the most common last names.[149]

The population of Fort Myers grew from 3,678 in the 1920 U.S. Census to an estimated 20,301 in 1926; 26,000 including the surrounding suburban area. There were 4,200 families and the demographics were 75% white, 20% black, and 5% foreign-born. Residences were mostly one- and two-story family houses, with many small apartments. There were many beautiful homes, valued at $50,000 or more in the city; 3,061 homes had electricity.

From the nearest large city, Fort Myers was a five-hour drive by auto, or a five-hour train ride. Train service to Fort Myers was possible by taking the A. C. Line, Seaboard Air Line or the Florida Railroad and Navigation Company. Plans were under way for cross-state waterway from Fort Myers on the West Coast to Stuart on the East Coast by way of the Caloosahatchee River, Lake Okeechobee, and St. Lucie Canal. There was local bus service in town.

The principal industries in Fort Myers included cigars, lumber, window shades, citrus fruit products such as canned grapefruit, and boat building. The leading industries surrounding Fort Myers were vegetable and fruit growing. The trading area was described as 50 miles in every direction for regular trading; and up to 75 miles east and southeast on special occasion.

Outgoing shipments included 300 train cars of vegetables annually and an estimated 1,500 cars of fruit.

There were four banks including three state and one national. The total resources of all banks were $7,500,000. There were $2,368,855 in total deposits, and the four banks combined for a profit of $812,610.

For entertainment, there were 5,000 total theatre seats, including two auditoriums, three moving pictures, and a vaudeville theatre.

The public schools in 1926 included one K-8 school, one junior high, and one high school. Worship services were available from any of Fort Myers 12 churches including Baptist, Christian Science, Episcopal, Presbyterian, Roman Catholic, and three Methodist churches. Medical needs were serviced by 12 medical doctors, 4 osteopaths, and 2 naturopaths.

Business offices were located at the cross streets on Jackson, Hendry, Lee, Monroe, and Broadway; and several businesses were located on Cleveland Avenue and Anderson Avenue. There were three outlying business districts that supported 20 to 50 additional businesses.

The retail shopping district extended from Lee Street on First Street to Monroe Street, on Main Street, on Jackson Street to Cleveland Avenue. Retail outlets for nationally advertised products included 14 automobile agencies, three commercial auto agencies, eight automobile accessory stores, and 13 tire stores. There were 21 cigar stores and stands, four bakers, 18 confectioners, four delicatessens, seven dressmakers, eight druggists (including one chain), seven dry goods, six furniture stores, five department stores, 15 public garages, 32 grocery stores (including three chains), six hardware stores, five jewelry stores, three meat markets, four men's furnishings, 12 men's clothing, four merchant tailors, five milliners, three opticians, four photographers, three piano (and other musical instrument) stores, four radio supplies, 15 restaurants (including hotels), nine shoe stores, three sporting goods stores, two stationers, and 10 women's apparel shops. There were 18 wholesale businesses including three groceries, seven fruit, three lumber, and five feed suppliers.[150]

In 1926, all residential and business addresses in Fort Myers were re-numbered consistent with a system recommended by the federal government. Duplicate street names were eliminated by renaming newer streets.[151]

In March of 1926, Hendry Brothers were conducting negotiations on behalf of Charles B. Zellner, formerly of the Tri-Pure Water and Bottling company of St. Petersburg, Florida, and his brother Thomas E. Zellner. The Zellner brothers were planning to open a NuGrape soda water factory in Fort Myers.[152]

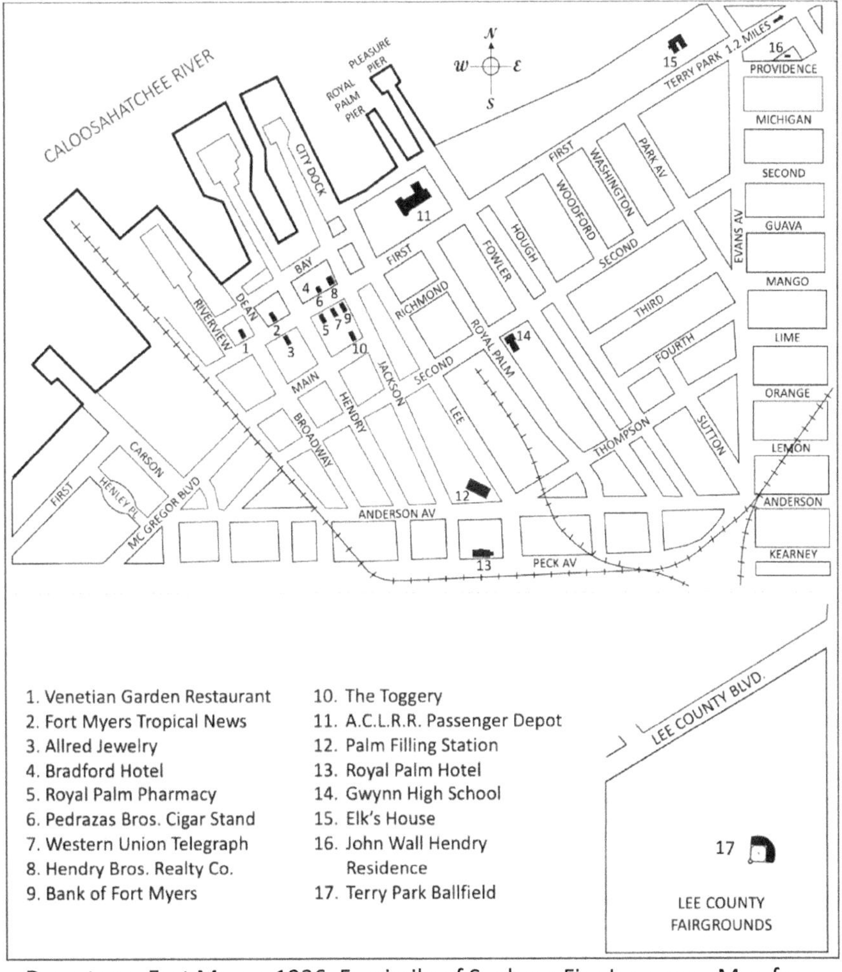

1. Venetian Garden Restaurant
2. Fort Myers Tropical News
3. Allred Jewelry
4. Bradford Hotel
5. Royal Palm Pharmacy
6. Pedrazas Bros. Cigar Stand
7. Western Union Telegraph
8. Hendry Bros. Realty Co.
9. Bank of Fort Myers
10. The Toggery
11. A.C.L.R.R. Passenger Depot
12. Palm Filling Station
13. Royal Palm Hotel
14. Gwynn High School
15. Elk's House
16. John Wall Hendry Residence
17. Terry Park Ballfield

Downtown Fort Myers, 1926. Facsimile of Sanborn Fire Insurance Map from Fort Myers, Lee County, Florida with select buildings and locations added.[153]

Picture of First Street in Fort Myers in 1926, taken from the southwest corner of Dean and First Streets, looking northeast. Two blocks down there is a banner hanging above First Street that reads "BASEBALL TODAY." The banner is upside down in the picture, which may indicate there was not a Fort Myers Palms baseball game on the day this photograph was taken. Photo courtesy of Cats Paw Prints.

John W. Hendry is Determined to Secure a Franchise in the Florida State League

On January 15, 1926, Al Lang, a former mayor of St. Petersburg, announced that after three years, he was stepping down as president of the Florida State League.[154] In the days that followed, there were reports the league had asked Mr. Mike H. Sexton, of Rock Island, Illinois, and president of the National Association of Baseball Leagues to replace Lang. There was discussion of an 8-team circuit in 1926, with 4 teams each in an East and West division. Preliminary franchise applications for the 1926 season were submitted by Jacksonville, Daytona, Palm Beach, and Miami in the East. Six applications were received from the West including

Tampa, St. Petersburg, Sanford, Orlando, Lakeland, and Fort Myers. "The latter city is understood to be anxious for a berth in the loop".

A representative from each team would need to attend the April 1 league meeting and present their proposed plans for fielding a team, and to provide assurance the team had adequate financial backing so there would be no chance of a mid-season withdrawal.[155]

Buck Conroy was hired by Hendry as the first manager of the Fort Myers Baseball Club on January 21, 1926. Conroy was recommended to Hendry by Mike Sexton.[156] Sexton told Mr. Hendry, "Buck is the man to put Fort Myers on the baseball map."[157] Conroy had many years of professional baseball experience as a minor league player and umpire and had worked as a scout for a major league club.[158] He moved to Florida in late 1925 to referee matches at the new Benjamin Field Boxing Arena in Tampa.[159] In December, 1925, he joined the B. L. Hamner Realty Corporation of Tampa as a salesman.[160]

On January 22, 1926, Hendry returned to Fort Myers from Tampa, where he had applied for a franchise in the Florida State League. He was confident the application would be accepted, stating he would personally finance the team. The one obstacle Fort Myers had was transportation – the ability for teams to get into and out of Fort Myers efficiently. Hendry believed Fort Myers would have these concerns addressed prior to the start of the 1926 season.[161]

On January 25, Buck Conroy visited Fort Myers and met with Hendry. Conroy was accompanied by Robert Cole, an associate from his Tampa boxing affairs, who believes he can help ensure Fort Myers a franchise in the Florida State League. Conroy believes Fort Myers would have no trouble securing a spot once enough players are lined up for the team.

A decision about Fort Myers would be made at a meeting of Florida State League officials on February 10. Assuming a positive decision, Conroy plans to return to Fort Myers to make further arrangements for the team. In the meantime, his plan is to travel to Chicago and other cities to sign up players for the team. Conroy is counting on help from Connie Mack when the Philadelphia Athletics come to Fort Myers for spring training in February.[162]

On February 10, 1926, Mike Sexton spoke at the meeting of the Florida State League officials and encouraged the leaders. "You have an opportunity to build one of the best minor leagues in the country here in Florida," he said. Mr. Sexton did not accept the opportunity to serve as president of the Florida State League but said he would attend the next meeting to help the league get organized.

John Wall Hendry, who has been negotiating for a Fort Myers franchise, said the matter would be decided on by club executives at their next meeting. He is unable to attend the next meeting due to previous business engagements. He was represented by Dr. H. E. Opre, a prominent Tampa sportsman, who has extensive property interests near Fort Myers. Hendry remained confident about the Fort Myers application for franchise but was concerned about the completion of the new cross-state highway, the inclusion of Miami and West Palm Beach may be preferred over Fort Myers.[163]

Athletics Spring Training Workouts Begin

February 20, 1926: Athletics President Thomas Shibe and his wife were expected to arrive in Fort Myers today, one day ahead of Connie Mack, his wife, and most of the ball players.

At the fairgrounds, the finishing touches were being made to the baseball park. Consistent with the contract signed by Connie Mack, a new hot water system had been installed in the Athletics' clubhouse, and the box office had been revised to help eliminate the pre-game congestion suffered last spring. The infield had been scraped and covered with three carloads of sand-clay from Bartow, Florida. Lumps in the outfield had been rolled to a level surface. All that remained to be done was the completion of a new seven-foot board fence surrounding the field.[164]

February 23, 1926:

In Fort Myers: The first week of spring training coincided with the annual Lee County Fair. As the Athletics players did their stretching and drills, they were often distracted by the attractions of the fair which were staged between the third base side of the baseball diamond and the grandstand. Among the attractions competing for the players' attention were galloping cowboys, trained dogs, and a performing elephant.[165]

In Tampa: Dr. H. E. Opre will represent John W. Hendry's application for franchise in the Florida State League tomorrow.[166] Dr. Opre expected there would be at least 10 cities represented at the meeting. "'Out of this number we expect little difficulty in selecting eight cities which will be able to support a franchise throughout the season,' Dr. Opre said. 'One of the prime factors to be considered in selecting these personnel will be financial stability. This new Florida State League will be one that will go through the season without a change, with no mid-season flops or withdrawals. Interested citizens in various cities are now arranging financial matters, and we expect a full report at Wednesday's meeting — 'yes' or 'no' — as to whether each will be able to make its club in the league a paying proposition. By keeping the league on the West Coast, we will eliminate a vast amount of expense in which would be incurred by long trips, and we believe that we will be able to organize a compact, sound loop that can furnish the West Coast good baseball throughout the season.'"[167]

February 24, 1926: In Tampa, at the meeting in Dr. Opre's office, Mike Sexton, president of the National Association of Minor League Baseball Clubs, announced he would be unable to accept the presidency of the organization. A monthly team payroll of $2,250, not to include the manager's salary which was not to exceed $500 a month, was agreed to. Buck Conroy represented Fort Myers. "We are ready," he reported.[168] Gilbert Freeman represented Avon Park, Florida, and reported liberal support.[169] "Fans in Wauchula, Sebring, and Frostproof have said they will help support a team at Avon Park." A final decision on the actual cities that will play in the league was deferred to the next meeting on March 4.[170] Each club would need to have half their entrance fee of $10,000 ready prior to the next meeting.[171]

Thomas Edison Meets Connie Mack

At the Lee County fairgrounds: The Philadelphia Athletics continued their workouts. "Practice often came to a dead stop today while the Athletics gazed on the lady in tights or watched the trained bear ring bells."[172]

Perhaps the greatest distraction of the day happened around 11 a.m. when an automobile pulled up along the third base side of the infield. An elderly gentleman with snow white hair carefully climbed out of his car and walked slowly over to Athletics Manager Connie Mack. The visitor was introduced. It was the world's greatest electrical genius, and Fort Myers most famous winter resident, 79-year-old Thomas A. Edison. "Mr. Mack asked him if he liked baseball and Mr. Edison responded that he was a 'crank,' a nickname for the present-day word 'fan' that was in use several decades ago." They spoke for about 20 minutes. Before leaving, Mr. Edison "was induced to take a bat and strike at a ball before a moving picture camera." Mr. Edison struck at a couple of underhanded pitches from Kid Gleason. He swung and missed the first but connected and hit the second pitch about four feet.[173]

March 3, 1926: In Orlando, a meeting of baseball fans was held and $10,000 of stock in the Orlando Baseball Club was underwritten.[174] Fans met in the parlors of the San Juan Hotel in Orlando, including scores of citizens that had yet to be approached, and pledged to purchase $100 shares of stock if the Orlando team was admitted into the Florida State League. Several businessmen in attendance offered to buy several shares of stock, but the goal was to limit each person to one share to enable as many fans as possible to participate in the organization. The fans voted to have Ernie Burke and Mike Kelly attend the league meeting in Tampa on March 4, and a follow-up meeting would take place the next day to hear the report of Burke and Kelly. There would be a mass meeting and baseball rally on Thursday, March 11, on the steps of the county courthouse to further interest in the local team.

March 4, 1926: In Tampa, newly elected President J. B. Asher, an Orlando real estate man and former statistician,[175] confirmed eight clubs would be included in the 1926 Florida State League. Tampa, Sanford, St. Petersburg, and Lakeland were all carry-overs from 1925, and Bradenton,

Sarasota, Orlando, and Fort Myers! Each team was required to post a $2,000 forfeit fee by March 15, and if any team dropped out, Miami or Ybor City would be allowed to take over the franchise. Each club would be limited to 13 players. Of the 13 players, five must be rookies who have no previous professional experience.[176]

Dr. George Cary Morfield attended the meeting representing Miami. He was disappointed when his application for admission was refused. The distance between Miami and the other cities in the league made it impractical to admit Miami to the league.[177]

March 9, 1926: Judge Landis, the commissioner of Major League Baseball, spoke with Florida State League President J. B. Asher. "'One of the best things that could be done for baseball in Florida,' said the judge, 'would be the permitting of Sunday games.'…Mr. Asher said that he would urge the adoption of such a law in Florida permitting Sunday baseball."[178]

March 15, 1926: Washington Senators ball players and comedians Nick Altrock and Al Schact performed their comedy act at the Lee County Fairgrounds before the exhibition game between the Baltimore Orioles and the Philadelphia Athletics.[179]

March 16, 1926: Bob Cole, son of F. H. Cole, a Tampa Jeweler, signed a contract with the Fort Myers club and will report to Manager Buck Conroy next week. Cole pitched for the Orlando Bulldogs of the Florida State League in 1922 and has since played semi-pro ball in Washington and Baltimore.[180]

March 18, 1926: A meeting of the Florida State League clubs is to take place on Friday March 19, Palms President John W. Hendry and team secretary C. Oren Smith, a real estate salesperson,[181] were expected to attend. The meeting agenda includes the formation of the 126-game league schedule that would begin on April 22 – the Palms are expected to host 66 home games.

Palms Manager Buck Conroy has signed several promising players and expects to pick up many more from the big league camps in Florida. Workouts will begin at the Lee County Fairgrounds (Terry Park) ball field on March 27, a few days before the Philadelphia Athletics leave. "Some of his men are expected in advance of that date and will have an opportunity to get in a little work with Connie Mack's crowd." Conroy has many friends in baseball throughout the country and has sent letters to them asking for any talent recommendations they might have.[182] Herbert Young, shortstop; Sam Mercer, catcher have been signed.[183] Faustino Casares and Philip Grandio are listed as probabilities for their positions according to Conroy.

"Local boys also will be given a tryout. Two of them having already been signed. They are Harry Kauffman and Robert Mawhor who have had some experience in semi-pro circles (Kauffman in Ohio and Mawhor in Iowa).[184] Conroy has also signed Joe Domingo, half-back of the Tampa high school team that played at the fairgrounds' football field last fall to play first base, and Joe Hernandez who pitched for St. Petersburg in 1925. 'Conroy is after Gene Davenport, a semi-pro twirler from Chicago who is said to be good.'"[185]

March 21, 1926: All eight teams submitted their $2,000 forfeit fee during the Florida State League meeting. Agreement on all matters was achieved except for the league schedule. Copies of two proposed schedules would be mailed to each club owner and each would vote on their choice.[186]

March 26, 1926: After watching the Philadelphia Athletics defeat the Philadelphia Phillies 10 to 8 at Terry Park, [187] a man, thought to be John Hayes, a Fort Myers businessman, found a lady's handbag that had been dropped behind the grandstand. He opened the bag and discovered it contained diamonds and other jewelry valued at $6,000.

Upon arriving at her hotel and realizing she had misplaced her bag, the owner immediately returned to the ballpark to look for the bag, but it was not there. Mr. Hayes had taken the bag to R. Q. Richards at the Royal Palm Pharmacy. Mr. Richards immediately sent the bag to its owner. Mrs. Connie Mack was very relieved that her bag had been returned to her.[188]

March 27, 1926: A schedule was adopted by mail vote for the Florida State League. Opening Day will be April 22, and Fort Myers first two games would be against Lakeland, in Lakeland.[189]

In Sanford, 200 baseball fans met for a rally at the Hotel Forrest Lake to commence a two-week campaign to raise $15,000 for the support of the local baseball club during the 1926 Florida State League season.[190] Prominent speakers included Judge Kennesaw Mountain Landis, commissioner of baseball, and Mike Sexton, president of the National Association of Minor League Baseball Clubs.[191]

March 29, 1926: "Buck Conroy has started his candidates, leading all of the clubs, in their spring training activities."[192]

March 30, 1926: Several players arrived for tryouts with John W. Hendry's Fort Myers Florida State team. They include Joe Domingo, an infielder who came down from Tampa where he is attending high school; Cody, an infielder from Michigan; White, an infielder from Columbus, Georgia. The Thielan brothers from Salina, Kansas, and Storey is from Lake Okeechobee at Moore Haven, Florida; Casendyke is from St. Petersburg, Florida, with Ridge League experience. Dutch Zwilling, manager of the Lincoln Links in the Western league sent Manager Buck Conroy a letter saying he would send two players down to tryout with the Fort Myers club.[193; 194]

March 31, 1926: The Philadelphia Athletics boarded the 3:55 p.m. train north and departed Fort Myers for Philadelphia.[195] The major league spring training of 1926 was complete, but a new season of professional baseball in Fort Myers was about to begin.

April 1, 1926: Manager Buck Conroy announced a partial lineup for the game against Macon next Tuesday. Philip Grandio, Joe Domingo, and Faustino Casares will play outfield; Mike Bouza will be the shortstop; Cliff Chancey at second; Joe Johnston and Dutch Bandera will catch; while Joe Hernandez, Gene Davenport, and Alonza will pitch. For next Wednesday's game against the House of David, it is likely Larry Thielen will pitch.

Manager Conroy also announced the unconditional release of five men who were trying out for the Palms. They are Cody, Storey, White, Tanner, and Tony Thielen. Joe Domingo has been shifted to the outfield because Manager Conroy believes he can hit more effectively as an outfielder than as a first baseman.[196]

April 2, 1926: Buck Conroy's contacts appear to be coming through for him. He was expecting several additional prospects to arrive for tryouts including an outfielder from Richmond, a first baseman from Kingston in the Virginia league, a third baseman from Asheville in the South Atlantic league, and a pitcher from Buffalo in the International league.

Already in camp is Gene Davenport, a highly regarded right-handed pitcher from Georgia who played for the famous Logan Squares in the Chicago Twilight League; Alonzo is from Tampa and has experience in the Ridge League; Catcher Joe Johnston has had minor league experience; Catcher Dutch Bandera who is a Philadelphia semi-pro; Cliff Chancey who is a second baseman from Gainesville, Florida, who has played in the Florida State League; Shortstop Mike Bouza is a 17-year-old rookie from Tampa; Robert Mawhor, who is playing third base for now, is a local boy with semi-pro experience in Iowa; Philip Grandio is a former Ridge leaguer.

Florida State League teams are allowed two "Classmen" who have played Class B or higher. Buck Conroy will be one of these two for the Fort Myers team. "The manager expects to be in a lot of games. He is either a first or third baseman and is known as a slugger."

Club President John W. Hendry ordered uniforms for the team. "Fort Myers" will be lettered across the front of the shirts. No name for the team had been decided on, but Hendry said it would probably be the Palms. "That is short and sweet and means something."[197]

April 5, 1926: "When the Fort Myers club of the Florida State League clashes at Terry Park tomorrow with the Macon club of the South Atlantic league, local fans will get their first opportunity to see in action the team which will uphold the honor of the city this summer."

April 6, 1926:

Off the field in Fort Myers: Conroy signed 4 players: Pitchers Leonard Mayo and Cy Williams of the Augusta club in the South Atlantic league, infielders Jack O'Reilly of Asheville, and Vincent Macey of the Richmond, Virginia, club. John W. Hendry announced ticket prices for the 1926 season. The Florida State League set prices for bleacher seats at 50 cents and grandstand seats at 75 cents. Children 14 and under would be admitted free.[198]

Off the field in Chicago: Judge Landis, commissioner of baseball, declared the decision by the rules committee last winter to allow pitchers to use a resin bag to dry their hands if they choose, must be upheld by all leagues.[199]

On the field: In the bottom of the ninth inning, Joe Johnston squeezed a bunt down the first baseline scoring Mike Bouza from third giving the Palms a victory over the Macon Peaches of the South Atlantic League 8 to 7 in a pre-season exhibition game.[200] The game was played before a small crowd.[201]

A large ad in *The Fort Myers Press* announced the April 7 game would be against the House of David[202] barnstorming team, but it turned out the House of David team had been rerouted and Macon stayed in Fort Myers for a second game.

April 7, 1926: Macon scored early and often and beat the Palms 10-7. Larry Thielan was impressive in relief in his pitching debut. Of note, Manager Conroy batted for Mawhor in the bottom of the ninth. Conroy struck out to end the game.[203] [This is the only time Buck Conroy appeared in a Palms box score.]

April 8, 1926: Conroy announced the arrival of three players including Third Baseman Jack O'Reilly of Asheville, North Carolina, who played for University of Washington at St. Louis; Bill Stanley, a utility player from Kingston, Virginia, played college ball at the University of Virginia; and Vincent Macey of Richmond, Virginia, who played with the Scranton club in the New York – Pennsylvania league last year. Cy Williams, purchased

BASEBALL!

FORT MYERS BASEBALL CLUB

Florida State League

vs.

House of David

Wednesday, April 7th

2 P.M.

TERRY PARK　　FAIR GROUNDS

Popular Prices

Facsimile of ad in *The Fort Myers Press* – USA TODAY NETWORK, April 6, 1926.

from the Augusta club in the South Atlantic league, was expected to report today.

Conroy also announced the release of three players: Pitchers Heflin and Alonzo and infielder Casendyke. President Hendry has tentatively scheduled games with the Jacksonville club in the new Southeastern League for three consecutive dates beginning April 15.[204]

The Season that Almost Wasn't

April 9, 1926: With the team coming together and opening day less than two weeks away, John W. Hendry announced he needed $20,000 to cover the projected cost of the team for the season, and he would be selling two-hundred $100 shares in the baseball club. Mr. Hendry would only require 25% (or $25 per share) immediately, with the remainder due as needed.

Last winter when he found he could get a franchise in the Florida State League, many fans advised him to proceed and made verbal commitments to support the team financially. $5,000 had been pledged but only $500 had been paid. The cost of assembling the team, providing uniforms and equipment cost $4,000, and Mr. Hendry said he is unwilling to proceed without support from the fans. Mr. Hendry believed there was a possibility that no further payments would be needed. "'If the attendance is good throughout the circuit, we can get by on a capital investment of about what we already have spent,' he said. 'On the other hand, we may run into bad luck as a business proposition. We want to be prepared for the worst.'"

The officers of the club (President John W. Hendry, W. H. Merrill secretary, and G. E. Hosmer treasurer) believe there is a good chance that an investment in the club will be a profitable one. Some of the players that have been signed will bring $15,000 when they are placed on the market.[205]

"'If the people in Fort Myers want the club, they must purchase the stock,' Mr. Hendry said. 'If they do not want it, I will sell the franchise to some other city in the state. I just want to arouse the people to the fact that the club must be supported if we are to have real baseball this summer.'"[206]

<u>April 10, 1926</u>:

Off the field: Pedrazas Brothers announced that returns from the American, National, and Florida State League games will be received by wire every three innings and posted on a chalkboard to be erected for fans at the Pedrazas Bros. cigar stand on First Street.[207]

After his appeal for help with financing the team failed to bring in the support he hoped for, John W. Hendry wired J. B. Asher, the president of the Florida State League, that the franchise, including players, uniforms, and equipment, was for sale and asked to be put in touch with prospective bidders. "Mr. Hendry and his associates made several calls on persons who were expected to give some help. Mr. Hendry says he got small encouragement and rather than suffer alone the grief he can see in the offing, he decided to throw the whole business overboard. "'I cannot finance the whole thing myself,' Mr. Hendry said. 'So far only a half dozen or so have actually come across though a great many others assured me that they would back the team when we had a chance to get the franchise…. The club is on the market. If there is any way to keep it in Fort Myers that would be fine, but something will have to be done immediately or it will go. I'm not going to be connected with a club that may blow up in the middle of the season. If it must come, it had better be now.'"[208]

On the field at Terry Park: The Palms new uniforms arrived today, and the team wore them for their workout at the fairgrounds. For the later portion of practice, Manager Buck Conroy took Jack O'Reilly's place at third base and "showed that he has not forgotten how to play baseball as well as teach it" After practice, Conroy talked about how pleased he was with the team and how confident he was about the season ahead. It is expected that Dexter Morgan, from Philadelphia, will be farmed out to a club in another league and Robert Mawhor will probably be released.[209]

<u>April 12, 1926</u>: Cy Williams arrived in camp today from Augusta. The hefty right-hand pitcher is a little overweight but will trim down before the season opens.

Buck Conroy is trying to establish a farm team partnership in the Ridge League where he can place prospects on 10-day options, but he has not gotten a team to agree yet.

"Baseball Magnate Holds Off to Give Fans Chance to Raise Money." John W. Hendry, president of the Fort Myers Baseball Club received an offer for his team, but delayed negotiations for the transfer of the franchise when local fans appealed to him to wait a few days while they work to raise money to keep the team in Fort Myers.   "Mr. Hendry consented to the delay though he remains pessimistic over the prospect of obtaining the proper support here." $500 in cash funds had been collected in the weekend scramble, but $6,000 in stock subscriptions had been pledged. The fans who were busily selling shares believed they could achieve their goal if given more time. "'Fort Myers cannot afford to lose the team after going this far with it,' said one of the fans. 'It would give us a black eye all over the state. Businessmen who have put money into the team are satisfied that the advertising it will bring is worth the investment even if they never get anything back in cash. Of course, nobody can promise a dividend in a minor league venture, but there is a good chance, nevertheless.'"[210]

<u>April 13, 1926</u>: Baseball fans crowded around the city's two scoreboards located at Pedrazas Bros. cigar stand and at the Royal Palm pharmacy, both on First Street, as Major League Baseball played opening day games. The Philadelphia Athletics and Washington Senators played 15 innings.[211]

<u>April 14, 1926</u>: The Palms worked out in their road jerseys and had their photo snapped in them. The team was prepared to face Rollins College at Terry Park the next day. Robert Mawhor and Bill Stanley were released by Manager Buck Conroy.[212]

<u>April 15, 1926</u>:

Off the field: Right-handed pitcher, Cecil McRae, arrived from Asheville, North Carolina, to join Buck Conroy's Palms. McRae remains property of the Ashville team but has been turned over to Fort Myers to be developed. This would be McRae's first start in professional baseball.[213]

On the field: The Palms scored 6 runs in the first inning and held on to beat Rollins College 10 to 6, in an exhibition game at Terry Park. With two outs in the top of the ninth inning, the Tars thought they scored a run, but the runner failed to touch home plate. Palms Catcher Dutch Bandera rushed all the way to the Tars bench to tag the runner. The umpire sided with Bandera and the game was over. Rollins College "showed a fairly good backstop in Overstreet" who led the Tars with three singles.[214]

<u>April 17, 1926</u>: H. B. Mayer, business manager for the Palms, announced that pledges for the necessary funds have been received and Fort Myers will retain a franchise in the Florida State League. "'Of course,' Mr. Mayer declared, 'this is conditional on the payment of these pledges; however, I am prepared to say that the club will open the season here Thursday against St. Petersburg at the fairgrounds.'"

The Palms continue daily workouts. Joe Hernandez has been dealing with a sore arm but is recovering and should be ready to pitch the season opener on Thursday. "Conroy will be a playing manager…. this means that only four hurlers may be retained."[215]

(Next page) Facsimile of "1926 Baseball Schedule for The Florida State League.," *The Fort Myers Press* – USA TODAY NETWORK, April 24, 1926[216]

1926 BASEBALL SCHEDULE FOR THE FLORIDA STATE LEAGUE

CATCH	AT BRADENTON	AT FORT MYERS	AT LAKELAND	AT ORLANDO	AT SANFORD	AT SARASOTA	AT ST. PETERSBURG	AT TAMPA
BRADENTON GROWERS	PALMS	May 31, June 1-2 July 15-16-17 September 2-3-4	May 17-18-19 June 24-25-26 August 12-13-14	May 13-14-15 July 19-20-21 September 13-14-15	June 7-8-9 July 22-23-24 September 9-10-11	April 24, May 27-28 July 5 PM 6 July 23-24-25 September 6 AM	April 26-27-28 June 14-15-16 July 29-30-31	May 10-11-12 June 21-22-23 August 9-10-11
FORT MYERS PALMS	April 29-30, May 1 July 8-9-10 August 26-27-28	GAMES	May 10-11-12 July 5-5-6 August 23-24-25	June 3-4-5 June 24-25-26 August 12-13-14	May 17-18-19 June 21-22-23 August 9-10-11	April 26-27-28 Jun 14-15-16 July 29-30-31	May 24-25-26 July 22-23-24 September 9-10-11	May 13-14-15 July 19-20-21 September 13-14-15
LAKELAND HIGHLANDERS	June 3-4-5 June 17-18-19 August 5-6-7	June 7-8-9 July 26-27-28 September 5-6-7	ALL	April 29-30 May 1 June 28-29-30 August 16-17-18	May 20-21-22 June 14-15-16 August 2-3-4	May 13-14-15 July 19-20-21 September 13-14-15	May 3-4-5 July 1-2-3 August 19-20-21	May 20-21-22 June 10-11-12 August 2-3-4
ORLANDO COLTS	May 6-7-8 July 12-13-14 August 30-31 September 1	May 3-4-5 June 17-18-19 August 5-6-7	May 27-28-29 July 22-23-24 September 9-10-11	SUMMER	April 22-23 July 5 AM July 26-27-28 August 23-24 September 6 PM	May 17-18-19 June 21-22-23 August 9-10-11	June 7-8-9 July 8-9-10 August 26-27-28	May 20-21-22 June 10-11-12 August 2-3-4
SANFORD CELERYFEDS	May 24-25-26 June 28-29-30 August 16-17-18	May 27-28-29 July 1-2-3 August 19-20-21	April 26-27-28 June 10-11-12 July 29-30-31	April 24 May 31, June 1-2 August 25 September 7 AM July 5 PM 6	LONG	May 10-11-12 July 15-16-17 September 2-3-4	May 13-14-15 July 19-20-21 September 13-14-15	April 29-30, May 1 June 24-25-26 August 12-13-14
SARASOTA GULLS	April 22-23, May 29 July 5 AM July 26-27-28 September 6 PM 7	May 20-21-22 June 10-11-12 August 2-3-4	May 6-7-8 July 12-13-14 August 30-31, Sept. 1	May 24-25-26 July 1-2-3 August 19-20-21	May 3-4-5 July 8-9-10 August 26-27-28	AT	June 3-4-5 June 17-18-19 August 5-6-7	June 7-8-9 June 28-29-30 August 16-17-18
ST. PETERSBURG SAINTS	May 20-21-22 June 10-11-12 August 2-3-4	April 22-23-24 June 28-29-30 August 16-17-18	May 31, June 1-2 June 21-22-23 August 9-10-11	May 10-11-12 July 15-16-17 September 2-3-4	May 6-7-8 July 12-13-14 August 30-31 September 1	April 29-30, May 1 June 24-25-26 August 12-13-14	TERRY	May 27-28-29 July 5 AM July 25-26-27 September 6 AM 7
TAMPA SMOKERS	May 3-4-5 July 1-2-3 August 19-20-21	May 6-7-8 July 12-13-14 August 30-31 September 1	May 24-25-26 July 8-9-10 April 26-27-28	April 26-27-28 June 14-15-16 July 29-30-31	June 3-4-5 June 17-18-19 August 5-6-7	May 31, June 1-2 July 22-23-24 September 9-10-11	May 17-18-19 July 5 PM 6 August 23-24-25 September 6 AM	PARK

Play Ball!

<u>April 19, 1926</u>: "MAYOR'S PROCLAMATION

In order that the people of Fort Myers may have an opportunity to thoroughly enjoy the opening of the baseball season on Thursday of this week, I hereby declare Thursday afternoon, April 22 from 1 p.m. to 6 p.m., a legal holiday in the City of Fort Myers, and urge everyone to attend the opening of the baseball season. Fort Myers has a team in the Florida State League and let us all show our appreciation by giving the team proper support.

FRANK KELLOW, Mayor
Fort Myers, April 19."

In addition to Mayor Kellow's proclamation, there was an announcement from H. B. Mayer, business manager of the Palms, that Thursday will be ladies' day, and ladies will be admitted free to the opening game. 50 to 100 cars were expected to come down from St. Petersburg carrying Saints fans. "'It is up to local fans,' according to Mr. Mayer, 'to prove to the visitors that Fort Myers is a baseball town. Our boys should be supported by a record-breaking crowd. Mayor Kellow has graciously done his part by declaring the day a holiday and the ball team management will add to that by admitting ladies free to the opening game.'"[217]

<u>April 20, 1926</u>: After spending more than 10 weeks at his residence on McGregor Boulevard, on April 20, 1926, Fort Myers most famous winter residents, inventor Thomas A. Edison and his wife Mina, left Fort Myers on the afternoon train, beginning their journey back to Menlo Park, New Jersey.[218] Thomas Edison would not be present for the inaugural game (or any game) of the 1926 Fort Myers Palms season.

Meanwhile, John W. Hendry announced everything was in place and ready for the opening game at Terry Park and the Palms starting lineup was announced.[219]

"Manager Buck Conroy thinks he has about the right crew for the class he will be in but has many friends in baseball who have promised to help him out if he needs it. Bill Clymer, of the Buffalo Internationals is ready to come to his rescue and Connie Mack said he would help all he could."[220]

<u>April 21, 1926</u>: Buck Conroy announced Joe Hernandez, veteran right-handed pitcher, will pitch opening day for the Palms against his former teammates from St. Petersburg. [221]

Top row (left to right)—W. H. Merrill, secretary; Davenport, Gibbons, Domingo, Bouza, Morgan and Williams. Middle row—Grandio, Chancey, Banderio, Manager Conroy, Hernandez, O'Reilly and Macey. Bottom row—Thielan and Casares. McRae and Johnston were absent at the time of the photograph.

"Buck Conroy's Palms in Formal Pose," *Fort Myers Tropical News* –
USA TODAY NETWORK, April 22, 1926.[222]

Top Row (left to right) W. H. Merrill, secretary; Gene Davenport, Bob Gibbons, Joe Domingo, Mike Bouza, Dexter Morgan, and Cy Williams. Middle row - Philip Grandio, Cliff Chancey, Dutch Bandera, Manager Buck Conroy, Joe Hernandez, Jack O'Reilly, and Vincent Macey. Bottom row - Larry Thielan, and Faustino Casares. Cecil McRae and Joe Johnston were absent at the time of the photograph.

April 1926 – Palms Start Strong!

<u>April 22, 1926</u>: Opening Day of the 1926 Florida State League!

The big day was finally here. Anyone in Fort Myers who was unaware of the significance of the day only had to pass by a newsstand and catch a glimpse of the two-inch tall headline across the top of the front page of the morning newspaper that proclaimed: *"BASEBALL SEASON TO OPEN HERE TODAY"* along with a team photo of the Palms. There were 4 subheadings including:

- FORT MYERS TO SEE FIRST LEAGUE BALL
- First Game in Florida Loop to be Played at Terry Park at 3 p.m.
- MARKS CIVIC EPOCH
- Half-holiday Proclaimed by Mayor; St. Pete Team Here.

The festivities for the day included an early afternoon parade the Palms players rode in and a flag raising ceremony at Terry Park.[223] Mayor Frank Kellow threw out the ceremonial first pitch to Commissioner Arthur Raymond. The pitch was high and wide, but Raymond caught it. The two then went to their seats in the grandstand and enjoyed free NuGrape.[224]

In front of 1,500 fans at Terry Park, the Palms won the first game in franchise history 3-0.[225] In the third inning, Mike Bouza tripled and then stole home. Joe Hernandez gave up nine hits and hit two batters (including beaning Saints Shortstop Dick Luckey in the sixth) but pitched nine shutout innings for the Palms.[226] In the top of the ninth, Pedro Dibut pinch hit for Wilhoit. [Dibut played for the Cuban Stars West of the National Negro League in 1923[227] and for the major league Cincinnati Reds in 1924.][228] Dibut grounded to the Palms shortstop, Mike Bouza, who threw to Joe Domingo at first.[229] The temperature in Fort Myers was 84 degrees.[230]

Front page of the *Fort Myers Tropical News* –
USA TODAY NETWORK, April 22, 1926.[231]

A total of 1,152 bottles of NuGrape were consumed by fans during the game. The drinks were donated by the Fort Myers NuGrape Bottling Company which began city-wide distribution of the new drink today.[232]

1926 NuGrape advertisement.[233]

<u>April 23, 1926</u>:

On the field: The Palms beat the Saints 7 to 5. With two outs and the Palms trailing 5-2 in the bottom of the seventh, Mike Bouza hit a pitch from former major leaguer Pedro Bidut 350 feet in the air to deep left field. The ball rolled to the fence, and the speedy Bouza made it all the way around the bases for the Palms' first home run of the season. A rally ensued and five batters later, Joe Hernandez drove in the tying and winning runs with a line shot to left. Manager Buck Conroy was so excited he began shadow boxing in the third base coaches' box. Bouza became the first of the Palms to win a free suit from the Toggery, a men's wear and boys' wear department store on Main Street in Fort Myers[234] that pledged a new suit to each member of the Palms who hit a home run at Terry Park.[235] This was a carry-over promotion the Toggery began in 1925 in support of the Philadelphia Athletics spring training.[236] The game-time temperature at Terry Park was 84 degrees.[237]

WE'RE BACKING

The

PALMS

TO THE LIMIT

We are Giving a Suit to Every Palm Who
Hits a Home Run on Terry Park Field.

ALWAYS AHEAD

THE TOGGERY

MAIN ST.

P.S. We clean and press. Call 336

Facsimile of The Toggery Ad in *The Fort Myers Press* –
USA TODAY NETWORK, April 23, 1926.[238]

Off the field: Palms Business Manager H. B. Mayer was canvassing businesses in town working to collect on financial pledges made prior to the start of the season and to secure new advertising revenue. He was using his advertising sales skills to help business owners understand the value of sponsoring prizes for hitting a home run or pitching a shut-out.[239]

April 24, 1926:

Off the field: To mark the closing of the Palms first home stand, the day began with a parade through downtown that included the Fort Myers Band. This was followed by a concert and parade at Terry Park before the game.[240]

Speaking with a reporter, Palms Business Manager H.B. Mayer said, "a good crowd of fans was on hand for the opener, but yesterday's attendance was disappointing. We need every citizen in Fort Myers back of the Palms." Mayer went on to guarantee a sweep of the Saints.[241]

On the field: The game-time temperature at Terry Park was 85 degrees.[242] The Palms beat the Saints 6 to 4 to complete their first series sweep in franchise history. Three games into the season, the Palms are alone at the top of the standings in the Florida State League.

After the game: The team met at the Venetian Garden; a restaurant located on First Street where Broadway ends in downtown Fort Myers.[243] They were treated to dinner by John W. Hendry. Palms Business Manager H. B. Mayer made an appearance at the dinner but left early to continue working to collect pledges and secure commitments for additional funds from businesses in the community.[244]

April 25, 1926: No game today.

April 26, 1926:

Off the field: The Palms left Fort Myers in the morning heading to Sarasota for their first road trip. The team traveled in their bus, an 18-passenger REO Pullman brand machine, that was acquired with the support of the Chamber of Commerce.[245] The bus was previously owned by the Elmer E. Jones (Transport) Company. The cost was $1,800 and required $750 down. Mr. James E. Hendry, prominent businessman and owner of the Everglades Nursery,[246] said that he would personally contribute $500 toward the down payment if the Chamber would commit to monthly payments of $100 each month toward the balance.[247]

On the field: Before play began, a few Sarasota Gulls players tried to frustrate the Fort Myers team by yelling demeaning and racial slurs at the Palms. A few of the fans in attendance joined in. In the early part of the game, the umpiring seemed to be extraordinarily biased in favor of the Gulls.[248]

The Palms lost their first game in franchise history 10-5 to the Gulls that afternoon. Joe Hernandez became both the first winning and first losing pitcher in Palms' history.[249] The highlight of the game for the Palms came in the fourth inning when Jack O'Reilly made a base hit that resulted in four runs. Mike Bouza led off the inning and reached first on an error by the Gulls shortstop, Faustino Casares was hit by a pitch, and Joe Domingo walked to load the bases. Jack O'Reilly lined the ball to center field where it got by a charging Harry Manush [brother of Detroit Tigers outfielder Heine Manush].[250] O'Reilly made it all the way around the bases on the play.[251]

April 27, 1926: The Palms beat Sarasota 14-3. Philip Grandio had two doubles and a three-run home run. Mike Bouza had a double and a triple. Palms Third Baseman Jack O'Reilly made several great plays[252] including the snaring of Gulls Left Fielder Joyner's line drive and force out of Meckley at second base in the seventh.[253]

April 28, 1926:

On the field: Cecil McRae allowed just four hits as the Palms pounded the Gulls 9-0 to win the three-game series. The Gulls' manager, former major leaguer, Ivy Olson, protested the game arguing Cecil McRae's uniform was a slightly different color than the rest of the team.[254]

After the game and back in Fort Myers: At the Chamber of Commerce meeting, H.B. Mayer explained to the membership that Mr. Hendry has already spent $4,000 prior to the start of the season and that it would take $27,000 to make it through the final game. Mr. Mayer asked the Chamber if they would donate $5,000 to support the team. Those present spoke only in support, but Walter S. Turner, chairman of the finance committee, pointed out the Chamber did not have that amount of money available. The Chamber was having trouble collecting pledges from business owners.

April 29, 1926:

On the field in Bradenton: Joe Domingo led the Palms with four hits, including a double, in a 9-7 victory over the Bradenton Growers.[255] Commentary in the *Bradenton Herald* referred to the Palms as "natives of Cuba, Spain, and other suburbs of Ybor City."[256] The paper also noted the crowd was small.

Off the field and back in Fort Myers: a comment on the sports page of *The Fort Myers Press* declared, "The sports department of this newspaper hereby goes on record as earnestly and devoutly opposing abbreviation of the word 'Fort' as it appears on the Palms uniform. Spell it out, every time."[257]

Facsimile of the Fort Myers Palms uniform lettering drawn by Ken Breen (2023).

April 30, 1926: Faustino Casares' two triples led the Palms to a 10-3 win over the Growers.[258] The Palms were alone in first place at the end of April.

END OF APRIL
FLORIDA STATE LEAGUE[259]

	W.	L.	PCT.
FORT MYERS	**7**	**1**	**.875**
Sanford	5	3	.625
Orlando	4	4	.500
Lakeland	4	4	.500
Tampa	3	5	.375
Sarasota	3	5	.375
Bradenton	3	5	.375
St. Petersburg	3	5	.375

May 1926 – Promised Financial Support
for the Palms is Slow to Arrive

<u>May 1, 1926</u>: The Bradenton Growers beat the Palms 5-1 to close out the series in Bradenton. Bradenton Left Fielder Mackie robbed Joe Domingo of a sure homer with a sensational running catch in deep left field.[260] After the game, the Palms boarded their luxury team bus and returned to Fort Myers.

<u>May 2, 1926</u>: No game today. The Palms were leading the Florida State League and there was anticipation of the week of home games ahead. It was suspected that businesses would find excuses to close early so owners and employees could attend the game at Terry Park. Mayor Frank Kellow was so confident there would be a large turnout to watch the Palms on Monday afternoon he said declaring a half holiday wasn't necessary.[261] H.B. Mayer, business manager for the Palms went so far as to say he expected an overflow crowd at Terry Park Monday afternoon.[262]

<u>May 3, 1926</u>:

Off the field: In accordance with Florida State League rules, each team was required to trim their rosters down to 13 players by Thursday May 6.[263] Only two of the 13 players may be classmen (having played Class B or higher baseball) and five must be rookies.[264]

Jack Doyle, a scout for Major League Baseball's Chicago Cubs, attended the game at Terry Park. He had been following the Palms for several days.[265]

On the field: The temperature at the start of the game was 86 degrees.[266] Cy Williams made his pitching debut for the Palms. He pitched all nine innings in the Palms 4-2 victory over the Orlando Colts.[267] The Palms scored their winning runs in the eighth inning, but not without controversy. The Palms Cliff Chancey was on first. With Philip Grandio at the plate, Chancey stole second. Orlando Manager Phil Wells believed Grandio stepped on home plate, and that interfered with his ability to throw the ball to second.   Umpire Dillon agreed Grandio stepped on the plate[268] but refused to change the call. Manager Wells stated he would protest the game.[269]

<u>May 4, 1926:</u>

Off the field: An article in the morning newspaper that described the attendance situation the day before as concerning. There were about 500 fans at the game, but the author felt there should be at least 1,000 people in attendance at every home game to properly reflect the appreciation of a very good baseball team, the sport itself, and the advertising value a professional baseball team provided for the community. The article mentioned that regular attendees Cozy Dolan, one-time coach with the New York Giants, and Jack Doyle, a scout for the Chicago Cubs, believed the Palms players were genuine prospects for the major leagues. The article noted the fans were excited about the Palms determination to win but were less impressed with Manager Buck Conroy's decisions throughout the game. There was plenty of interest and buzz about the Palms throughout the city, even when the team was away, but attendance when the Palms are home was light and financial support was lacking. Money paid as admissions or as contributions were needed to keep the team afloat.[270]

H. B. Mayer, the team's business manager, continues to try to collect on pledges made to support the team and to secure additional commitments. He made a series of announcements on behalf of the team beginning with the news that Thursday May 6 would be Ladies' Day at Terry Park; women would be admitted free as part of the team's effort to have record attendance for the game against the Tampa Smokers. Next, Mayer reminded fans the Palms were the only team in the Florida State League to admit all visitors 14 and under for free, but this is a privilege, and it would be taken away if the boys continue to steal foul balls. Finally, he announced that the practice of fans simply taking their seats and a ticket taker coming around to collect a ticket or fee from them would be discontinued beginning with today's game and everyone coming to the game would be required to purchase a ticket at the box office prior to entering the stands.[271]

On the field: Playing under sun-soaked skies and a temperature of 88 degrees,[272] the Palms came from behind to beat the Colts 9-8.[273]

<u>May 5, 1926</u>:

Off the field: To meet the required thirteen player roster, Buck Conroy released Larry Thielan, Dexter Morgan, and Bob Gibbons. Thielan was expected to be picked up by the Tampa Smokers who would be arriving in Fort Myers to begin a three-game series the following day.[274]

It was announced today the Smokers series would be the final games fans under 14 years old would be admitted into Terry Park for free. A 25-cent admission charge would go into effect the following week.[275]

On the field: The temperature in Fort Myers at game time was 90 degrees.[276] Gene Davenport pitched a complete game, three-hitter for the Palms, but the Colts took advantage of poor fielding to win the final game of the series 3-2.[277] For no apparent reason, fans were very vocal in their criticism of Palms Catcher Joe Johnston and Manager Buck Conroy in the second inning.[278]

<u>May 6, 1926</u>:

Off the field: H.B. Mayer announced that a watch would be awarded to the Palms player with the most home runs by Saturday, courtesy of Allred Jewelry store.[279]

On the field: The temperature at game time was 84 degrees.[280] For the first time in Fort Myers Palms' history, the team lost back-to-back games. Tampa took game one of the series 7 to 4 at Terry Park.[281] The game was heavily attended and included many Tampa fans who traveled to Fort Myers to attend. "The grandstand was in a state of continuous uproar from the beginning of the game until the locals had sent their last man to bat." Hundreds of visiting and local ladies were in attendance taking advantage of the Ladies' Day free-admission promotion.[282]

<u>May 7, 1926</u>:

Off the field: H. B. Mayer, business manager for the Palms, appealed to the Fort Myers City Commission for funds to keep the team in business for the remainder of the season.   Agreeing the Palms were an excellent advertising feature for the city, the commission voted to allocate $1,500 from the publicity fund to the Palms.[283]

Believing they've figured out Babe Ruth's secret to success, several Palms players have begun eating two to five barbecue sandwiches just prior to game time.[284]

On the field: The temperature at Terry Park was 78 degrees.[285] In the second inning, Bob Gibbons, who was released by the Palms two days earlier, appeared in a Smokers' uniform and singled to center field. He stole second and scored two batters later. Gibbons singled again in the third. The Palms scored in the bottom of the tenth inning to beat the Smokers 9 to 8.[286]

Palms Left Fielder Faustino Casares was distracted by certain Smokers throughout the game – the ongoing debate was in Spanish.

It is believed Philip Grandio was cheated out of a sure home run because of something related to the condition of the right field foul line.[287]

<u>May 8, 1926</u>:

Off the field: Palms Business Manager H. B. Mayer, who has made many public pleas for pledges to be paid, surprised everyone when he announced that while almost none of the pledges have been paid yet, he would not be attempting to collect on the pledges until the Palms begin winning again.

On the field: The game-time temperature was 78 degrees.[288] Philip Grandio hit a line drive down the right field line that the Smokers were comfortable was foul, but it was called fair by Umpire McCarthy. By the time the Smokers reacted and played the ball, Grandio had made it all the way around the bases. Smokers Manager Charlie Allen, who was playing center field, ran to home plate and began an emphatic argument with the umpire. McCarthy tossed Allen out of the game, but Allen refused to leave, and began to walk back to his position in center field. After McCarthy stopped the game and pulled out his watch, Allen decided to leave the field and sit on the Smokers' bench. Not satisfied, McCarthy ordered Allen to leave the field. Allen took his time changing shoes before he finally left.

Grandio's home run secured him the watch offered by Allred Jewelry store, and a new suit from Toggery.[289] The home run wasn't enough though; excessive walks and nine errors cost the Palms the deciding game to the Smokers 10 to 9.[290]

After the game: Palms Secretary W. H. Merrill confirmed a newcomer, McGruger, had been added to the Palms' roster, and Vincent Macey, who was sent to the Palms under option by Richmond,[291] was released by the Palms back to Richmond. Poor hitting and inconsistent fielding were the reasons cited for Macey's release, but some suggested his mouth got him in trouble. Macey consistently complained and boasted off the field. Manager Buck Conroy has been trying to find a second baseman since the season began and is likely to put himself in the lineup and shift the infield around until he fills the role.[292]

May 9, 1926: No game today. Players boarded the luxury team bus in the afternoon and took off for Lakeland to begin a three-game series with the Highlanders who are tied for first place with the Palms.

May 10, 1926:

Off the field: Manager Buck Conroy knows where the weak spots are on his team and is working to strengthen the club but must do so within the financial constraints that paid attendance at Palms home games will permit.

On the field: Rather than inserting himself into the lineup, Palms Manager Buck Conroy shifted Mike Bouza from shortstop to third base, Jack O'Reilly from second base to shortstop, and inserted Joe Hernandez at second base. Both Bouza and O'Reilly made errors at their new positions in a 6-run Lakeland first inning. The Highlanders beat the Palms 7 to 5.[293]

This was the first day since the Florida State League opener on April 22 the Fort Myers Palms were not in first place in the league standings.[294]

<u>May 11, 1926</u>:

Off the field: The towns of Eustis, Mt. Dora, and Tavares are discussing the feasibility of joining forces to field a Florida State League team. The "Golden Triangle" cities would pool equal resources to defray the expense of having a team in the Florida State League, and the team would play home games in each of the three cities' primary fields.[295]

On the field: Every player in the lineup for the Palms got a hit – 17 in total, including triples by Dutch Bandera, Joe Domingo, and Jack O'Reilly. The Palms beat Lakeland 10 to 4 and share first place in the Florida State League with the Highlanders.[296]

<u>May 12, 1926</u>:

Off the field: An op-ed in the morning paper appealed to fans to accept and embrace the Palms with all their imperfections. The citizens of Fort Myers have been spoiled the past two springs watching Connie Mack's Philadelphia Athletics, one of the best teams in the major leagues, and expect the Class D Palms to perform with the same precision. The writer went on to explain the organization has been challenged in securing enough pledges to cover the cost of operating the team and is continuing forward on promissory notes. All things considered, the team is doing quite well, and the manager and players deserve praise.[297]

On the field: Joe Hernandez hit a home run in the seventh inning, but it wasn't enough. The Highlanders beat the Palms in 10 innings 5 to 4, dropping the Palms to third place behind Lakeland and Sanford.[298]

After the game: Buck Conroy placed a long-distance call to Doc Opre, the owner of the Tampa team, to let him know there were about 125 cars in the Fort Myers delegation on their way from Lakeland to Tampa where the Palms intend to win the series with the Smokers.[299]

<u>May 13, 1926</u>:

Off the field: W. H. Merrill, Palms team secretary, announced the Palms had cast a "no" ballot in response to a Florida State League proposal that would raise the player limit from 13 to 14 and raise the team salary limit from $2,250 to $2,400 per month.[300]

On the field: With the Palms leading 4 to 1 in the top of the fifth inning, Smokers Pitcher Cesare Alvarez threw a fastball inside at Palms Right Fielder Cliff Chancey. Chancey and Alvarez exchanged words and Chancey eventually walked. Chancey took off to second when Mike Bouza hit an infield grounder. Chancey passed second but got caught in a run-down between second and third. After trying to get back to second twice, Chancey turned toward third and saw Alvarez standing on third holding the ball and waiting to tag him out. Chancey ran straight into Alvarez standing up and the two got into a fistfight. Chancey was removed from the park by a police officer. Alvarez was escorted by a police officer to the Smokers' bench; he had a grin on his face. Chancey returned later announcing his bond had been signed. He was expected to have to explain what happened in police court the next morning.

The fight between Chancey and Alvarez was the highlight of the game for the Tampa fans, until the bottom of the ninth inning came along. Palms Pitcher Cy Williams threw a curve ball that Tampa First Baseman Bill Jesmer lined to right field for a triple. Manager Buck Conroy was furious with Williams whom he had instructed to throw a fast ball. After Williams threw four more curves, Conroy yanked him, and Cecil McRae took over on short notice. The Smokers scored a total of 4 runs in the bottom of the ninth inning to win the game 5 to 4.[301]

<u>May 14, 1926</u>:

Off the field: Dr. H. E. Opre, president of the Tampa club, announced he had submitted a "no" vote via telegraph on St. Petersburg's proposal to increase the player limit and salary allowance in the Florida State League. Only one "no" is required to defeat a vote that is taken by telegraph.

Sanford Manager Lee Crowe filed a protest with the league president charging that St. Petersburg has three "class" men on their team (players that have played higher than Class C) when only two are allowed. St. Petersburg Manager George Block filed a counter protest that Sanford also has three.[302]

On the field: The Palms out hit the Smokers 14 to 12, but the Smokers were aggressive on the bases and handed the Palms their third consecutive loss, 8 to 5. In the seventh inning, Joe Hernandez turned his ankle going into first base and had to be carried from the field.[303] Former Palm, Larry Thielan, struck out Rich Porter in the top of the ninth to end the game.[304]

After the game: Buck Conroy and the Palms, along with Manager Charley Allen and the Smokers, were guests of the 116th Field Artillery for boxing matches. More than 4,000 were in attendance.[305]

May 15, 1926:

Off the field: Palms Manager Buck Conroy announced the release of Joe Hernandez and the signing of infielder Tommy Condon, who was previously with the Bradenton Growers.[306] Condon hailed from St. Louis, Missouri.[307]

Florida State League President J. B. Asher released umpires, Dillon and Graham, citing lack of experience.[308]

On the field: Palms first baseman and former Tampa High School football star, Joe Domingo, made his pitching debut. Domingo pitched a complete game shutout giving the Palms a 3 to 0 victory.[309]

May 16, 1926: No game today. The Palms rode in the luxury team bus to Sanford to prepare for a three-game series with the Celeryfeds.

<u>May 17, 1926</u>:

Off the field: "J.B. Asher, president of the Florida State League, today announced he had allowed the protest by the Orlando club of the game played at Fort Myers on Monday, May 3. He has thrown the game out and ordered it to be replayed as part of a double-header at Fort Myers on June 17."[310] Asher's decision was made based on the fact the umpire Dillon admitted he made the wrong call and did not correct the decision. Fort Myers was given ten days to respond to the protest and provide reason why the protest should not be upheld but the Palms did not reply. Asher's ruling was supported by Mike Sexton, president of the National Association of Professional Baseball Clubs.[311] The Palms won the game on May 3, so one win was removed from the Palms record. "Buck Conroy has a scrapping, corking good outfit, but the boys at times seem a bit too anxious."[312]

Asher also reported the result of the votes to raise the player limit to 14 and the salary limit to $2,400, exclusive of the manager. Team presidents voted these proposals down 5 to 2. St. Petersburg and Orlando voted for the increases; Lakeland abstained.

Finally, Mr. Asher acknowledged he was aware of protests claiming violations of the two-class-men rule. He cited the penalties for violations and said his office would enforce the penalties if any violations occurred.[313]

In Bradenton, Larry Lariscy stepped down (or otherwise) as manager of the seventh-place Growers. Dixie Parker, Bradenton catcher [who played for the major league Philadelphia Phillies in 1923],[314] was named temporary manager. Fans disappointment with the Growers' performance on the field has led to a dramatic reduction in attendance.[315]

On the field in Sanford: The Palms rally for three runs in the ninth to beat the Sanford Celeryfeds 5 to 3 and are tied with Lakeland and Sarasota for first place in the Florida State League.[316]

May 18, 1926:

Off the field: The Palms acquired Hal Fisher from Augusta in the South Atlantic League.

Palms Business Manager H. B. Mayer was with the team in Sanford. Concerned about attendance for the home series against Sarasota, he wired home an incentive for fans.[317] Palms team secretary, W. H. Merrill, announced a $25 prize would be given to a lucky fan during the Sarasota series this week at Terry Park. The winning number will be drawn from the stubs of all tickets redeemed on Thursday, Friday, and Saturday, and the ticket holder will receive the prize. The winning number will be announced at Saturday's game.[318]

On the field: For the first time in franchise history, the Palms were shut out 8-0, by the Celeryfeds. Sanford Pitcher Ben Cantwell [who would spend the next 10 years in the major leagues with the New York Giants and Boston Braves][319] limited the Palms to four hits.[320]

The highlight of the game was a triple play made by the Palms. Sanford Third Baseman Lee Crowe led off the bottom of the fifth inning with a double; then Center Fielder Otto Dumas beat out a bunt. First Baseman Frank Bailey hit a hard bouncer to the Palms' Jack O'Reilly at short. O'Reilly tossed to Cliff Chancey at second, retiring Dumas. Chancey threw to Joe Domingo at first and Bailey was out. Domingo then fired the ball to Joe Johnston at the plate who tagged out Crowe trying to score.[321]

May 19, 1926:

Off the field: Palms President John W. Hendry, returned to Fort Myers from New York. He was there negotiating to acquire another pitcher for the Palms but was unable to close the deal. Mr. Hendry expects to make an announcement during the Sarasota series.[322]

On the field: Palms Center Fielder Philip Grandio made a great catch on a short fly ball to center and doubled up a Sanford runner at second. The game was delayed due to both teams arguing with umpires. Sanford Pitcher John Wilson [who would make pitching appearances for the major league Boston Red Sox in 1927 and 1928][323] four-hit the Palms, helping to ensure a 5 to 1 victory for the Celeryfeds.[324]

After the game: The Palms boarded their deluxe bus to begin the journey back to Fort Myers. It was expected the team would ride as far south as Lakeland or Bartow and spend the night; then complete the journey to Fort Myers in the morning.[325]

<u>May 20, 1926</u>:

Off the field: The Palms' luxury team bus came to a stop in Fort Myers at 4:00 a.m. The fourth-place team made the trip directly from Sanford, skipping the planned stopover in Lakeland or Bartow. The players went to their quarters to get some sleep before they would board the bus again and head out to Terry Park to begin a series against the Sarasota Gulls.

Palms Business Manager H. B. Mayer arrived in Fort Myers an hour ahead of the team bus. Mayer announced that Tommy Condon, who had been acquired from Bradenton on May 15, had been released.[326] Mayer also confirmed Palms' home games will begin at 4:00 p.m. instead of 3:00 p.m. from now on to accommodate businessmen who want to attend the games.[327]

The Gulls will begin the series without their manager, Ivy Olson, former Brooklyn major leaguer, who was indefinitely released last night by league President J. B. Asher. In the ninth inning of yesterday's Sarasota and Orlando game, Umpire Walker and Manager Ivy Olson were both placed under arrest and later released on bond.[328] After Umpire Walker called a third strike on Olson in the ninth inning, Olson hit Walker, knocking him to the ground. This triggered bleacher fans to rush out onto the field, and police had to be called to restore the peace. Olson claimed Walker used foul language.[329]

Ivy Olson was seated in the stands for this afternoon's game at Terry Park. Olson knew the umpires had instructions to enforce his suspension and he would not cause any trouble. He spoke with reporters, telling them his side of the story about the argument with Umpire Walker.[330]

Leonard Mayo, a right-handed pitcher acquired from Augusta, joined the Palms yesterday. In addition, Joe Casares, brother of Palms Left Fielder Faustino Casares, is at Terry Park for a pitching tryout.[331]

On the field: The game-time temperature in Fort Myers was 89 degrees. Home plate Umpire George Tandy took the brunt of three foul tips during the game. Tandy seemed unphased by the shots. When he was not behind the plate, Tandy was a center on Jim Thorpe's Tampa Cardinals barnstorming football team. Sarasota scored in the tenth inning to beat the Palms 4 to 3.[332]

After the game: Palms President John W. Hendry released Buck Conroy as manager of the team. Mr. Hendry explained that he and Conroy had been on friendly terms, but Conroy no longer had the support of the fans. Hendry believed a change in manager was in the best interest of the team and the city. Not all fans were surprised to hear Conroy had been fired. They cited the use of profane language, accusation of throwing games, gamblers influencing games, and severe criticism by fans about how games were being managed.[333] Conroy said he had no hard feelings toward anyone. Hendry said, "We are all grateful to Conroy for his pioneering work here and for assembling the club which we are determined to support with every means at our disposal." When asked about reports that Conroy was replaced at the insistence of gamblers who have lost money during the Palms' slump, Hendry made an emphatic denial, claiming he made the decision himself and it was not influenced by the opinions of fans or stockholders of the club. Catcher Joe Johnston was named temporary manager of the team.[334]

May 21, 1926:

Off the field: Former Manager Buck Conroy left Fort Myers on the afternoon train. He was headed for his home in Wichita, Kansas. Conroy expects he'll find work as a major league scout.[335]

Palms Vice President S. W. Lawler addressed fans before the start of the game. He asked them to refrain from betting.[336] Mr. Lawler explained that betting in the ballpark was prohibited, and anyone caught betting would be arrested and prosecuted to the fullest extent of the law.[337]

On the field: The game-time temperature in Fort Myers was 84 degrees. Gene Davenport pitched a five-hit shutout. In the seventh inning, Davenport smashed a triple to deep center field. He was completely exhausted by the time he reached third base. Leonard Mayo went to the bullpen and began warming up, but Davenport stayed in the game and blanked the Gulls in the final two innings. Manager Johnston's Palms won 2 to 0.[338] [The losing pitcher for Sarasota was Jumbo Brown. Brown appeared in two games in 1925 for the major league Chicago Cubs. After spending the 1926 season with the Sarasota Gulls, Brown moved through several major league rosters from 1927 – 1941 including the Cleveland Indians, New York Yankees, Cincinnati Reds, and New York Giants.][339]

After the game: The Sarasota Baseball Club released Ivy Olson as manager of the Gulls citing public opinion. Harry Manush was named interim manager.[340] Mr. Olson planned to return to Orlando in the morning.

May 22, 1926:

Off the field: Orlando Manager Phil Wells resigned citing an illness in his family. Wells becomes the fourth of eight league managers to be replaced during the week. Local businessman Jim Black has been working out with the Colts the past three weeks and will serve as manager on an interim basis.[341] Black pitched for Orlando (then the Caps) in 1920, then pitched the following two years for the Tampa Smokers.[342]

Palms Business Manager H. B. Mayer sent an unprecedented telegraph to President J. B. Asher of the Florida State League complimenting the work of umpires Tandy and Rollins; they were the most competent officials Mayer had seen this season.[343]

Mr. Alvin Gorton, a Fort Myers Realtor and member of the Chamber of Commerce, won the $25 cash prize and generously donated it back to the club.[344]

On the field: Afternoon rain delayed the start of the game until 4:10 p.m. The game-time temperature in Fort Myers was 88 degrees. Cliff Chancey, Philip Grandio, and Faustino Casares hit consecutive singles in the bottom of the twelfth inning to give the Palms back-to-back wins, 7 to 6.

<u>May 23, 1926</u>: No game today. The Palms boarded their luxury bus and left Fort Myers at 1:00 p.m. headed to St. Petersburg for a three-game series with the Saints.[345]

<u>May 24, 1926</u>:

Off the field: John W. Hendry announced Fridays would be Ladies' Day for the rest of the season. He also announced a number of improvements that would be made to the Terry Park stadium including: An elevated press box would be built behind home plate to provide news reporters an enhanced view of the game; bleachers would be relocated from the left field line to opposite first base (though they would be placed far enough down so as not to block the view from cars parked next to the club house); and canvas awnings would be placed behind the grandstand to protect spectators' backs from the hot afternoon sun.[346]

Palms Business Manager H. B. Mayer claimed several citizens had sent letters to him indicating their interest in purchasing stock in the team. The letters had been lost when they were forwarded to him while he was traveling. He implored these fans to see him at once.[347]

On the field in St. Petersburg: The final out of a Mike Bouza to Cliff Chancey to Hal Fisher double play was captured by a *St. Petersburg Times* photographer and appeared in the newspaper the following day. In the photo, Saints Manager George Block is running full speed through first base. Included in the photo are Umpire Meikle and Palms First Baseman Hal Fisher.[348]

Saints Pitcher Vivi Hewitt limited the Palms to four hits; St. Petersburg beat Fort Myers 9 to 0.[349]

<u>May 25, 1926</u>:

Off the field: The St. Petersburg Saints had to cut Third Baseman Kitty Wickham, and Palms Manager Joe Johnston was quick to sign him up.[350]

On the wet field: For the first time in franchise history, the Palms game was rained out in St. Petersburg. The day off cost the Palms one spot in the standings. Now in the sixth position of eight teams, the Palms are only one-and-one-half games out of first place. It was not clear if the rained-out game would result in a double-header the next day or not.[351]

May 26, 1926:

Off the field: Florida State League President J. B. Asher, with the approval of Mike Sexton, president of the National Association of Professional Baseball Clubs, threw out six victories of the St. Petersburg Saints that were protested by the managers of the opposing teams, alleging St. Petersburg violated the two-class player rule. Sanford would have three losses removed, Tampa two, and Orlando one.[352]

The league confirmed the Palms and Saints will play the first double-header of the season today beginning at 2:30 p.m. at Waterfront Park.[353]

On the field: Gene Davenport pitched seven shutout innings in the first game but weakened in the eighth, giving up four runs to the Saints. St. Petersburg won the first game 4 to 3.

In the second game, Joe Domingo three-hit the Saints. The Palms won 3 to 1. The two teams agreed to end the second game after seven innings.[354]

May 27, 1926:

Off the field: The Bradenton Growers filed a protest with Florida State League President J. B. Asher claiming Sanford played more than two class men in the three-game series just completed. Bradenton requested the two games the Growers lost be thrown out.[355]

Palms President John W. Hendry announced he obtained Pat Doran, a third baseman from Knoxville in the South Atlantic league. Hendry also shared that he had been offered two players by Lakeland in a trade for Cecil McRae, but he was not willing to part with McRae.

Mr. Hendry also announced improvements to Terry Park had been completed, including the first-base side bleachers and new press box and would be available for use during the next home game.[356]

On the wet field: The game-time temperature at Terry Park was 88 degrees.[357] The Celeryfeds' Ben Cantwell, the best pitcher in the Florida State League, was in complete control of the game. With the Celeryfeds leading 4 to 0 in the top of the fourth, an intense downpour came over Terry Park. After waiting 30 minutes, the umpires ruled the field too slippery to play, and the game was called off and a double-header was scheduled for Saturday.[358]

May 28, 1926:

Off the field: H. B. Mayer, business manager of the Palms, announced May 31 and June 1 would be Merchant Days in Fort Myers. On those days, Mr. Mayer or another club official will visit each merchant in town requesting they give $5 to support the Palms. In exchange, the merchant will be given a complimentary admission ticket for each person the merchant employs.[359]

"'The Fort Myers franchise is in grave danger,' declared Mr. Mayer. 'We must have money and have it quick. The buying of new ball players to give Fort Myers a pennant winner has practically exhausted our funds,' he said. Mr. Mayer was very emphatic in his appeal declaring, 'This is not my ball club or your ball club, but it is ours, and everyone must put his shoulder to the wheel.'"[360]

On the field: The temperature in Fort Myers was 90 degrees.[361] Newcomers Pat Doran and Kitty Wickham were solid at the plate leading the Palms 17-hit, 13 to 4 trouncing of the Celeryfeds. 1,500 fans at Terry Park enjoyed seeing Umpire Walker eject Sanford Catcher Wallace from the game for arguing loudly in opposition of a call.[362]

May 29, 1926:

Off the field: H. B. Mayer, business manager for the Palms, announced he had 25 local baseball fans enlisted to call upon Fort Myers merchants

Monday. The goal was to solicit $5 from each Merchant during Merchant Days Monday and Tuesday, to support the Palms. The group would meet at the Hendry Brothers office on Monday to divide the city into sections.[363]

On the field: The game-time temperature in Fort Myers was 90 degrees.[364] The first game of double-header began at 2:30 p.m. A heavy downpour interrupted the game in the eighth inning. The teams would eventually complete the first game with Sanford winning 6 to 4. Rain persisted and the field was too wet to play the second game.[365]

May 30, 1926: No game today. The Pedrazas Brothers hosted a party Sunday afternoon at Fort Myers Beach for the Palms, their wives, and friends. A chicken dinner was served.[366]

May 31, 1926: The game-time temperature at Terry Park was 88 degrees.[367] Joe Domingo pitched shutout ball through three innings. In the fourth inning, the thumb on Domingo's pitching hand was injured on a toss back to the mound from Catcher Joe Johnston. Domingo struggled through the next few batters and Johnston was forced to replace him with Leonard Mayo who blanked Bradenton the rest of the game. The Palms beat the Growers 6 to 2.[368]

"With the team's infield, outfield, batting, and pitching strength greatly improved during the last few days, President John W. Hendry is getting mighty optimistic concerning the Palms. It's early yet, but he can even now see visions of a pennant flapping out at Terry Park."[369]

END OF MAY
FLORIDA STATE LEAGUE[370]

	W.	L.	PCT.
Sanford	18	9	.667
Lakeland	18	12	.600
FORT MYERS	**17**	**15**	**.531**
Bradenton	18	16	.529
Tampa	16	15	.516
Orlando	15	15	.500
St. Petersburg	11	17	.393
Sarasota	10	24	.294

June 1926 – Financial Insecurity is Exactly What the League was Trying to Avoid

<u>June 1, 1926</u>: The temperature at Terry Park was 88 degrees.[371] Cecil McRae held Bradenton to four hits leading the Palms to a 3 to 1 victory over the Growers. In the bottom of the fifth inning, Cliff Chancey doubled down the left field line scoring Cecil McRae. Chancey advanced to third on a passed ball. Faustino Casares walked putting runners at the corners. Casares and Chancey flawlessly executed a double steal, giving the Palms their second run of the inning.[372]

<u>June 2, 1926</u>:

Off the field: Florida State League President J. B. Asher announced former Sarasota Manager Ivy Olson is suspended for the remainder of the season for striking Umpire Walker on May 19.[373]

On the field: The temperature in Fort Myers was 88 degrees.[374] The Palms combined for 16 hits to complete a series sweep of the Bradenton Growers. The score was 7 to 2.

Jack O'Reilly had an amazing day in the field including participating in three double plays. In the fourth inning, Gene Davenport hit a triple that rolled to the Orangewood sign on the fence in left field. In the sixth inning, Faustino Casares did the same, rolling his shot to the Russel Park sign.[375] [Orangewood and Russel Park were real estate developments in Fort Myers.]

After the game: The Palms were treated to another meal at the Venetian Garden restaurant courtesy of President John W. Hendry and his business partner and real estate broker, L. Budde Shilling.

W. W. Way, a local fan, spoke about the winning spirit. Umpire Mielke, who called the game at Terry Park the previous day, had joined the team for dinner. The umpire limited his comments to thanking Mr. Shilling and Mr. Hendry for the meal.

John W. Hendry, the Palms' president, spoke, and "declared that he wanted a fighting team, winning or losing. 'If you fight and lose, I am satisfied; and if you fight and win, I appreciate it that much more.'"

H.B. Mayer, the Palms business manager, was not at the dinner. He was busy collecting money to cover the cost of the teams' trip to Orlando. "'We are working with our backs to the wall,' Mr. Mayer said. 'Yesterday's attendance was the poorest of the season, yet we swept the series from Bradenton. Fort Myers fans must support the club or do without baseball.'"[376]

"The Palms left immediately after dinner for Orlando."[377]

June 3, 1926: The Palms rallied for 3 runs in the eighth inning beating Orlando 3 to 1 and running their current winning streak to four games.[378]

June 4, 1926:

Off the field in Fort Myers: John W. Hendry announced the Palms had signed Pitcher Larry Schacht, the brother of Washington Senators comedian, Al Schacht. If Schacht is added to the roster, the Palms will have to release a member of the team, but Hendry did not have any thoughts as to who that would be.[379]

On the field in Orlando: Philip Grandio hit a two-run home run, but it was one of only five Palms' hits. Orlando beat the Palms 5 to 2.[380]

June 5, 1926:

Off the field in Fort Myers: H. B. Mayer announced "'None of the passes now out will be honored at the gate Monday. Because of losses, all holders of passes must call at the business office before game time and receive new ones, which are of a different color.'"[381]

On the field in Orlando: Gene Davenport hit a solo home run in the top of the 12th to win the final game of the series for the Palms, 3 to 2.[382]

After the game: The Palms boarded their luxury team bus and began the journey home to Fort Myers.

June 6, 1926: No game today.

The Palms bus arrived from Orlando into Fort Myers at 6 a.m. Sunday morning. Howard Johnson, a tall right-hander that pitched for Lakeland last season and who has been working out with Jacksonville in the Southeastern League, accompanied the team on the journey.

Larry Schact, the pitcher signed last week, wired team President John W. Hendry asking to postpone his trip from New York a couple more days; Mr. Hendry agreed.[383]

June 7, 1926:

Off the field: After speaking at the Fort Myers Rotary luncheon at the Elks Club[384] earlier in the day, A. A. Coult, the secretary of the Fort Myers Chamber of Commerce, enjoyed the Palms game from the press box. He met with club officials including team President John W. Hendry and "pledged the moral support of the chamber to the Palms."[385]

On the field: The game-time temperature in Fort Myers was 88 degrees.[386] Gene Davenport gave up just 5 hits and the Palms beat the

Highlanders 4 to 1. It was Davenport's third consecutive victory. Pat Doran scored the Palms fourth run in the third inning – this was the Palms 200th run of the season.[387]

A spectacle developed in the second inning when Lakeland Manager Roy Ellam charged the press box and nearly got into a fistfight with Charley Kline, the official scorer of the game. Ellam tried one of the oldest tricks in Minor League Baseball – sending in a good hitter where a weak hitter was scheduled to bat. The official announcer called this to Ellam's attention, and the Palms questioned Umpire Walker. It turned out the umpire had not been given a copy of the batting order, but the official scorer had, and Dean was listed before Cusack. Umpire Walker sided against Ellam and Dean had to bat. Dean forced Ellam at third.[388] [389]

"The game was played before the smallest crowd of the season".[390]

<u>June 8, 1926</u>: The game-time temperature at Terry Park was 88 degrees.[391] The Highlanders scored four runs in the first inning and chased Palms starter Howard Johnson from the mound. Leonard Mayo relieved Johnson and held Lakeland to no runs on four hits the rest of the way, but Frank Sproul, the Highlanders rookie pitcher, held the Palms to the same. The Highlanders beat the Palms 4 to 0.

"The game was again played before one of the smallest crowds of the season."[392]

<u>June 9, 1926</u>: The temperature in Fort Myers was 92 degrees.[393] Pitching prospect Larry Schacht arrived from New York and worked out with the Palms. The Highlanders and Palms waited out an early afternoon shower, but in the end, Umpire Walker called the game off.[394]

<u>June 10, 1926</u>: The temperature at Terry Park was 78 degrees.[395] Rain delayed the start of the game between the Sarasota Gulls and the Fort Myers Palms. When the rain dissipated and sawdust had been spread around the bases, the two teams agreed to play a seven-inning game.

In the second inning, Palms Left Fielder Faustino Casares hit a two-run home run that rolled to the Alvin Gorton [Realtor] sign in left field.

At the end of the seventh inning, the Sarasota players began gathering their bats to leave. Umpire Walker informed them the score was tied 2 to 2 and the game must continue. Pitchers, George Lanning of the Gulls and Cecil McRae of the Palms, each pitched another four innings of shutout baseball before Umpire Walker called the game due to darkness.[396]

"The game was played before a handful of people."[397]

June 11, 1926: The temperature at Terry Park was 90 degrees,[398] but rain prevented baseball from being played.[399]

June 12, 1926:

Off the field: Palms Pitcher Cy Williams is suspended from the team roster so that Pitcher Larry Schacht can be evaluated.

On the field: The temperature in Fort Myers was 90 degrees.[400] Two games were scheduled for today. Thursday's rained-out game was to begin at 10:30 a.m., and the regularly scheduled game for today would start at 4:00 p.m.[401]

The Palms won the first game 11 to 8. In the bottom of the fourth inning, Palms Pitcher Gene Davenport hit into an inning-ending double play, short to third to second. In the bottom of the fifth, Palms Left Fielder Faustino Casares scored when he and Right Fielder Kitty Wickham pulled off a double steal. Turner, the Gulls' first baseman, tripled to the Tamiami City [development] sign in left center. In the bottom of the eighth inning, with bases loaded, the Palms Third Baseman Pat Doran stole home on a called third strike to McRae.

The heat was a factor during the later innings of the game.[402] When Gene Davenport left the game in the seventh inning, "there was only a slight difference between the color of his face and the color of his dark red sweater."

The Palms lost the second game, a seven-inning contest, 1 to 0.[403]

June 13, 1926: No game today.

June 14, 1926: The Palms left in the morning for Sarasota.[404] Palms Pitcher Joe Domingo held the Gulls to 3 hits; Palms win 3-0.[405]

June 15, 1926:

Off the field: H. B. Mayer, Palms business manager, announced a battle royal championship will take place tomorrow at 8:00 p.m. at Terry Park in Fort Myers for the benefit of the Fort Myers Baseball Club. Eight men will battle in an 18-foot ring, winner takes all. Mayer explained the team is hard-pressed for money, and something must be done to save the franchise. Mayer extended a special invitation to ladies. "The show will be fast and furious, but clean," said Mayer. "A small admission fee is required, and no passes will be honored." [406]

On the field: First Baseman Mike Bouza's two doubles combined with Cecil McRae's solid pitching led the Palms to a 4 to 2 victory over Sarasota.[407]

June 16, 1926:

On the field: The start of the game was delayed an hour while a terrific downpour soaked the field.[408] Back in Fort Myers, "the Arcade Cigar stand didn't get the returns because Western Union thought the affair had been called off." Sarasota beat the Palms 5 to 2 to avoid a series sweep.[409]

After the game and back in Fort Myers: More than 200 boxing fans made the trek to Terry Park to witness a battle royal for the benefit of the Fort Myers Baseball Club. After a few fast rounds of boxing, the men got down to the main event. A no-holds-barred, no-weight-limit, free-for-all in an 18-foot ring. H. B. Mayer indicated there would be another battle royal soon for the same cause. Mayer believed attendance was less than anticipated due to unfavorable weather.[410] [The temperature at 8:00

p.m. in Fort Myers that evening was likely 83 degrees, having peaked at 88 degrees during the afternoon.]

June 17, 1926:

Off the field: Two games were scheduled to be played at Terry Park today between the Orlando Colts and the Palms. One is the replay of the game Orlando successfully protested on May 3.

Allred Jewelry company announced they will give a silver baseball to each Fort Myers player making a safe hit during today's games.[411]

On the field: The temperature in Fort Myers was 86 degrees.[412]

The Palms scored nine runs in the third inning of the first game. The offense was led by Mike Bouza, who hit a home run to right center field and Jack O'Reilly, who tripled to the Tamiami City sign in left center.[413] In the field, the Palms turned four double plays. The Palms won the first game 15 to 5.

The Palms won the second game 2 to 1. Palms Manager and Catcher Joe Johnston felt ill and took himself out of the lineup for the game, inserting Second Baseman Cliff Chancey in his place. Chancey cut down four Colts trying to steal second base during the game. Chancey had caught 102 games in the Louisiana State League in 1925.[414]

The games were played before a large and enthusiastic crowd of fans.[415]

[A quick scan of the box scores indicates 10 of the Palms earned a silver baseball from Allred Jewelry company.]

June 18, 1926:

Off the field: Palms Pitcher Larry Schact was suspended until either he or another member of the team is released.[416]

On the field: The game time temperature at Terry Park was 92 degrees.[417] The Colts' Haskell Verble, a former Orlando high school pitcher, made his

Florida State League pitching debut. The rookie walked two, struck out two, and gave up 15 hits, including a triple to Cy Williams. The Palms scored 6 times in the fifth inning and beat the Colts for the third time in two days, 7 to 4. [418]

June 19, 1926: The temperature in Fort Myers was 92 degrees.[419] The Colts hammered Gene Davenport for all the runs they would need in the first inning and beat the Palms 3 to 2. Leonard Mayo relieved Davenport in the third and pitched shutout baseball the final seven innings. Mike Bouza and Jack O'Reilly both hit triples.[420]

June 20, 1926: No game today.

June 21, 1926: Beneath blue skies and a 90-degree[421] sun, approximately 250 fans were gathered in front of the Arcade cigar store in downtown Fort Myers to hear the play-by-play returns of the Palms game in Sanford via a special Western Union service arranged by the Pedrazas brothers, the owners of the store. The crowd was disappointed to learn the game was postponed due to rain.[422]

June 22, 1926:

Off the field: In Fort Myers, Palms Business Manager H. B. Mayer announced a second boxing bout at Terry Park would take place Thursday night at 9:00 p.m. for the benefit of the Fort Myers Baseball Club. General admission seats cost $1.00 and box seats $2.00.

Mayer also announced a carload of clay arriving from Bartow, Florida, would be added to the infield dirt at Terry Park to help prevent standing water after rains. The placement of the clay will be supervised by E. N. Stanley, a Fort Myers city engineer. "When we do that, we will have one of the fastest diamonds in the state," said Mayer.[423]

On the field: The first game of the scheduled double-header between the Palms and the Sanford Celeryfeds was interrupted twice by rain. Philip Grandio was called out on his third attempt to bunt.[424] The teams were tied 0 to 0 after five innings when a heavy downpour persisted, and the game was called. The second game never began.[425]

<u>June 23, 1926</u>:

On the field: The Palms split a double header with the Celeryfeds. In the first game, the Celeryfeds two-hit the Palms in a 9-inning 6-0 shutout. Larry Schact pitched in relief for the Palms. Domingo three-hit Sanford in the 7-inning second game giving the Palms a 2-0 victory and ending Sanford's 13 consecutive game winning streak.[426]

The Palms boarded their luxury bus and headed to Orlando to prepare for their series with the Colts that would begin the next day.

After the game: Palms President John W. Hendry made a formal announcement that the Fort Myers Baseball Club franchise would be surrendered at the end of the first half of the Florida State League season on July 3. Hendry explained the club was costing more than the money that was coming in, and he did not have confidence ticket sales would achieve the volume needed to cover the expenses during the second half of the season. Mr. Hendry said the team had canvassed the town for contributions, and he had spent every penny he had available in advancing money to cover team expenses.

"'It will take $5,000 to carry us through the second half and the only prospect we have is an appropriation of $2,000 by the county commission when it meets July 7 to prepare its budget,' Mr. Hendry said. 'We have exhausted every other source of contributions and can see no hope of getting the necessary funds.' The club is now in debt, but Mr. Hendry thought it would be possible to settle all obligations by quitting July 3. He has a $2,000 forfeit posted with the league treasury to guarantee finishing the season and hopes to get this money back. A number of the players are also saleable. From funds received for them and with the league guarantee, it is thought all debts can be discharged.'"

Another possibility would be the outright sale of the team. Mr. Hendry announced that H. B. Mayer sent wires offering the team to officials in Clearwater and Leesburg who are known to have been negotiating with Sarasota to acquire the Gulls' franchise. The Sarasota team has been on the market for some time and the owners have made clear they intend to exit the league at the end of the first half.[427]

<u>June 24, 1926</u>:

Off the field: Baseball fans were reminded of the opportunity to support the Palms at Terry Park this evening. They could "hear the impact of gloves against jowl or ribs instead of the smack of the bat against the horsehide" during the second boxing match and battle royal for the benefit of the Fort Myers Baseball Club.[428]

OH BOYS!

A Big Treat for You and the Girls at the Ball Park

THURSDAY NIGHT, JUNE 24

A Real Boxing Exposition and Battle Royal--Your Money's Worth, and Some Side Splitting Laughs

A REAL CURE FOR THE BLUES

Benefit

Fort Myers Baseball Club

Facsimile of advertisement in *The Fort Myers Press* –
USA TODAY NETWORK, June 23, 1926.[429]

John W. Hendry was asked to appear before the Lions Club. Mr. Hendry explained the financial situation the club was in because of poor attendance at their home games at Terry Park. He explained that $3,000 was needed to ensure the club could make it through the second half of the season. The Lions Club immediately began a campaign to keep the Palms franchise in Fort Myers. The Lions pledged $150 and appointed a committee of Dr. B. Whisnant, Dr. E. P. Bugg, and C. J. Andel to appear before the Chamber of Commerce board of governors at 7:30 tonight to seek their cooperation.

After learning of the Lions commitment to the Palms, Hendry sent a wire to J. B. Asher, president of the Florida State League, protesting all games won by Sanford in which Catcher Wallace had participated. Asher had announced the day before that Wallace had been determined to be a "class man," having played more than 20 games higher than C League. The result was the league-leading Celeryfeds had more than two class men on their roster in violation of league rules.

While Hendry was at lunch, he received wires from the Leesburg Chamber of Commerce asking the price to purchase the franchise, and from the club in Augusta, Georgia, asking if Hendry had a good outfielder for sale.

Mr. Hendry will travel to Orlando tomorrow to meet with league President J. B. Asher.[430]

On the field In Orlando: Prior to the start of the game, Field Day events were conducted by the American Legion. Palms Shortstop Jack O'Reilly won a base-running contest. Cecil McRae tossed a two-hit shutout and the Palms beat the Colts 4 to 0 in a rain-shortened 5-inning game.[431]

After the game in Tampa: After losing ten of eleven games, Tampa Smokers Manager Charlie Allen resigned. He was replaced by Tommy Leach[432] [who played Major League Baseball from 1898 – 1918 for the Louisville Colonels, Pittsburg Pirates, and Chicago Cubs.][433]

After the game in Fort Myers: At a meeting of the Chamber of Commerce board of governors and the Lions' committee, John W. Hendry explained the predicament the team was in. Mr. Hendry explained it would take $3,000, plus the $2,000 expected from the county commission to cover the costs of the team through the second half of the season. Hendry emphasized the benefits to the city of having a Florida State League franchise.

"'In my belief, the city could get no better advertising than it has got and will get through having the baseball team,' Hendry said. 'I do not want Fort Myers to lose the team,' he said repeatedly, 'but I cannot carry the burden as I have been doing the first half. I must have aid.'"

Mr. Hendry said he had put $2,400 into the team and was willing to let it stay if arrangements could be made to finance the team during the remainder of the season. When the season was over, if the team turned a profit, he would accept reimbursement for his investment; but if there was not a profit, he would be satisfied.

Mr. Hendry explained the average daily income and expenses and believed that with several saleable players on the roster, the Palms' books would show a profit at the end of the year.[434]

The Governors agreed that to lose the ball club would be a blow to the city, but they were unable to adjust their budget to provide the full amount needed. The Governors appointed a committee including Clifford Heath, Tom Phillips, J. E. Crafton Jr., A. E. Raymond, and Wm. Silver. The Chamber's committee would meet with the Lions' committee the next day and outline a plan to raise the $3,000 needed to finish the season. Mr. Hendry agreed he would not sell the team or any of the players until the committees had the opportunity to present their plan.[435]

[There is no mention of how successful the Boxing event scheduled for this date was.]

June 25, 1926:

On the field in Orlando: The Colts put newly acquired Pitcher Robert Vines on the mound for the first time. He pitched a complete game.[436] [Vines had made pitching appearances for the major league St. Louis Cardinals in 1924 and the Philadelphia Phillies in 1925.][437]

The Palms rallied for four runs in the first and Jack O'Reilly hit a solo home run in the ninth, but Orlando managed to score six runs in-between to defeat the Palms 6 to 5.[438]

After the game and back in Fort Myers: John W. Hendry hosted a meeting of the committees of the Chamber of Commerce and the Lions Club at his Hendry Brothers Real Estate office. A proposal to reorganize the Fort Myers Baseball Club into a non-profit to be financed by popular subscription and gate receipts was adopted. Members of the two committees told Mr. Hendry they would act as trustees of the club and would work to raise the funds needed to finish the season on the condition that the present owners of the club turn over their interests to the new organization. Mr. Hendry agreed to the plan and stated he did not need to be reimbursed for the money he had already put into the venture.[439]

The drive will come to an end at 5 p.m. on Tuesday, June 29. If, at that time, sufficient funds have been raised, Mr. Hendry would turn over his interest to the trustees of the reorganized club. If the funds are not raised, Mr. Hendry would be free to sell the club.

A committee led by the Lions had already collected $150, largely from Lions Club members, to send to Palms Manager Joe Johnston to cover the current expenses of the team. Another payment will be needed to cover the teams' bills in Orlando where they are currently playing.[440]

Dr. E. P. Bugg, a member of the Lions Club committee explained that donations from citizens would be held until the drive was completed. If the full amount was not raised, all money would be returned to the subscribers. If the desired amount was achieved, the club will be able to finish the season. Any surplus at the end of the season would be carried over to aid in financing the team in 1927.[441]

June 26, 1926:

Off the field in Fort Myers: $895 had been collected by the end of the day by the Lions Club and Chamber of Commerce committee members. The first contributor to the fund was L. M. Stroup, Chief of Police, who donated $25.[442] [$25 in 1926 is about $432 in 2023.[443]]

On the field in Orlando: Cliff Chancey was out when he was hit by a batted ball. The Palms took advantage of three errors by Second Baseman Joe Tinker, Jr., to beat the Colts 6 to 5. The game was played under protest by Palms Manager Joe Johnston because the game was started during a drizzle that continued through the fourth inning.[444]

June 27, 1926: No game today.

Yesterday's donors to the Lions Club Baseball Fund were listed in the *Fort Myers Tropical News.* They included:

L. M. Stroup	$ 25
William F. Grogan	10
C. J. Andel	10
Grand Central Hotel	25
K. C. Hasringer Co.	10
D. M. Parker	5
Chapman-Shirley Electric Co.	10
L. Williams	5
I. D. Hancock	10
James J. McCool	5
George Hyatt	25
S. T. Barlow	5
Princess Coffee Shop	5
Broadway Toggery	5
Pollock Lumber Co.	50
Builders Supply Co.	100
M. Flossie Hill Co.	25
Leon D. Smith	5
Anonymous	10
Roy Cochran	10
Owen L. Lee	5
J. W. McWilliams	50
Piggly-Wiggly	20
Ladies' Haberdasher	25
Vance Will	10
Gorton Realty Co.	25
E. E. Watson	25
W. R. Davis	25
Elmer E. Jones	5
H. A. Stahn	10
J. Harold Davis	15
Rev. J. H. O'Keefe	10
J. D. Lynn	25
Coca-Cola Bottling Co.	25
Schlossberg's Store	5
Walter O. Sheppard	100
Evans Pharmacy	50

Harold Bundy	5
W. A. Sheppard	15
P. W. Irvine	5
H. W. Cramer	5
Anonymous	5
T. J. Swain	5
J. R. Randle	50
Pedrazas Bros.	15
Lee County Motor Co.	5

First Day Total	$ 895 [445]

June 28, 1926:

Off the field: Members of the Lions Club and Chamber of Commerce continued to energetically pursue raising the funds needed to fund the Palms through the second half of the season.[446]

A meeting of Florida State League team presidents would be held in Tampa the next morning to determine whether Sanford will be penalized for playing too many class men. It is possible the games Sanford won during the period they used an extra class man will be thrown out of the standings. "Throwing out of enough games might mean a pennant for the Palms in the first half."[447]

On the field: The temperature in Fort Myers was 84 degrees.[448] McRae picked up his 10th win of the season. The Palms defeated St. Petersburg Saints 5 to 1.[449]

June 29, 1926:

Off the field in Fort Myers: Yesterday's list of donors to the baseball fund appeared in the *Fort Myers Tropical News* and included:

Gonyea and Vanboy	$ 5
Charlie Wolf	10
S. O. Godman	50
Fort Myers Lumber Co.	20

J. S. Gillientine	10
Ray Morgan	5
R. D. Liddell	5
W. M. Harley	10
O. H. Leifeste	25
Bill Moger	5
F. M. Castleberry	10
E. O. Darrow	25
N. G. Stout	25
Mrs. Holland McCormick	5
F. D. Hibble	5
A. D. Moore	5
J. F. Garner	25
N. O. Scott	5
E. P. Shelton	10
W. A. Cornell	2
Fort Myers Produce Co.	5
Order of Owls	25
R. C. Lang Jr.	10
W. F. Gordon	5
Russell Hardin	5
Wilson Starnes	5
W. H. Graham	5
O. S. Poer	5
M. F. Flynn	5
Foy Durrence	5
Boston Store	20
Thompson Grocery	5
J. W. Furen	6
A Friend	10
The Toggery	5
The Vogue	10
W. B. Graham	5
E. M. Goss	5

Yesterday's Total	$422
Saturday's Total	$895

Total to date	$ 1,317[450]

H. B. Mayer, Palms business manager, announced the team will provide fans who do not have automobiles available to them at game time free transportation to Terry Park. The luxury team bus, purchased to transport the players to away games, will be used for this promotion. The first bus will leave from the Hendry Brothers Real Estate office at First and Jackson streets at 3:30 p.m. The second trip at 3:50 p.m. The bus will circle the block bounded by First, Jackson, Main, and Hendry streets and stop at hotels to pick up any out-of-town patrons who would like to attend the game.[451] [The distance from the corner of First Street and Jackson Street in downtown Fort Myers to Terry Park in East Fort Myers is 1.9 miles.[452] It is unclear if the entire stretch of road then known by section as First Street / Dixie Highway / Tamiami Trail / Lee County Boulevard[453] (now known as First Street / Palm Beach Boulevard) from downtown to the fairgrounds was paved in 1926 or not.]

The Lions Club and Chamber of Commerce committee would have a busy day ahead of them. Fundraising efforts through the previous night indicated their efforts were $1,683 short of the $3,000 needed to keep the baseball franchise in Fort Myers. After voting to continue the drive all summer if needed to raise the $3,000, the Lions asked team President John W. Hendry for an extension, but Hendry said he did not consider that advisable. "'It is impossible for me to grant further time,' he said. 'I must meet the payroll of the ball club Thursday morning. If the committee is unable to raise the money, I shall have to obtain the funds in some other way.'"

In Tampa: At a meeting of Florida State League team presidents, six victories of the Sanford Celeryfeds were stricken from the standings because of Catcher Wallace having been a Class A player in violation of league rules. The victories that were disallowed included three wins against St. Petersburg and three against Fort Myers. More victories could have been disallowed but Sanford demonstrated Wallace had been signed without intention of violating the rule.

There was discussion about the distribution of the victories to be overturned. Bradenton, Lakeland, St. Petersburg, and Fort Myers all protested but the decision of which games to disallow considered that Fort Myers was struggling to remain in the league, and St. Petersburg had recently lost several games because of a penalty.

The league boosted salaries from $2,250 a month to $2,400 a month for each team consistent with the national Class D league salary limit.

It was reported by the Associated Press that "the award of the league directors puts Fort Myers in second place with a standing of .615, having 32 victories to 20 defeats. Sanford leads with 27 wins and 14 losses. There are four games to play. If Sanford should lose three and Fort Myers win three out of four, the championship would go to the Palms."[454]

On the field: The game-time temperature in Fort Myers was 88 degrees.[455] Joe Domingo pitched eleven strong innings for the Palms, but he tired in the final stanza. The Saints scored three runs in the top of the twelfth to defeat the Palms 5 to 2.[456] A scout for the New York Yankees was reported to have been in attendance for the games at Terry Park on June 28 and 29.[457]

After the game: Late in the evening, members of the Lions and Chamber committees met in disappointment. They had only collected $1,740.50 of the $3,000 needed. They decided there was nothing more they could do and made plans to return the money to each donor. They waited until after midnight for John W. Hendry to arrive back in town from the league meetings in Tampa, where the Palms had been moved into second place and mathematically could win the first half pennant. Mr. Hendry met with the committee for more than an hour. They decided the president of the Baseball Club should accompany the committee as they return the money to each person. Mr. Hendry would ask each donor to transfer their donation from the trust fund to the ball club itself. If most or all donors agreed to this plan Mr. Hendry believed the Palms could be financed for the remainder of the season.[458]

June 30, 1926:

Off the field: Yesterday's list of donors to the baseball fund appeared in the *Fort Myers Tropical News* and included:

Donald S. Foley	$ 10
A. J. Kelley	5
A. Friend	25
Henry Bartley	10

W. B. Gibson	5
N. J. Reid	5
N. D. Griffis	5
Cash	25
G. E. Jones	5
P. O. McGinley	5
A. N. Strickland	5
John Bomar	5
Cash	5
Anonymous	5
J. C. Tucker	5
Palmee Park Corp.	50
Joe Sandberg	5
H. E. Yelvington	5
Broadway Barber Shop	5
J. B. Garfunkle	25
M. T. Reed	10
C. G. Langford	10
Cash	10
G. C. Coyer	5
W. J. James	2.50
Roy Hanchey	15
C. M. Foxworthy	10
J. M. Barron	5
Foxworthy & Lee	10
E. L. Evans	15
Allan Moseley	10
Grover Hackney	5
Earl Blackman	10
J. E. Shaefner	5
W. W. Shiver	5
H. H. Burns	10
J. S. Tarrer	10
A. D. French	5
H. B. Turner	5
T. Schmidt	5
D. H. Lamons	10
Ernest Shipman	25
Chapman & Shirley	25
F. M. Lanier	5

Royal Palm Cafeteria	25
"Jiggs"	10
The Grocerteria	10
S. Loeb	5
R. T. Branham	5
Cash	1
Seminole Cafe	5
Palace Billiard Hall	10
Jackson J. Sells	10

Total	$ 423.50
Previously Received	1,217.00

Total	$ 1,740.50[459]

On the field: The temperature at Terry Park was 90 degrees. The Palms piled on five runs in the bottom of the eighth and beat the Saints 8 to 2 to close out the three-game series.[460] The crowd was one of the best and most enthusiastic of the season.[461]

After the game: After spending the day requesting donors to the Lions Club fund transfer their subscriptions to the Fort Myers Baseball Club, John W. Hendry felt enough encouragement to retain the franchise for the second half of the season. Most donors approved the request. Many donors offered words of encouragement to Mr. Hendry and the Palms. A few supporters went so far as to suggest he come around again if the effort falls short and additional funds are needed. More than $1,000 had been moved into the ball clubs account, and Mr. Hendry believed after they called on the remainder of the donors the next day, they would end the campaign with between $1,600 and $1,700. "'I think it is a sure go,' said Mr. Hendry, 'and the credit belongs to the Lions. The work of the committee has been invaluable. They saved the ball club after I had abandoned hope.' … 'I have found that Fort Myers really wants league baseball, a point on which I have frequently of late had some doubt.'"[462]

END OF JUNE
FLORIDA STATE LEAGUE[463]

	W.	L.	PCT.
Sanford	28	14	.667
FORT MYERS	**33**	**20**	**.623**
Lakeland	31	19	.620
St. Petersburg	28	23	.549
Bradenton	26	33	.441
Orlando	24	32	.429
Tampa	23	31	.426
Sarasota	18	38	.321

July 1926 – Play On, Palms!

<u>July 1, 1926</u>:

Off the field: The Lions Club held their weekly luncheon at the Elks Club yesterday. Ernest Shipman congratulated the members on their efforts to raise a fund to carry the Fort Myers Baseball Club through the season. Shipman acknowledged the Lions had fallen short of the quota set, but the enthusiasm the effort aroused was an invaluable benefit to the club and it showed the people of Fort Myers the club was really in danger of having to drop out of the league and needed the support of the community.[464]

Florida State League President J. B. Asher clarified the league standings are:

	W.	L.	PCT.
Sanford	31	17	.646
Lakeland	30	19	.612
FORT MYERS	**33**	**23**	**.589**

This meant the punishment to Sanford was not as had been reported in newspapers the past couple of days. It had been reported that six victories were taken away from Sanford and three losses each from St. Petersburg and Fort Myers. Instead, the club owners took away three

Sanford wins and added three Sanford losses but did not alter the standings of the other teams.

The implication for Fort Myers was that to win the first half pennant, the Palms would need to win all four games against Sanford, and they needed St. Petersburg to win at least one game in their series against Lakeland.[465]

On the field: The temperature at Terry Park was 88 degrees.[466]

The Palms learned via telegram prior to the game they needed to win all four games against the visiting Celeryfeds to win the first half pennant. They approached the game with great determination. Doran was out on the base paths when he was hit by a batted ball.

The Palms argued every call that was debatable and even a few that were not. In the eighth inning, Palms Shortstop Jack O'Reilly made an error on a ground ball that resulted in two runs for Sanford. O'Reilly claimed he was interfered with, and a long argument with the umpires ensued. Palms Manager Joe Johnston protested the game on the grounds that the interference that prevented O'Reilly from making a play which might have changed the result of the game.

When the dust settled, Sanford had won the game 10 to 7 and in doing so, had mathematically eliminated Fort Myers from the pennant race.[467]

After the game: A few passionate fans at Terry Park were unable to control their frustration, and one of them threw a pop bottle at the umpires. The bottle struck Umpire Rollins in the back of the neck, and a noisy argument followed. A newspaper reporter reminded fans that throwing bottles or razzing umpires after the game is over does nothing to change the outcome of the game and risks giving Fort Myers a reputation for poor sportsmanship.[468]

July 2, 1926:

Off the field in Sarasota: A mass meeting of all civic bodies was scheduled to determine the fate of the Sarasota Baseball Club. An effort to raise the $6,000 needed for the Gulls to remain in the Florida State League for the remainder of the season will be sponsored by the Kiwanis Club of

Sarasota, in cooperation with all other civic organizations. The Gulls have been in last place for nearly the entire season and attendance at home games has suffered as a result. A drive for funds was opened two weeks ago but was unsuccessful.[469]

On the field in Fort Myers: The temperature at Terry Park was 90 degrees.[470] A double and triple by Mike Bouza, a double by Cliff Chancey, and a pretty throw from deep left field by Faustino Casares to get Sanford Left Fielder Dunbar at the plate were among the highlights of the Palms' 6 to 3 victory over the Celeryfeds.[471]

July 3, 1926: The game-time temperature at Terry Park was 90 degrees.[472] The Palms played with a nonchalant and indifferent disposition. Sanford won the first game 5 to 0. The loss mathematically eliminated the Palms from the possibility of a second-place finish. There was discussion about calling off the second game because of the time, but the crowd raised a commotion and the umpires and managers decided to play a 5-inning game. The game was tied at the end of five innings, so the teams played a sixth. Both teams scored a run in the sixth inning. Sanford refused to play additional innings and the game was declared a tie by the umpires.[473]

July 4, 1926: No game today. The City of Fort Myers celebrated the 150th anniversary of the signing of the Declaration of Independence.

The Sanford Celeryfeds won the first half of the 1926 season. The Fort Myers Palms finished in third place.

FIRST HALF FINAL STANDINGS
FLORIDA STATE LEAGUE[474]

	W.	L.	PCT.
Sanford	33	18	.647
Lakeland	30	22	.577
FORT MYERS	**34**	**25**	**.576**
St. Petersburg	30	27	.526
Orlando	27	32	.458
Bradenton	28	34	.452
Tampa	24	33	.421
Sarasota	18	41	.305

The Race for the Second-half Pennant!

<u>July 5, 1926</u>: The Fort Myers Baseball Club traveled to Lakeland to open the second half of the 1926 Florida State League season with a double-header at Lakeland. The Highlanders defeated Fort Myers 8 to 1 in the first game. Cecil McRae led the Palms to a victory over Lakeland in the second game 4 to 1.[475]

<u>July 6, 1926</u>: Fort Myers won the final game of the series against Lakeland 3 to 1. In the bottom of the ninth inning, Highlanders First Baseman Roy Ellam, a former Pittsburg Pirate,[476] hit a line drive that struck Palms Pitcher Gene Davenport in his pitching shoulder before Davenport was able to react. Joe Domingo relieved Davenport and salvaged the win for the Palms.[477]

<u>July 7, 1926</u>: No game today.

<u>July 8, 1926</u>:

On the field in Fort Myers: The Kiwanis Club and Lions Club baseball teams met in battle on the diamond at Terry Park. Tied after six innings, a Kiwanis Club rally in the seventh, combined with errors by the Lions, gave the Kiwanis a 10 to 7 victory.[478] Carl J. Andel served as soft drink dispenser. All proceeds from the game were donated to the Fort Myers Baseball Club.[479]

On the field in Bradenton: The Growers acquired several players recently and appeared to be a much different team than the Palms had seen previously. The Growers beat the Palms 5 to 2.[480] The highlight of the game for the Palms was Pat Doran's home run to deep right field.[481]

<u>July 9, 1926</u>:

Off the field: It was announced today in Fort Myers that passes to the Palms games at Terry Park will no longer be honored unless the season pass holder has paid their subscription in full.[482]

On the field: Palms Third Baseman Pat Doran was ruled out when he was hit by a batted ball while running the bases. Shortstop Jack O'Reilly tripled, and Left Fielder Faustino Casares hit a two-run home run.[483] The Palms broke Mike Kelly's eight-game winning streak defeating Bradenton 7 to 4.[484]

<u>July 10, 1926</u>:

On the field: Dick Richards, the Growers' rookie centerfielder who arrived in Bradenton five days earlier in the week from Wrightsville,[485] Georgia, hit his third home run of the week. Richards hit the ball to deep center field, and he crossed the plate just ahead of the relay arriving to Palms Catcher Joe Johnston. Bradenton fans spontaneously collected $38 to present to Richards for his performance. It was the first time during the 1926 season the Growers fans had honored a player in this way. Bradenton beat Fort Myers 3 to 1.[486]

After the game: The Palms boarded their luxury bus and returned to Fort Myers for the first time in a week. The team would have tomorrow off to rest before playing 7 games in 6 days next week.

<u>July 11, 1926</u>: No game today.

<u>July 12, 1926</u>: The temperature at Terry Park was 92 degrees.[487] Gene Davenport, pitching for the first time since a line drive hit him in his pitching shoulder six days earlier, was in prime condition. He struck out one Tampa Smoker each inning and allowed only five hits. Davenport doubled in the seventh and scored the Palms' only run when Philip Grandio doubled. The Palms beat the Smokers 1 to 0.[488]

July 13, 1926: The temperature in Fort Myers was 92 degrees.[489] The Tampa Smokers' catcher, Al Lopez, had two doubles in the game. [Lopez and Buck Stanton, Smokers first baseman, would both go on to play Major League Baseball. Stanton played for the American League St. Louis Browns in 1931.][490]

In the bottom of the fourth, Cliff Chancey fouled a pitch back that hit Umpire Bradley in the ribs. As Bradley fell to his knees, his ball/strike indicator fell to the ground. After recovering from having the wind knocked out of him, Bradley had to recall the pitch count. The Tampa players argued there were two balls and two strikes on Chancey, while the umpires believed the count was three and two. Umpire Bradley finally turned to the official scorer, and everyone in the press box, including Claude Lee (the local manager of Universal Picture Corporation),[491] and Palms Business Manager H. B. Mayer agreed with the umpire, "that being the first time in history either of them had ever done so."[492]

In the top of the ninth, with two outs and runners on second and third, Smokers Manager, and former Pittsburg Pirate, Tommy Leach, tried to get into Domingo's head when he inserted himself as a pinch-hitter. Unphased, Domingo took a bouncer back to the mound and tossed Leach out at first to end the game.[493] Making the most of just four hits, the Palms handed the Smokers their fifth consecutive loss, 3 to 1.[494]

July 14, 1926:

Off the field in Sarasota: The baseball directors of the Gulls announced they have only been able to raise 20% of the $6,000 needed to cover player salaries and expenses for the remainder of the season. Unless assistance is provided, Sarasota will forfeit its franchise in the Florida State League. Sarasota fans appear to have lost interest in the team due to their poor performance during the first half of the season.[495]

On the field in Fort Myers: The game-time temperature was 92 degrees.[496] In the bottom of the eighth inning, with Kitty Wickham on first, Pat Doran singled to right advancing Wickham to second. Wickham and Doran advanced on a double steal before Mike Bouza grounded out to end the inning. The Palms made it three in a row over the Smokers, sweeping the series with a 5 to 3 victory. Nine games into the second half of the season, the Palms and the Lakeland Highlanders were tied atop the Florida State League standings.[497]

<u>July 15, 1926</u>:

Off the field – the good news: After a conference between Sarasota city officials and leaders of the Sarasota Chamber of Commerce, an announcement was made that local capitalists would underwrite the Gulls, and Sarasota would retain its Florida State League franchise for the remainder of the 1926 season.[498]

Off the field – the bad news: While the Bradenton Growers were arriving in Fort Myers, a headline on the front page of the *Bradenton Herald* newspaper read "BALL CLUB END IS NEAR." The article spelled out for the citizens of Bradenton the sad financial state of the town's professional baseball franchise. E. A. Rood, a director of the Bradenton Baseball association, sent a telegram to Florida State League President J. B. Asher explaining the team had not been able to collect on subscriptions [season tickets] sold at the beginning of the season. The team owed the bank eight hundred dollars; player salaries were paid up to date and the team was in Fort Myers with money to cover their expenses. Beyond that, Mr. Rood saw no path forward other than to quit the league.

Like the situation in Sarasota, officials attributed the financial embarrassment to the failure of local citizens to attend the Growers' home games. Other than opening day and the Fifth of July, attendance in Bradenton had not exceeded 200 fans a game. It was hoped the Chamber of Commerce or other interested citizens might come forward with ideas about how to save the franchise.[499]

On the field: The temperature at Terry Park was 92 degrees.[500] An early afternoon rain shower poured a lot of water on the field, and at 4 p.m., it was still soaking wet. A brief conference was held, and all agreed to wait 45 minutes to see if the field might dry out. In the meantime, Palms Business Manager H. B. Mayer, team President John W. Hendry, Manager Joe Johnston, a couple of kids, the umpires, and some of the ball players worked together to remove the accumulated water from the field. Combined with the sunshine and hot air, the field was ready to play on by 4:45 p.m.

"Just before the game started, an umpire announced a collection would be taken up for Joe Farrar, a former member of the Bradenton team, who has been stricken with tuberculosis and so is very much out of the struggle for a while. The fans responded to the tune of $61.75."[501]

The Palms jumped on the Bradenton Growers with four runs in the bottom of the first and coasted to a 5 to 1 victory.[502]

July 16, 1926: The temperature in Fort Myers was 86 degrees.[503] The Palms faced Bradenton ace Mike Kelly [who, on August 30, 1926, would be sold to the major league Philadelphia Phillies].[504] The Palms could only manage 4 hits against Kelly, but one was by Manager Joe Johnston in the bottom of the ninth. With the Palms down 2 to 1 and bases loaded, Johnston hit a single that scored Pat Doran from third. Mike Bouza tried to score from second but was thrown out at the plate to end the inning. The teams played a scoreless tenth. Dark, overcast skies had been hovering over Terry Park for some time and a heavy rain developed in the tenth inning. The umpires declared the game a tie, 2 to 2, and a double-header was scheduled for the following day beginning at 2 p.m.[505]

The Growers were making so much noise during the game that at one point Umpire Frederick had to shut them up. Manager Parker came out of the dugout to challenge the umpire contending his team had the right to holler, and the umpire agreed.[506]

July 17, 1926:

On the field In Sanford: The Celeryfeds protested in the fourth inning that the Sarasota Gulls were stalling. Umpires agreed and awarded the Celeryfeds a 9 to 0 forfeit victory over the Gulls.[507]

Before the game in Fort Myers: Umpires Frederick and Bradley addressed the crowd announcing there would be a boxing show at Terry Park the following Tuesday, July 20. Palms Business Manager H. B. Mayer confidentially advised those in the press box that two experts were booked, but he could neither confirm nor deny that Jack Delaney, the World light heavyweight champion, was one of them.[508]

On the field in Fort Myers: The game-time temperature was 86 degrees.[509] Bradenton Second Basement Gene Elliott [who played for the major league New York Highlanders in 1911][510] was hitless in four plate appearances.

Suspecting the Growers Pitcher Bucky Wilson had forgotten about him, the Palms' Faustino Casares stole second with Wilson holding the ball in his hand. The Palms beat the Growers 6 to 2 in the first game.

Just three innings into the second game, with the score tied 2 to 2, the drizzle became more intense. Umpire Frederick called the game off and got the crowd out just in time to avoid a severe downpour.[511]

After the game in Bradenton: The Growers returned to Bradenton having played what everyone assumed was their final game of the season. Team officials had notified Florida State League President J. B. Asher they were out of money. Word came from President Asher who was in Asheville, to "hang on until he returns from the mountains of North Carolina."[512] This created angst for Elon Rood, director of the club, who stated the Growers needed $240 immediately to fund their road trip to Orlando this week.[513]

July 18, 1926: No game today.

July 19, 1926: About 30 minutes before the first pitch was scheduled to be thrown in Tampa, a heavy downpour began. The dark clouds moved away by game time, but Plant Field resembled a swimming pool. A double-header was scheduled for the next day between the Palms and the Smokers.[514]

July 20, 1926:

Off the field in Fort Myers: Tonight's featured welterweight boxing match is announced – Young Del Pino of Tampa and Slim Chino of Atlanta will go ten rounds at Terry Park. Kid Alonzo of Tampa and Anderson Avenue Kid of Fort Myers will go four rounds in a featherweight bout. Kid Brown of Tampa and Special Delivery Jones of Fort Myers will face off in the lightweight bout. The program will begin at 8:30 p.m. in a ring erected in front of the grandstand.[515]

Off the field in Tampa: The Palms paused for a team photo that appeared in the *Tampa Daily Times.*

Taking the lead in the Florida State loop for the second half the Fort Myers Palms are making a flying dash for the pennant. Reading from left to right (standing): Davenport, McRae, Bouza, Wickham and Grandio; (sitting) Williams, manager, Johnston, Domingo, Doran, Chancey, O'Reilly and Casares; (kneeling) the mascot.

Standing (from left to right) Gene Davenport, Cecil McRae, Mike Bouza, Bob Wickham, and Philip Grandio. Sitting are Cy Williams, Manager Joe Johnston, Joe Domingo, Pat Doran, Cliff Chancey, Jack O'Reilly, and Faustino Casares. Kneeling is the mascot. Photo from *Tampa Daily Times*. ©1926 Tampa Bay Times. All rights reserved. Used under license and used with the permission of Newspapers.com.[516]

On the field in Tampa: The Palms were leading 6 to 5 when the game went to the bottom of the ninth. With one out, Tampa loaded the bases. Pinch hitter Blackstock doubled to left. Tanner scored from third followed by Al Lopez with the winning run from second. The Smokers beat the Palms 7 to 6.[517]

The second game was tied until the bottom of the sixth. After the Smokers Second Baseman Tanner doubled to left, Tampa Center Fielder Stanton singled to center. As Tanner rounded third and ran for the plate,

Palms Center fielder Philip Grandio heaved the ball to Johnston at the plate. Umpire Ery called Tanner safe. Grandio was furious with the call. He ran in to the Palms bench, grabbed a bat and began running toward the umpire. Grandio was restrained by a half dozen policemen and some of the Palms players. Grandio was ejected from the game and assessed a $25 fine. Umpire Ery had assessed a $10 fine on one of the Palms players for spewing foul language from the bench during the first game.[518]

After the game and back in Fort Myers: A crowd of 500 fans waited out a delay to watch the boxing match for the benefit of the Fort Myers Baseball Club. Another 500 left Terry Park before the fights finally got started, thinking the fight had been postponed. The delay was a result of Del Pino's car breaking down on the way to the fight.

Once things got started, Young Del Pino knocked out Slim Chino. Anderson Avenue Kid won a decision over Kid Brown of Tampa, and Black Hawk beat Kid Marales. A jazz band from Safety Hill entertained the fans between matches. Despite the delay, the boxing match was the first financially successful one staged by the ball club.[519]

July 21, 1926:

On the field: Philip Grandio was in the lineup. Each time he stepped into the batter's box, the Tampa fans engaged in loud booing and catcalling. Grandio focused on the pitch and went three for four and batted in both Fort Myers runs. The Palms beat the Smokers 2 to 1.[520]

After the game: Palms Manager Joe Johnston announced all of the games played between Fort Myers and Tampa at Plant Field this week had been protested. "They've got a flock of class men…It isn't right men, and we're going to see what can be done about it." Tanner, Blackstock, Whitman, and Tommy Leach are the four Smokers in question.[521]

Off the field: The Tampa newspapers were unimpressed with the Palms' behavior in Tampa this series. *The Tampa Daily Times* wrote: "Amid a hail of protesting from Manager Johnston and a volley of disputing from the entire Fort Myers aggregation of ball players, Tommy Leach's Tampa Smokers dropped the third game of the series to the Palms. Come what may, the Palms left a bad taste with the local fans as far as baseball goes.

And it is supposed that the two umpires who handled the series feel the same way about it."[522]

Off the field in Sarasota: Florida State League President J.B. Asher waived the fine and suspension of Gulls Manager Manush that was applied because of his reaction to the forfeiture of the game in Sanford on July 17. This was at the recommendation of Umpire Ery who said he did not believe Manush intended to attack him when he jumped onto the umpire's car after the game. President Asher threw out the game, which removed a Sanford victory and a Sarasota loss, and will require the teams to play a double-header on September 22.[523]

July 22, 1926: Philip Grandio hit a two-run home run over the right field fence and hit a hard shot to center that rolled to the fence for a triple, but it was not enough to make up for a seven-run rally the Saints managed in the fifth inning. St. Petersburg defeated the Palms 9 to 7.[524]

July 23, 1926:

On the field in Sanford: Celeryfeds Pitcher John Wilson pitched a no-hitter. Sanford beat Bradenton 2 to 0.[525]

On the field in St. Petersburg: Philip Grandio and Faustino Casares tripled, and Casares, Joe Johnston, and Jack O'Reilly doubled. Gene Davenport was solid on the mound. The Palms defeated the Saints 3 to 1.[526]

July 24, 1926:

Off the field in Orlando: J. B. Asher, president of the Florida State League, announced the Manatee County commissioners had given the Bradenton Growers sufficient funds that, when combined with the $1,500 presented by local fans, would finance the Growers through the end of the 1926 season.[527]

On the field in St. Petersburg: Charley Allen, former Tampa Smokers manager, played his first game as a Fort Myers Palm today. Pat Doran, the Palms third baseman was suspended to make room on the roster for

Allen. The Palms staged a ninth-inning rally, but the three runs they achieved in the final stanza fell just short. St. Petersburg defeated Fort Myers 4 to 3.[528]

July 25, 1926: No game today.

July 26, 1926:

Off the field: Cecil McRae has been out with the stomach flu. Pat Doran has been out with an injured hand. Doran suffered a badly torn finger on a barbed wire fence in St. Petersburg and has been out for a week. "He won't say whether or not he got the watermelon."[529]

Fort Myers formally submitted their protest to Florida State League President J. B. Asher claiming Tampa had three, or four "class" men on their roster. St. Petersburg Manager George Block wired Florida State League President J. B. Asher to protest the Saints recent games against Tampa for the same reason, naming the same four Smokers as being "class" men.[530]

On the field: The temperature at Terry Park was 94 degrees.[531] In the seventh-inning, Kitty Wickham lined a sure double down the right field line. Home plate Umpire Tandy ruled the ball foul. The crowd disagreed and booed Tandy loud and long. A few excited fans yelled threats at Tandy.[532]

The Lakeland Highlanders and Fort Myers Palms combined for 24 hits. Philip Grandio had a triple and a double. Charlie Allen had four hits and a sacrifice in five plate appearances. The Palms loaded the bases in the ninth inning but were unable to score. Philip Grandio hit a high pop foul behind the plate. The fans yelled loudly trying to cause Lakeland Catcher Francis to miss the ball, but he did not. After making the catch, Francis placed his thumb beneath his nose and waved his fingers at the fans. The Highlanders beat the Palms 8 to 6.[533]

<u>July 27, 1926</u>:

Off the field: Palm Beach, on the east coast of Florida, took the brunt of a tropical storm that approached land then turned north. People attending the ball game today enjoyed a refreshing breeze with wind gusts up to 24 miles per hour.[534]

"H. B. Mayer, business manager of the Palms, personally attended to the chalking of the first base foul line before the game." This was likely a measure to prevent another occurrence like Umpire Tandy's decision the previous day on Kitty Wickham's smash.[535]

On the field: The temperature in Fort Myers was 84 degrees.[536] Down by a run in the seventh, Charlie Allen doubled to center. After Mike Bouza struck out, Jack O'Reilly hit a fly ball to right field. Allen tagged up on the play and advanced to third. Cliff Chancey hit a fading liner to right center field. The ball got by Brazier and Chancey ended up on third. With Joe Johnston at bat, Chancey stole home to the delight of "the handful of loyal rooters."

Lakeland outfielder Futvoye led off the ninth inning with a triple, but his teammates were unable to bring him across the plate. The Palms beat the Highlanders 3 to 2.[537]

<u>July 28, 1926</u>:

Before the game: there was standing water on the field at Terry Park thanks to a hard rain in the early afternoon and a three-minute power-soaker just before game time. After a brief meeting, it was decided the game would be played.[538]

On the field: The game-time temperature was 88 degrees.[539] It was an uneventful game. Mike Bouza hit another triple. Charlie Allen used a batting stance where he faced the pitcher. He has hit safely in four straight games with the Palms and is carrying a .642 batting average. Fort Myers fans were satisfied with the umpiring of Tandy for the first time during the series. The Palms beat the Highlanders 6 to 4.[540]

After the game: Palms President John W. Hendry announced the team has signed left-handed pitcher, Clarence Spurgeon, and right-handed pitcher, Jim Moore, formerly of the Muskogee team in the recently disbanded Western Association.[541] Cy Williams is released while Pat Doran (injury) and Cecil McRae (illness) are suspended. Moore and Springer accompanied the Palms on their luxury bus to Sarasota while Doran and McRae remained in Fort Myers.[542]

July 29, 1926: Leonard Mayo gave up nine hits and five runs in the first three innings. Clarence Spurgeon relieved Mayo and pitched five shutout innings. Philip Grandio went three for four at the plate. The Palms lost the first game of the series in Sarasota 5 to 1.[543]

July 30, 1926:

On the field in Sarasota: Charlie Allen and Palms Pitcher Gene Davenport both hit safely in two out of three trips to the plate, one of Davenport's hits was a double. Davenport also pitched nine innings of shutout baseball, giving up just five hits. The play of the game came in the seventh inning when Manager Joe Johnston executed a perfect squeeze play scoring Jack O'Reilly from third for the only run of the game. The Palms beat the Gulls 1 to 0.

Elsewhere in the Florida State League: Sanford lost to Lakeland and Orlando lost to Tampa. The Palms victory combined with the Celeryfeds and Colts losses resulted in Fort Myers sitting alone at the top of the league standings.[544]

In the Florida State League office: League President J. B. Asher announced Tampa had not played more than two class men in the games protested by Fort Myers and St. Petersburg, and no penalty would be assessed.

Mr. Asher advised all teams that no changes to rosters would be allowed beginning August 25, including in a post-season series, if needed to determine the league championship.

Finally, Mr. Asher advised that all postponed games needed to be made up at the first opportunity, or he would take action to forfeit the games to the non-offending team.[545]

<u>July 31, 1926</u>:

Before the game in Fort Myers: Palms Business Manager H. B. Mayer announced the team's first-place standing will be recognized with a dinner party at Fort Myers Beach tomorrow night. In addition to the players, local sports writers are invited, and team management will be in attendance.[546]

On the field in Sarasota: Eight Fort Myers' hits combined with eight Gulls' fielding errors resulted in the Palms beating Sarasota 6 to 4.[547]

After the game: The Palms arrived back in Fort Myers tired but happy. Team President John W. Hendry announced that Charlie Allen, who had been with the team since Pat Doran was injured, would return to Tampa, and Doran would be back in the Palms lineup. Mr. Hendry noted one pitcher would need to be released but said he would not make any announcement until Monday. Mr. Hendry was looking forward to the Palms' dinner party at the casino on Fort Myers Beach.[548]

END OF JULY
FLORIDA STATE LEAGUE[549]

	W.	L.	PCT.
FORT MYERS...................**14**		**9**	**.609**
Lakeland...........................14		10	.583
Sanford............................12		9	.571
Orlando............................12		9	.571
Tampa 12		11	.522
Bradenton........................10		13	.435
Sarasota 9		14	.391
St. Petersburg 9		14	.391

August 1926 – O'Reilly to Chancey to Bouza!

<u>August 1, 1926</u>: No game today.

<u>August 2, 1926</u>: The temperature at Terry Park was 93 degrees.[550] With the permission of league President J. B. Asher, Home Plate Umpire Ed "Bugs" Ery was calling balls and strikes from behind the mound because he did not have his mask and chest protector.[551]

In the second inning, Faustino Casares hit a line shot down the first base line. Umpire Ery, from his vantage point behind the mound, called the ball foul. Palms fans disagreed and gave Ery an extended earful while Manager Johnston protested the call.

In the top of the third, with the Gulls Left Fielder Hogan on third, Sarasota Manager Manush grounded the ball to Jack O'Reilly at shortstop. O'Reilly threw to Joe Johnston at home to get Hogan. Umpire Ery, from his position behind the mound, called Hogan safe. Again, the fans disagreed with the call and "Ery was the object of a verbal onslaught."

After the entire Gulls team batted in the third, and they had scored their fourth run of the inning, a rain shower interrupted the game. Several fans rushed the field and surrounded Umpire Ery. A few fans threatened Ery with their fists, but park police got the situation under control. The rain persisted and the game was called off. The two teams would play a double-header the following day.[552]

<u>August 3, 1926</u>:

Off the field: Florida State League President J. B. Asher reassigned Umpire Ery, and his partner, Umpire Frederick to Bradenton. They were replaced by umpires Weaver and Kane.

Palms Pitcher Leonard Mayo was suspended. The Palms' pitching staff includes right-handers Cecil McRae, Jim Moore, and Gene Davenport; and left handers Joe Domingo and Clarence Spurgeon.[553]

The first-base side bleachers held the largest and loudest crowd of the season.

On the field: The temperature in Fort Myers was 94 degrees.[554] In the first game, Palms Pitcher Cecil McRae, returning from a two-week bout with the flu, went against Sarasota's Jumbo Brown. The Palms won game one 2 to 1.

In the second game, Palms Pitcher Gene Davenport had a no-hitter through four innings. In the fifth inning with Gulls Right Fielder Denton on first, Gulls Third Baseman Thorn hit a line shot that skyrocketed off Davenport's knee and rolled to the Sarasota bench. Denton scored on the play and Thorn ended up at third. Sarasota defeated the Palms 2 to 1.[555]

August 4, 1926:

Off the field: Florida State League President J. B. Asher was visiting Fort Myers to attend the afternoon game at Terry Park. He attended the Kiwanis Club luncheon at the Elks Club. Mr. Asher was introduced as a Kiwanian who had not missed a luncheon in five years.[556]

H. B. Mayer, business manager for the Palms, is expecting record-breaking attendance for the Orlando series beginning tomorrow.[557]

On the field: The game-time temperature was 94 degrees.[558] League President J. B. Asher watched the Gulls take on the Palms from the press box.[559] Asher had brought Umpire Meikle with him. Meikle called balls and strikes from behind the plate while umpires Kane and Weaver managed the base paths. In the bottom of the fifth, the Palms made the most of four hits, a walk, and an error putting five runs on the board. Joe Domingo hit a triple and was the winning pitcher. The Palms (who J. B. Asher picked to win the second half) beat the Gulls 7 to 3 in their final meeting of the season.[560]

August 5, 1926:

Off the field: Palms President John W. Hendry and Vice President S. Watt Lawler watched the game from the press box. They were observed to be in very good moods discussing the prospect of the Palms being in first place in the league.

"A fight between two youngsters behind the press box almost stopped the game. As usual the red-headed scrapper won."[561]

On the field: The temperature at Terry Park was 94 degrees.[562] Jim Moore made his pitching debut for the Palms. Moore turned in a three-hit complete game. The Palms beat the Orlando Colts 2 to 1.[563] Orlando nearly lost the game in the eighth inning. Colts Third Baseman Foss grounded to Shortstop Jack O'Reilly. O'Reilly fielded the ball, stepped on second base to force out Formby, then fired the ball to Mike Bouza at first. When Umpire Kane called Foss out, the Colts immediately surrounded him and began a lengthy protest. Umpire Kane finally took out his watch and gave the Colts a limited amount of time to either get back to work or forfeit the game.

After the game: Palms management announced there had been one of the biggest crowds of the season on hand at Terry Park. It was further noted the gate receipts of the day were large enough to cover the daily cost of the ball club operations for the first time during the 1926 season.

At the luncheon yesterday, the Kiwanis discovered that during the off-season, Umpire Kane is 'the Kane' of the Lovett and Kane team in Keith's vaudeville circuit. Mr. Kane offered to perform a juggling act at Mr. Claude Lee's Omar theater tomorrow evening. Mr. Lee is donating 50 percent of the receipts of the evening to the Fort Myers Baseball Club.[564]

August 6, 1926:

Off the field: Leonard Mayo's suspension is expected to be lifted Monday and one of the Palms will be released.[565]

On the field: The temperature in Fort Myers was 92 degrees.[566]

In a wild third inning, the Palms combined four hits with four Colts errors, a base on balls, and a passed ball to post seven runs. With Clarence Spurgeon on second, Philip Grandio hit one back to Colts Pitcher Culbreath. Culbreath juggled the ball then threw it to the plate, apparently thinking there had been a runner on third. There was not. A few minutes later, with Grandio now on third, Pat Doran walked to load the bases. Apparently thinking the bases were already loaded, Grandio began to jog home. They were not. Grandio was an easy out.[567]

In the same inning, Pat Doran lined a sharp grounder to Foss at third. Foss fired the ball to Shortstop Viau at second, and the Palms Mike Bouza was trapped between second and third. Bouza broke for third, Viau threw the ball back to Foss who missed when he tried to tag Bouza as he raced past him; Bouza was safe at third.

In the top of the sixth inning, the Colts' center fielder, Formby, was knocked unconscious when he was struck on the cheek by a foul ball off his own bat. His teammates carried his limp body into the shade of the Colts' bench. A doctor was summoned from the stands to examine Formby. Water splashed on his face brought him to after four to five minutes. Formby got to his feet and walked to the clubhouse.

Clarence Spurgeon struck out 7 Colts. The Palms beat Orlando 8 to 1.[568]

After the game: Umpire J. B. Kane performed in front of a packed house at the Omar theater for the benefit of the Fort Myer Baseball Club. "'We took in more money on Kane than we do at the ballpark,' said H. B. Mayer, the Palms business manager, after the show.... 'Kane has absolutely refused to take a penny for his services. The officials of the ballclub cannot thank him too much,' Mayer said."[569]

August 7, 1926: The game-time temperature was 92 degrees.[570] In the third inning, Colts Center Fielder Sam Johnson ran a long way to the center field fence and made a great back-handed catch to rob Faustino Casares of an extra base hit.[571] The Palms turned double-plays in the seventh and eighth to shut down potential Colts' rallies. The Palms beat the Colts 5 to 3 to sweep the series.[572]

August 8, 1926: No game today. The Palms left on the luxury team bus for Sanford in the morning.[573]

The Palms turned nine double plays during the past week bringing their total to nineteen so far in the second half. The most common Fort Myers combination is O'Reilly to Chancey to Bouza.[574]

August 9, 1926: In one of the best pitchers' duals of the 1926 Florida State League season, Fort Myers was held to three hits. Cecil McRae hurled all eleven innings for the Palms and limited the Celeryfeds to just six hits. In the bottom of the eleventh inning, with two runners on and two out, Sanford Second Baseman Herman Myers hit a long drive to right field. Philip Grandio made a great running catch to end the inning. The game was called due to darkness. The final score was 0 to 0.[575]

August 10, 1926:

Off the field in Fort Myers: It was announced today there will be another boxing show at Terry Park this week for the benefit of the Fort Myers Baseball Club. Young Louis, Tampa lightweight, will meet Billy Earns of Miami in the 10-round main event. Battling Kid will take on Jimmy Gore in an eight-round featherweight match. Local boys will go six rounds to start the night and a battle royal is scheduled.[576]

The Palms announced that Pitcher Leonard Mayo was returned to Augusta of the South Atlantic Association. Mayo's professional baseball debut came in May when he arrived in Fort Myers. He became a fan favorite by winning his first three games, but his current record was six wins and seven losses.[577]

On the field in Sanford: The Palms and Celeryfeds split a double header. Davenport led the Palms to a 4 to 3 victory in game one. Sanford won the second game 4 to 1.[578] During the second game, Home Plate Umpire Moore was injured by a foul tip. Sanford Pitcher Williams and Palms Pitcher Joe Domingo assisted Umpire Weaver to finish the game.[579]

August 11, 1926: Pat Doran batted three for four, but it wasn't enough. The Celeryfeds beat the Palms 4 to 3.[580]

<u>August 12, 1926</u>:

On the field in Orlando: "A near capacity crowd including several Ft. Myers rooters filled the Tinker field stands."[581] Cecil McRae held Orlando to seven hits. The Palms beat the Colts 8 to 3.[582]

After the game in Fort Myers: Lightweights Young Louis of Tampa and Billy Earnso of Miami, battled 10 rounds to a draw in the main event of the boxing match for the benefit of the Fort Myers Baseball Club at Terry Park. In the featherweight match, Battling Kid of West Tampa, scored a knockout of Jimmy Gore, of West Palm Beach.[583]

<u>August 13, 1926</u>:

On the field in Orlando: Former major league Pitcher Bob Vines limited the Palms to seven scattered hits. For the first time in their last five meetings, the Colts beat the Palms 8 to 2.[584]

On the field in Tampa: Sanford Celeryfeds manager, "Lee Crowe and Umpire Simmons had a run in...during the sixth inning that resulted in Crowe leaving the field and a half-hour argument that marred the interest of players and spectators alike. President J. B. Asher, of the State league, probably will receive a request for better umpiring as a result."[585]

<u>August 14, 1926</u>:

Off the field in Fort Myers: it was announced that the Palms would board their luxury team bus after today's game and return to Fort Myers early Sunday morning. The team would have the day to rest before attending a dinner in their honor at Nelson's Casino at Fort Myers beach.[586]

On the field in Orlando: Thirteen Orlando hits and six infield errors by the Palms made for a difficult afternoon. The Colts pounded the Palms 10 to 4 in their final meeting of the season.[587]

<u>August 15, 1926</u>: No game today.

The Palms arrived in Fort Myers early in the morning, leaving the memory of the 17 fielding errors of past week behind them. "In crowing wildly over the fact that the Colts won their first series of the year from the Palms, the *Orlando Sentinel*, in its account of Saturday's game, declares that 'the Fort Myers delegation exhibited many old and several new ways of booting the ball.'"[588]

The *Orlando Morning Sentinel* also noted "local fans comfortably filled the stands…Saturday. The club has received better backing during the Ft. Myers series than for several weeks."[589]

The fact that today was payday for the Palms, combined with one of Dr. Thomas' amazing steak dinners at Nelson's Casino, put the Palms in a positive mindset as they looked ahead to the final month of the season.[590]

August 16, 1926: The temperature at Terry Park was 92 degrees.[591] The summer rains of Southwest Florida rolled in just before the start of the game. The Saints and Palms game was postponed. A double-header was scheduled to begin at 2:30 the next afternoon.[592]

August 17, 1926: The temperature in Fort Myers was 82 degrees.[593] In the bottom of the fifth inning, Cecil McRae was hit on the ankle by a pitch, but Umpire Fredericks disagreed. McRae had a large bump on his left foot, and Umpire Fredricks got an earful from the Palms and their fans.[594] The Palms' field woes continued in the first game. Four fielding errors contributed to Pitcher Cecil McRae's first loss of the second half. The Saints beat the Palms 6 to 2.[595]

The Palms committed four errors in the second game, but the Saints topped them with six errors. When the Palms exploded for seven runs in the fifth inning, Saints Manager George Block replaced Pitcher Lanning with Vivi Hewitt who had pitched all nine innings in the first game of the day. The Palms won the second game 10 to 5.[596]

August 18, 1926: The game-time temperature was 92 degrees.[597] With two out in the top of the first inning, the Palms committed three fielding errors, gave up two stolen bases, and spotted the Saints four runs. The

Palms scored three in the second and four in the third and led the Saints 7 to 5 at the end of the third inning. In the bottom of the fourth inning, Pat Doran walked then went to third when Mike Bouza was safe on an error by Saints Third Baseman Frank Austin. Bouza and Doran executed a double steal to give the Palms their eighth run. Neither team had a hit during the final three innings. The Palms beat the Saints 8 to 7.[598] It was Pitcher Gene Davenport's 16th victory of the season.[599]

Charlie Allen, the former Smokers manager, who played with the Palms while Pat Doran was injured, was now with the Saints. He was one of the league's best hitters, but the Palms pitching held him to just one single during the three-game series.[600]

August 19, 1926:

On the wet field at Terry Park: The temperature at game time was 88 degrees.[601] "More than 2,000 fans, who gathered at Terry Park...to watch the opening game of the crucial series between Fort Myers and Sanford, went away disappointed when the weatherman turned loose one of his wettest August showers."[602]

Sanford Manager Lee Crowe announced he was planning to have Ben Cantwell and John Wilson pitch against the Palms the next day. Crowe wanted to give his team every advantage in trying to win the second-half title for Sanford. Cantwell and Wilson are the top pitchers in the Florida State League. Wilson has been sold to the major league Philadelphia Phillies for a reported $5,000. Milwaukee of the American Association has been trying to acquire Cantwell for a similar amount.[603]

That evening, the Palms players and officials were guests of Nick Cornish, Charles Hinnelbauch, and Dick Ede for a chicken dinner at Aunt Saline's restaurant at Punta Rassa. In thanking the hosts, Palms Business Manager H. B. Mayer promised another dinner for the team if they won the series against Sanford.[604]

August 20, 1926: The temperature in Fort Myers was 88 degrees.[605] For the second day in a row, Palms' fans turned out in force only to be deprived of the opportunity to see the crucial series with the Celeryfeds begin.

The first game was declared rained out at 3 p.m., but team officials hoped they could get the second game in at 4 p.m. More than 500 fans waited until 3:50 p.m. when President John W. Hendry, Business Manager H. B. Mayer, and Manager Johnston abandoned the idea.

The weather didn't just disappoint those on hand at Terry Park, but there was an estimated crowd of 600 outside Joe's Smoke Shop in Sanford at the other end of a leased wire that were waiting to hear the call of the game. The final edition of the *Sanford Herald* was held past press time until the sports department was notified over another special leased wire that both games had been called off.

Palms' officials made numerous attempts to try to get all three games of the series in. Proposals were made to play a third game early Saturday morning or to play on Sunday. Celeryfeds Manager Lee Crowe responded with an emphatic "no" to each suggestion.

While the Palms and Celeryfeds were idle, the Tampa Smokers kept winning and were in contention for the second-half pennant. "It has been pointed out that should Tampa or Orlando capture the second half, the post-season series would be more profitable to the winners of the first half. Both cities are located closer to Sanford and, as a result, the crowds and the receipts would be larger than they would be if Fort Myers meets Sanford. The attendance at Tampa has been better throughout the season than at any other league city."[606]

The Palms have been in first place in the Florida State League for 16 consecutive days.

<u>August 21, 1926</u>:

On the field in Fort Myers: The game-time temperature was 88 degrees.[607] "The Palms lost two heart-breaking ball games to Sanford."

Cecil McRae held the Celeryfeds to two hits in the first game, but the Palms made five fielding errors and Sanford defeated the Palms 3 to 1. In the second game, Palms Pitcher Jim Moore hurled ten scoreless innings, but 4 hits and an error in the eleventh resulted in a 4 to 0 Celeryfeds victory.[608]

By winning both games, Sanford moved into first place in the league standings and the Palms dropped to the third position.[609]

On the field in Orlando: The Orlando Colts moved into the second spot in the league standings when the Sarasota Gulls forfeited the game. "The forfeiture was made when Sarasota players protested a decision of Umpire Moore at the plate in the fifth inning."[610] In the bottom of the fifth, with one out, Dent and Viau of the Colts singled. Foss was walked. Then Cox walked, forcing in Dent. When Cox walked, the Gulls' catcher, Miller, threw the ball into the outfield in protest of Umpire Moore's pitch calling. Viau, Foss, and Cox all trotted around the bases and went to their bench. Gulls Manager Manush ran in from the outfield protesting the judgment of the umpire. He gathered his players as he made his way to the plate. After several minutes of arguing, "the game was forfeited with the Colts in the dugout and the ball somewhere near the left field fence."[611]

August 22, 1926: No game today. The Palms boarded the luxury team bus and left Fort Myers at 1:30 p.m. headed for Lakeland. H. B. Mayer, business manager for the Palms, said that First Baseman Mike Bouza is still on the club's payroll after he was removed from the lineup yesterday and replaced by Joe Domingo. Mr. Mayer said the team is working to sign a new, hard-hitting first baseman by the name of Daniels from Chipley, Florida, who was recommended by Dr. B. Whisnant. As of this morning, there was no confirmation from Daniels as to whether he would join the team in Lakeland.[612] John W. Hendry, team president, said "he still considered Bouza 'a most promising youngster.'"[613]

August 23, 1926:

Off the field: It was announced today the play-by-play details of the three games between Lakeland and Fort Myers would be announced at the office of Hendry Bros. Realty company at First and Jackson Streets. All fans were invited to listen in. The returns would be made possible through a special arrangement between Hendry Bros. and Western Union. [614]

On the field in Lakeland: Palms Center Fielder Kitty Wickham was ruled out when he was hit by a batted ball. Lakeland put together four hits with a walk to put up three runs in the fourth inning. That was all the Highlanders needed. Lakeland defeated the Palms 5 to 2.[615]

August 24, 1926:

Off the field in Tampa: The sports editor of the *Tampa Daily Times* wrote: "As the [tail] end of the season comes on, it begins to look as if Fort Myers is out of it. The team enjoyed a comfortable lead a couple of weeks ago, only to sluff it away in a manner that makes losers out of potential champions."[616]

On the wet field in Lakeland: The Highlanders were leading the Palms 3 to 2 in the third when rain began to pour down on the field. By the time the rain stopped, the field was unplayable. A double-header was scheduled for the following day.[617]

August 25, 1926:

Early morning in Fort Myers: Both games of today's double header will be received via a special Western Union wire and announced outside of Hendry Brothers Realty office at First and Jackson Streets.

"John W. Hendry, president of the Fort Myers Baseball Club, left this morning for Lakeland to talk things over with Manager…Johnston…prior to this afternoon's double bill."[618]

Before the games in Lakeland: H. B. Mayer, business manager for the Palms, announced all passes to games at Terry Park for the remainder of the season were recalled. No outstanding passes will be honored at the gate for any remaining games. Fans who have paid their pledges in full may pick up new tickets at the Hendry Brothers office at First and Jackson streets. Mayer stated the club has more than $1,900 remaining due on these passes.[619]

Hendry announced Joe Johnston's dismissal from the Palms and the hiring of Pete Doyle, a former Florida State League catcher and manager of Lake Wales, a team in the West Coast League, as the new manager of the club. Mr. Hendry had been negotiating with Doyle for the past six weeks and considers him an excellent manager.[620] Fort Myers fans may remember seeing Doyle play at Terry Park last fall when he caught[621] for "the old 'Palms' to vanquish the champion Tampa Smokers in a three-game series at Terry Park."[622]

Hendry also announced that Mike Bouza had been suspended and Earl Daniels, a former semi-pro from Alabama, had been signed. Daniels was scouted by Dr. Baker Whisnant and Palms Pitcher Cecil McRae is a former teammate.

No official reason was given for the dismissal of Johnston, though many believe it was due to lack of discipline. It was rumored that several players had been staying out almost the entire night prior to important games and this showed in their performance on the diamond.[623]

On the field in Lakeland: As his first order of business as the new team manager, Pete Doyle rearranged the lineup and moved Faustino Casares to the top of the batting order. Casares stepped up to the plate to lead off the first and hit a home run that carried more than 50 feet beyond the left field fence. New First Baseman Earl Daniels singled in his first trip to the plate in the second inning. Manager Doyle was solid behind the plate. The Palms made zero errors in the field, and Pitcher Cecil McRae picked up a 6 to 1 victory in a rain-shortened six-inning game. The scheduled second game of the double header was rained out.[624]

Off the field in Bradenton: the Bradenton Growers took out a full-page ad in the *Bradenton Herald* newspaper promoting the series against the Palms that would begin the next day.

August 26, 1926: Faustino Casares went four for five (now seven in his last eight at bats) including a triple and three singles and the Palms' new first baseman, Earl Daniels, went three for five. The Palms combined for 16 hits in all. Kitty Wickham made several impressive catches in center field and Joe Domingo picked up his 14th win of the season. The Palms beat the Bradenton Growers 13 to 1.[625]

Facsimile of ad appearing in *The Bradenton Herald* on August 25, 1926.[626]

August 27, 1926: Casares and Daniels continued their hitting exhibition, each getting a single, Daniels a double, and Casares a triple. The Palms scored the go-ahead run in the top of the ninth inning. In the bottom of the ninth, with two outs, Palms Pitcher Jim Moore walked two Growers,[627] then intentionally walked Gene Elliott, before Wheeler grounded to Jack O'Reilly at short, who tossed the ball to Pat Doran at third base for the final out of the game. The Palms won their second straight over the Growers 5 to 4.[628]

August 28, 1926: Bradenton ace Mike Kelly held Fort Myers to four hits, but that was all the Palms needed. Philip Grandio tripled in the third inning and scored when Earl Daniels doubled. The Palms scored again in the sixth by leveraging two walks and a fielder's choice. Gene Davenport pitched a complete game shutout for the Palms. The Palms beat the Growers 2 to 0.[629]

The Palms win over Bradenton combined with the Orlando Colts' loss to St. Petersburg meant the Palms were in first place in the Florida State League by one-half game over the Colts. Bring on the Smokers!

August 29, 1926: No game today.

Off the field (literally) in Bradenton: Florida State League President J. B. Asher announced the Growers series with the Colts scheduled to begin Monday will be moved from Grower Park in Bradenton to Tinker Field in Orlando. The change was made at the request of Bradenton officials.[630]

The Growers had less than 50 paid admissions at the Friday and Saturday games with Fort Myers. This continued the season-long trend of the failure of fans to turnout for games in Bradenton. Not knowing whether they would be paid or not has led to a "don't care" attitude among the players.

Bradenton President W. B. Kirby and Manager "Dixie" Parker announced that Pitcher Barron and Catcher Bauerlein had been released to reduce expenses. "There are now but eleven men on the team and it may be found necessary to cut them down to nine; this, however, will be the last recourse."[631]

Joe Domingo. Photo credit: *Fort Myers Tropical News* –
USA TODAY NETWORK, August 29, 1926.

Off the field in Fort Myers: A rare feature article appeared on the sports page of the *Fort Myers Tropical News* celebrating Palms Pitcher Joe Domingo.[632]

August 30, 1926:

Off the field: Palms team President, John W. Hendry, announced that Mike Bouza, who had been with the Palms since opening day, was released. Bouza was immediately signed by Lakeland to fill in for Third Baseman Freddie Heck who was out of the lineup with an illness.[633]

On the field: The temperature in Fort Myers was 94 degrees.[634] The Palms led 1 to 0 at the end of the third when rumbling thunderclouds and a drizzling rain caused Umpire Tandy to pause the game for 15 minutes.[635] The Smokers scored a run in the fourth and managed two unearned runs in the eighth. The Palms complained repeatedly in the eighth and ninth innings that it was too dark, and they could not see the ball, but Umpire Tandy refused to call the game. The Smokers beat the Palms 3 to 1. The loss caused Fort Myers to fall to third place in the league standings, just one-half game behind the lead leading Orlando Colts.[636]

August 31, 1926: The temperature in Fort Myers was 92 degrees.[637] In the second inning, Tampa Right Fielder Lee stole second. Palms Second Baseman Cliff Chancey jumped high to try to catch the throw from Doyle. As he came down, one foot landed on the edge of the base, and he rolled his ankle. He remained in the game through the fifth inning.[638] The middle of the Palms' batting order had been in a collective slump, and Shortstop Jack O'Reilly made his second mental error on the base paths in the same number of days. The Smokers beat the Palms 5 to 2. The Palms remain in third place, one game behind the Colts.[639]

END OF AUGUST
FLORIDA STATE LEAGUE[640]

	W.	L.	PCT.
Orlando	27	18	.600
Sanford	25	18	.581
FORT MYERS	**27**	**20**	**.574**
Tampa	27	21	.563
Lakeland	27	22	.551
St. Petersburg	21	27	.437
Sarasota	17	29	.370
Bradenton	15	31	.326

September 1926 – Can the Palms Stay Healthy in the Sprint for the Pennant?

<u>September 1, 1926:</u>

Off the field: J.B. Asher, president of the Florida State League, was in town for a previously scheduled meeting with officials of the Palms. Commenting on the Palms' third-place standing in the league, Mr. Asher said, "Things are going fine. I don't see any reason for worry, it is only a temporary setback. As I said when I was here before, I believe you have the strongest team in the league if they can get down and play ball."[641]

The starting time of the game was delayed 30 minutes to 4:30 due to the funeral service of Walter O. Sheppard which began at 3:30. Mr. Sheppard was an attorney and one of Fort Myers most prominent citizens. Mr. Sheppard died Sunday evening when his car overturned while he was racing to Jacksonville to be at the bedside of his dying brother. All businesses in Fort Myers were closed at 3 p.m.[642; 643]

On the field: The game-time temperature was 92 degrees.[644] "A small crowd of local fans and President J. B. Asher, Florida State League head," attended the final game of the series between the Palms and the Smokers at Terry Park.

In the top half of the fourth inning, Tampa Third Baseman Salvatz doubled to right field. Palms Third Baseman Pat Doran caught a steal sign. The next Tampa batter, Blackstock, hit a roller to Doran. Doran turned around and tagged Salvatz, who had started for home.

Joe Domingo picked up another win as the Palms beat the Smokers 7 to 3. With the win, the Palms fell back one-half game in the standings because of the Orlando Colts winning both games of a double-header with Bradenton.[645] The second game in Orlando was forfeited in the seventh inning when Pitcher Peel was hit in the shin by a line drive. The Growers are now down to nine players and rather than play with only eight men, Manager Parker forfeited the game to the Colts.[646]

<u>September 2, 1926</u>: The temperature at Terry Park was 92 degrees.[647] "Several local players from Bradenton came down to Fort Myers…to enable the Growers to play their series here."[648] Wallame and Wyatt were introduced as new Growers for the game.[649] After a 20-minute rain delay in the top of the seventh inning, Cecil McRae replaced Jim Moore on the mound for the Palms and held the Growers scoreless from the eighth inning on.[650] In the bottom of the tenth, Faustino Casares and Joe Domingo walked. Kitty Wickham laid down a perfect bunt, moving Casares and Domingo to second and third. Pat Doran walked to load the bases. Philip Grandio singled, scoring Casares. The Palms won 7 to 6.

Rain prevented the second game from being played, but Orlando and Sanford both lost, so the Palms moved up in the standings to second place, one-half game behind Orlando.[651]

<u>September 3, 1926</u>: The temperature in Fort Myers was 92 degrees.[652] An ironman competition of sorts took place at Terry Park when Gene Davenport of the Palms and Manager "Dixie" Parker of the Growers both pitched complete games of a double header. The result was Davenport ringing up his 18th and 19th victories of the season. The Palms won the first game 3 to 0 in what was suspected to be a record time of 73 minutes. The pace continued in game two with the Palms winning 4 to 2 in a rain-shortened five-inning game that lasted just 50 minutes.

Orlando lost to St. Petersburg and with 12 games remaining, the Palms reclaimed first place in the Florida State League standings by one-half game.[653]

<u>September 4, 1926</u>:

Before the game: Umpire Fredericks made an announcement that the NuGrape and Nehi bottling companies had donated several dozen bottles of drinks to the Growers and Palms.[654]

On the field: The game-time temperature was 92 degrees.[655] The Palms put up four runs in the bottom of the first and never looked back. Joe Domingo collected another win. The final score was 6 to 1. The Palms are atop the league standings by one and one-half games.[656]

<u>September 5, 1926</u>: No game today.

<u>September 6, 1926</u>: The temperature at Terry Park was 92 degrees.[657] In the morning contest, the Palms committed five errors but managed to stretch the game to 12 innings before losing 5 to 3. Manager Doyle made a wild throw that resulted in two Highlander runs. Doyle benched himself in the second game—Chancey, still recovering from a fractured ankle, agreed to catch for the Palms.

In the afternoon game, Cecil McRae gave up three runs in the top of the third inning. Jim Moore struck out ten Highlanders in six and two-thirds innings of relief. Only one Highlander, former Palm Mike Bouza, managed to hit one of Moore's pitches out of the infield. Bouza flew out to Philip Grandio in right field. After nine innings, the score was tied 3 to 3 and Umpire Fredricks called the game due to darkness. The teams agreed to make up the tie Wednesday the 8th at 2:30 p.m.[658; 659] In losing the first game, the Palms dropped to second place behind Sanford.

<u>September 7, 1926</u>:

Before the game: An x-ray revealed a broken bone in the middle finger of Manager Doyle's throwing hand. Cliff Chancey was assigned catching duties.[660]

H. B. Mayer announced that Palms Pitcher Cecil McRae and Shortstop Jack O'Reilly were recalled to the Asheville [North Carolina] club of the [South] Atlantic League. Mr. Mayer explained that McRae and O'Reilly had been playing with the Palms under option. It was rumored the major league Cleveland Indians were eyeing McRae in the draft. Both players were to report to spring training with Asheville in 1927.[661]

On the field: The temperature in Fort Myers was 94 degrees.[662] Lakeland beat the Palms 4-2, but Sanford also lost, and the Palms moved back into first place by percentage points calculated to the fourth decimal.[663]

	W.	L.	PCT.
FORT MYERS	**32**	**22**	**.5925**
Sanford	29	20	.5918
Orlando	30	22	.577
Tampa	31	24	.564
Lakeland	31	24	.564

After the game: John W. Hendry announced that Manager Pete Doyle was released by the Palms. Pat Doran, Palms third baseman, was named as the Palms fourth manager. The reason given for the release of Doyle is he failed to measure up to expectations as a manager and player. The release of Doyle opens a position, and the Palms are trying to secure a catcher to make a run at the second-half championship. [664]

"Tomorrow's encounter will be the last appearance of the Palms at home this year unless they should crash through the opposition for the second-half pennant."[665]

September 8, 1926:

Every remaining player on the 1926 Fort Myers Baseball Club roster played in the final game of the regular season at Terry Park, but it was two former Palms, now with Lakeland, that were the stars of the diamond.

Former Palm Mike Bouza scored two runs and was the middleman in two Highlander double-play combinations, and former Palms pitcher, Howard Johnson, turned in a five-hit complete game performance for Lakeland.

The Highlanders were leading 5 to 0 after four innings when rain began to pour down, but the game was able to resume after a 30-minute delay.

"Ed Overstreet, catcher-manager of the pennant-winning Arcadia club in the Ridge circuit, reported shortly before game time, but local officials were not able to reach President J. B. Asher in order to sanction the signing of Overstreet in the place of Doyle...An answer from the league's head came later." Mr. Asher's approval proved timely because Cliff

Chancey had to leave the game in the seventh when he reinjured his ankle.

Rain came again in the eighth inning, and it was too dark to continue the game. The Highlanders defeated the Palms 9 to 2 in their final meeting of the season and the final regular season game of the 1926 season at Terry Park.[666]

September 9, 1926:

Off the field in Fort Myers: "Local baseball fans who are backing the Fort Myers entry in the State league race to the last pitch, have arranged for a special telegraphic play-by-play report of the series between the Palms and the Saints at St. Petersburg beginning this afternoon. The special wire has been installed in Hendry Brothers' office."[667]

On the field in St. Petersburg: Gene Davenport held the Saints to six hits. The Palms defeated the Saints 3 to 2. It was Davenport's 20th win of the season.[668]

September 10, 1926: Cecil McRae's pitching was solid, but the Palms only managed four hits. In the top of the seventh inning with Cliff Chancey on second, Cecil McRae drove a single to right field. Chancey rounded third and attempted to score, but former Palm Charlie Allen threw him out by a yard. The Saints beat Fort Myers 3 to 0.[669] The Palms dropped to fourth place in the league standings, three full games behind Sanford.[670]

September 11, 1926: The final meeting between the St. Petersburg Saints and the Fort Myers Palms was rained out. The Palms moved up a position in the league standings when Lakeland lost to Orlando. The final series of the regular season at Tampa would decide everything.[671]

September 12, 1926: No game today.

In Orlando, real estate developer Joe Tinker, announced he, in cooperation with businessman H. B. Stevens of Sanford, was completing arrangements for a best-of-seven game All-Star series involving the Sanford Celeryfeds.[672] Tinker (a retired major league shortstop of "Tinker to Evers to Chance" lore) would coach an All-Star Nine made up of select players from seven teams in the Florida State League, provided the Celeryfeds win the league championship. The players would share 90% of gross receipts of the first four games. The series would begin at Tinker Field in Orlando and shift to Sanford beginning with the third game.[673]

September 13, 1926: Cesare Alvarez pitched a masterful game for the Smokers. The Palms managed just four hits and were shut out in Tampa, 5 to 0. The Palms remain in fourth place, three games behind the league-leading Celeryfeds. The win moved Tampa into a tie for the league lead with Sanford.

September 14, 1926:

On the field in St. Petersburg: The Fort Myers Palms were mathematically eliminated from the second-half pennant race when the Sanford Celeryfeds defeated the St. Petersburg Saints in the first game of a double header.[674]

On the field in Tampa: Pitcher Red Craig held the Palms to just four hits. Tampa Catcher Al Lopez crossed the plate in the bottom of the ninth to give the Smokers a 2 to 1 victory over the Palms.[675]

September 15, 1926: The Fort Myers Palms lost the final game of the 1926 season to the Tampa Smokers, 5 to 0. Clarence Spurgeon relieved Cecil McRae in the fourth inning. Spurgeon threw the final pitch for the Palms in the bottom of the eighth inning, and Palms Manager Pat Doran was at the plate for the final out of the game.[676]

Sanford won the second half of the 1926 season, and combined with having won the first half, the Celeryfeds won the Florida State League Pennant. The Fort Myers Palms finished the second half in fifth place, three-and-a-half games behind Sanford.

SECOND HALF FINAL STANDINGS
FLORIDA STATE LEAGUE[677]

	W.	L.	PCT.
Sanford	33	20	.623
Tampa	38	24	.613
Orlando	34	24	.586
Lakeland	36	26	.581
FORT MYERS	**33**	**27**	**.550**
St. Petersburg	25	32	.439
Sarasota	21	36	.368
Bradenton........................	15	46	.246

And with that, the 1926 season was over...*or was it?*

Tampa ended the second half of the season with a half-game lead over Sanford, but Sanford was placed above Tampa in the standings based on ten percentage points. This frustrated Dr. H. E. Opry, president of the Tampa Smokers, because Tampa played all 62 games while Sanford only played 53 games due to rainouts and ties.

Dr. Opry sent a letter of protest to Florida State League President J. B. Asher suggesting (former Major League Baseball player) Joe Tinker's organizing of an All-Star series may have influenced the outcome of the season. Opry argued players invited to play in the All-Star series had a financial incentive to throw games, ensuring Sanford would win the title and dates reserved for a Florida State League playoff series would be available for the All-Star series. Opry requested that Sanford be required to replay several games that were rained out or ended in tie scores in hopes that would result in Tampa finishing above Sanford. What Opry really wanted was a playoff series between the Sanford Celeryfeds and the Tampa Smokers to take place in Tampa.

Lee Crowe, manager of the Celeryfeds initially agreed to a playoff series between Sanford and Tampa and league President J. B. Asher sanctioned the series, but Crowe quickly changed his mind and chose to play Tinker's All-Stars instead.

Dr. Opry decided not to pursue the matter further. He declared the season was over, and the Sanford Celeryfeds were the champions of the 1926 Florida State League.[678]

<u>September 16, 1926</u>: The Palms rolled into to Fort Myers on the luxury team bus for the final time. Each member of the team signed for their pay and then departed for their homes throughout the country.[679] They were fortunate to be leaving Fort Myers on that day.

The Great Miami Hurricane of 1926

In the early morning hours of Saturday, September 18, 1926, a catastrophic hurricane advanced rapidly from the Bahamas and came ashore in Miami, Florida. The storm, known as the Great Miami Hurricane, brought winds of more than 150 miles per hour and a storm surge of 11 feet. Hundreds were killed and thousands were injured. The storm cut a path of destruction across South Florida.

In Fort Myers, the wind "which is conservatively estimated to have reached a 75-mile-an-hour-gale," increased through the morning and was most severe during the middle of the afternoon. The storm slowly died out about 2:30 Sunday morning. The wind and accompanying rain inflicted damage throughout the city – business, churches, and residences alike. Roofs were ripped off and hundreds of houses and stores were flooded. Trees, telegraph, telephone, and power lines had been knocked down and were out of commission. Automobiles were wrecked, many flipped, and some blown into the river.[680] Sanibel and Captiva Islands were flooded by the surge, and the bridge connecting the two islands was out.[681] In the days that followed, the devastation and death toll from the storm and the surge would be better understood. The clean-up effort would be massive.

"The devastation left in the wake of the hurricane prompted one Weather Bureau official to call the storm the 'most destructive in the history of the United States.' Officials estimated the storm destroyed 4,700 homes in South Florida and left 25,000 people without shelter. The Red Cross reported that 372 people lost their lives, and more than 6,000 people were injured in the storm. The long-term impact of the Great Miami Hurricane became apparent in the months and years to come as the real estate bubble burst and Florida plunged into an economic depression some three years in advance of the rest of the nation."[682]

On Friday, October 8, it was announced that H. B. Mayer had volunteered to champion the remaining clean-up effort in the City of Fort Myers.[683] On Tuesday, October 12, Mr. Mayer reported there was great interest by citizens in having their trash removed, and he called on anyone with a truck not being used to donate it to the clean-up effort.[684] On October 16, Mr. Mayer quit his volunteer job citing a lack of trucks needed to complete the work. During his week of volunteer service, Mr. Mayer supervised the hauling of 110 loads of debris which cost the city about $1.20 per load to compensate the drivers for their time and gasoline expense. City forces would continue the clean-up effort.[685]

In November of 1926, Hendry Brothers Realty Company moved their offices from First and Jackson streets to the new Collier building, diagonally across the street. There was no change in policy or personnel.[686] The Heitman building at the corner of First and Jackson Streets was being remodeled in anticipation of United Markets opening in January.[687]

1927

Discussion about the 1927 season began in December of 1926 with the City of Sarasota trying to figure out how to retain its Florida State League franchise. Citizens were determined to have a team in the league, and a delegation planned to appear before the city council to ask for an appropriation of $5,000 to guarantee the financing of the club.[688]

Even though Tampa had strong attendance at Plant Field during the Smokers' second-half surge, Doc Opre claimed to have lost $5,000 during the 1926 season.[689]

On January 15, 1927, Florida State League President J. B. Asher confirmed the mid-winter league meeting would take place at 10 o'clock the morning of Tuesday, January 18, at the Forrest Lake Hotel in Sanford. Agenda items would include the schedule for 1927, the possibility of moving the league from Class D to Class C, the rookie and class man rules, the cities to be represented in 1927, and the election of league officers.[690]

Fort Myers Franchise Forfeited

On January 18, 1927, the mid-winter meeting of the directors of the Florida State League was held in Sanford, Florida. Representatives from Tampa, St. Petersburg, Lakeland, Orlando, and Sanford were present.[691] A message was received from Sarasota indicating the city would support any decisions made at the meeting. A message received from Bradenton indicated the city would not enter the 1927 campaign and requested its franchise be transferred to West Palm Beach.

League officials praised the city council of Sanford for appropriating $15,000 for the use of the Sanford Celeryfeds Baseball Club in 1927. "Nearly every club in the circuit receives some aid from their respective city councils, but it was believed that the Sanford council is the first to fully provide for the baseball club throughout the season."[692]

"The Fort Myers franchise was forfeited due to failure to meet league assessments and to pay players during the latter part of the 1926 season, it was said at the meeting."[693]

Enthusiastic Fans Rally to Save the Fort Myers Franchise

After publishing an open letter in the newspaper, L. A. Wingate, a city commissioner and prominent Fort Myers businessman, was urged to act by enthusiastic fans to try to ensure Fort Myers retained its Florida State League franchise. He called for a meeting of baseball fans to take place on Thursday, February 10 in the Chamber of Commerce offices.

"'I think we should get together right now and find out where we stand,' said Mr. Wingate. 'I understand it is a case of "put up or shut up." Let's meet and decide what to do while there still is time to do something.'"

"Minor League Baseball has always been and will continue to be in the small cities of the country a speculation. In cities where club owners have made money, this profit can be directly traced, in most cases, to the development and sale of promising young players. In other cities, the financing has been taken care of by the civic organizations such as Kiwanis, Lions, or similar clubs, and a few cities having municipality-owned teams have been successful. However, in no instance has financial success come from the season's attendance alone."

Unable to reach John W. Hendry, who headed the 1926 club, Charley Klein, reporter for the *Fort Myers Tropical News* confirmed with S. Watt Lawler the costs involved in operating a team include a $2,000 forfeit fee, $1,500 dues to the Florida State League, the National Association, and the Commission; $12,000 for player salaries and $2,500 manager salary. Additional expenses including a bus, traveling expenses, transportation to bring players to Fort Myers, changes in management, groundskeeper, bookkeeper, telegrams, water, lights, baseballs, uniforms, and equipment brought the projected expenses to more than $20,000.

Mr. Lawler cautioned the Fort Myers' franchise was forfeited for nonpayment of players and dues, and any budget for team operations would need to include the purchasing of a franchise. "Provided Fort Myers can again secure a franchise, not less than $15,000 must be raised and banked before the opening day. Past experience proves that the money must be raised first.

'Local fans who believe that a franchise could be obtained, point to the great advertising value of having a team in organized baseball. Some of them go as far as placing the value of a league from an advertising standpoint equal to the benefit obtained by having the Philadelphia Athletics train at Terry Park."[694]

At the start of the meeting at the Chamber of Commerce offices on February 10, John W. Hendry spoke and told those present he felt confident that he "could assure" that Fort Myers could regain her franchise in the Florida State League by the payment of $5,600 in back dues and the posting of the $2,000 forfeit required of all teams.

"'I feel sure that the people of this city have been educated to baseball and will turn out in larger numbers another year. I might add, too, that profiting by one year's experience another team can be run cheaper than the one last season,' Mr. Hendry declared."

After Mr. Hendry finished speaking, L.A. Wingate, city commissioner and prominent businessman who called the meeting, nominated Mr. A. A. Coult to be chairman of the effort to secure the franchise. His nomination was seconded by Bard L. Hendry, and Mr. Coult's election was unanimous.

Retired manufacturer, T. J. Garganous, of Norfolk, Virginia, now living in Fort Myers, shared that he has been a ballplayer, manager, and a part-owner of the Norfolk team in the Virginia league. Mr. Garganous offered his services as a "citizen who wants baseball."   John W. Hendry asked him for a definition of "services" he would provide, he said he would return to baseball as an active manager and take charge of the team if asked, but he preferred not to do so unless it was absolutely necessary.

It was decided a general mass meeting would be held at the courthouse on Monday evening, February 14, at 8 o'clock to determine whether the city will be represented in the league. Action to regain the franchise would need to be made before the meeting of league officials on February 23.[695]

Following several optimistic speeches by prominent businessmen, L. A. Wingate named a committee who would be responsible for ensuring a large turnout at the courthouse the following Monday.[696]

On February 12, 1927, President J. B. Asher of the Florida State League announced that negotiations for the purchase of a franchise by Miami and West Palm Beach were nearly completed. "The East Coast cities would replace Bradenton and Fort Myers under the present plans."

On February 14, 1927, 13 people showed up at the Lee County courthouse to support the idea of organized baseball in Fort Myers. The 13 enthusiasts came early and spent some time discussing the situation among themselves, but their enthusiasm began to wane by 8:15 p.m. Several people who had pledged to take part in the work and lend financial support failed to appear. At 8:30 p.m., Chairman A. A. Coult adjourned the meeting on the grounds of "lack of attendance and absence of any tangible population that would give the city organized baseball."

"H. B. Mayer, former business manager of the Palms, offered to raise $5,000 toward the financing of the team and turn this amount over to 'any committee or group that will operate the club.' No action was taken on the offer."[697]

Let's Try This Again

On February 21, 1927, "after a week or so of hemming and hawing about baseball for Fort Myers," a group of fans met at the Chamber of Commerce offices. They organized a club, elected officers, and outlined a plan to finance the team. The revival of baseball talk after it had gone quiet following the recent mass meeting was inspired by James E. Hendry and a few others.

J. R. Randle, manager of the Bradford Hotel, was elected president; A. E. Raymond, city commissioner was named vice president; and C. C. Pursley, vice president of the First National Bank, was chosen as treasurer. A board of directors was elected including James E. Hendry, Dr. Baker Whisnant, E. M. Goss, L. J. Van Duyl, Mrs. Sara C. Douglass, L. A. Wingate, George E. Hosmer, and Harrison Fuller.

During the meeting, it was shared that when Florida State League President J. B. Asher was informed by the *Fort Myers Tropical News* of the developments in Fort Myers, he confirmed over the phone from his home in Orlando that Fort Myers could get its franchise back, provided it pays up its debt of about $6,000 and posts the required $2,000 forfeit fee.

The opinion of those at the meeting was that $12,500 would be enough to carry the club through the season. Previous estimates were that $15,000 would be required. It was estimated that gate receipts would be about $7,500 for the season and the cash outlay for all purposes would not be more than $20,000. They agreed on a plan to raise the $12,500. $5,000 would come from public subscriptions by 50 citizens at a rate of $100 each, which leaders at the meeting believed they would have no difficulty achieving. $5,000 from the city treasury and $2,500 from the county. Jim C. Clements was appointed to draw up papers incorporating the club.[698]

On March 2, a meeting of the newly formed Baseball Club to back a Fort Myers entry in the Florida State League was called by President J. R. Randle for the purpose of obtaining a definite financial guarantee for a team.[699] "It was decided that no action would be taken by the club until after the meeting of the Florida State League to be held in Tampa on March 21. Dr. Baker Whisnant will represent Fort Myers at the meeting in Tampa."[700]

On March 19, 1927, the Associated Press released three wires in quick succession:

From Orlando: J. B. Asher declared that ten cities were seeking entrance into the Florida State League. Mr. Asher called a meeting of the league at 11 o'clock Monday morning [March 21] in Tampa to select the eight clubs that would comprise the league and to approve the 1927 schedule. Mr.

Asher said the Fort Myers franchise was forfeited at the annual league meeting in Sanford in January, but the Palm city is seeking readmission, and it is possible that franchise will be reinstated at Monday's meeting. Mr. Asher considered the applications of Miami, West Palm Beach, Lakeland, and Daytona were "doubtful."

From Lakeland: Clare Henley, president of the Lakeland Baseball Club, the oldest member of the Florida State League, stated that after being represented in the league for eight years, he will return his franchise at the meeting on Monday. Lakeland has withdrawn from the league.

From Fort Myers: James E. Hendry, spokesman for the group of fans backing the proposed reorganization of the Fort Myers Baseball Club announced the committee tonight decided to drop the project and will not have a representative at the meeting in Tampa on Monday.[701]

"Although the Florida State League is holding a place open for Fort Myers as the sixth member of the reorganized circuit, the fans of this city have abandoned interest in the prospect of obtaining a franchise, J. R. Randle, president of the proposed club said." Mr. Randle's statement was made after the league announced it had decided to reinstate Fort Myers and would ask a committee from this city to meet with President Asher this week to review the details. "'The group which had under consideration the matter of arranging to re-enter the league has definitely abandoned the project,' said Mr. Randle. 'We decided several days ago that it was too late in the season to try to finance the club or recruit a team that could give the fans here the quality of baseball they demand.'"[702]

At the meeting of Florida State League officials in Tampa on March 21, plans to have an eight-club league were abandoned. Fort Myers, Bradenton, and Lakeland forfeited their franchises when they failed to have a representative at the meeting. West Palm Beach had not settled their finances. Miami has financial support but would not be admitted without West Palm Beach because of the cost of transportation from the west coast to the east coast. Mr. Asher said Lakeland may reclaim its franchise before the season opens; Winter Haven and DeLand were other applicants for admission.[703]

On March 28, President J. B. Asher announced that Fort Myers appeared to be the sixth city in the Florida State League. "Under a complete local reorganization, the Palm City is seeking reinstatement in the league, and it is probable the Palm City will be included. Officials of the Fort Myers club are expected here this week to complete details with league officials for entrance into the league."[704]

In response to the announcement from Mr. Asher, J. R. Randle announced, "There has been no renewal of interest on the part of Fort Myers in obtaining a franchise in the Florida State League and no arrangements have been made to discuss this matter with President J. B. Asher."[705]

On April 5, 1927, after hoping for several weeks that Fort Myers might reconsider its decision and join the Florida State League, President J. B. Asher announced he had abandoned the idea.[706] Mr. Asher sent a telegram to Louis MacReynolds in Miami offering the city the sixth spot in the Florida State League.[707]

In the days that followed, it was learned that at the league meeting in March the representative from Miami had a check in his pocket for $5,000 to cover the admittance fee, but the West Palm Beach delegate informed the league officials the money his club had raised was unavailable due to the recent failure of several West Palm Beach banks.

League officials voted to award the Fort Myers franchise to Daytona Beach, but that city failed to support the movement, and J. B. Asher was scrambling to secure a sixth team for the league.

Fans in Lakeland who were trying to retain their franchise hoped Mr. Asher would meet with them on April 7, but Mr. Asher did not appear in Lakeland and his whereabouts were unknown. Dr. Opre, the Tampa president, explained that Mr. Asher was a fan of adding a team from the East Coast and suspected he might be in West Palm Beach or Miami.[708]

On April 11, 1927, Miami accepted a franchise in the Florida State League ensuring the league would have six teams. President J. B. Asher announced that baseball officials in West Palm Beach and Fort Myers were being approached once again to consider entering the league.[709]

On April 12, 1927, J. B. Asher returned to Orlando from Miami. After reviewing the prospects for getting West Palm Beach and Fort Myers to join the league, the league president decided it best to begin the season with six teams. He left open the possibility that two teams might join the league for the second half of the season.

"Mr. Asher is confident that the Palms will again cavort on league greensward."[710]

Growers' Franchise Turned Over

In 1927, Miami fielded its first team in the Florida State League. The team was known as the Miami Hustlers. This was made possible by W. B. Kirby, the new head of the Miami organization. Kirby was the former president of the Bradenton Growers, and turned the Bradenton franchise over to Miami as his investment in the new club.[711]

The 1927 Florida State League included the Miami Hustlers, Orlando Colts, St. Petersburg Saints, Sanford Celeryfeds, Sarasota Tarpons, and the Tampa Smokers.[712]

Connie Mack's Assessment of the Real Estate Market

On the evening of February 17, 1927, Connie Mack, manager of the Philadelphia Athletics, and Athletics President Thomas Shibe arrived in Fort Myers ahead of the 1927 spring training season. They had been relaxing and golfing with Clark Griffith, owner of the Washington Senators, and others in Tampa, Florida.[713]

The next morning, the two men visited Terry Park and were very pleased with the condition of the field. Mr. Mack decided he needed to find a new straw hat, so they left the ball field and headed to downtown Fort Myers to shop.

"The famous manager, cornered late yesterday afternoon in the Royal Palm Pharmacy by a group of fans of this city, said that he had two homes and one of them was Fort Myers.

'I had the time of my life at Tampa, but Tampa doesn't measure up to Fort Myers,' he assured them. 'Let me say here, that there is more activity in your city and more real progress than in any other Florida city I have seen. The real estate business is in a slump in Philadelphia as well as in Fort Myers.'"[714]

John Wall Hendry – The Later Years

John Wall Hendry spent 1927 trying to salvage his real estate business. For recreation, he participated as a member of one of the teams in the Elks bowling league.[715]

In 1928, Hendry sold his house on Providence Street to Lucius C. Curtright, president of Fort Myers Real Estate.[716] John and Gladys Hendry traveled to New York and spent the summer there with their children and returned to Fort Myers in October.[717]

Tragedy struck the Hendry family on December 31, 1928, when John Wall Hendry's father, Louis Asbury Hendry, was hunting with a nephew, Fred Hendry. The pair had separated to pursue a deer and when Fred thought he heard the deer, he aimed his gun and shot into the brush. When he went to see the deer, he discovered he had shot his uncle Louis. He ran to get help, but the shot was fatal.[718]

In May of 1929, Hendry and his family left Fort Myers and traveled back to Jacksonville to spend the summer at the Needham home.[719] By the second half of 1929, the United States had fallen into the Great Depression, and in October that year the stock market crashed. His wealth was still largely tied up in real estate. He was over-extended, and he lost his fortune during the depression.[720]

Hendry was determined to work and to provide for his family. He was able to secure a job managing two mines in Havana, Cuba, in the early 1930s. One was zinc and the other bauxite (the main mineral used in aluminum). Mrs. Hendry and their three children thought Cuba was beautiful, but the area was a mining town, and Mrs. Hendry chose to live with her parents in the Needham family estate in Jacksonville, Florida, until Hendry was able to return to the States. The Needham estate included a magnificent three-story home fully staffed with servants who would care for their every need.[721] Hendry used his vacation time to visit the family in Jacksonville and Fort Myers, and Mrs. Hendry would occasionally visit Mr. Hendry in Havana. By November of 1934, Hendry had left Havana for good, and he and his family moved from Jacksonville back to Fort Myers.[722]

Hendry was very involved with the Elks in his later years. In December of 1934, he was managing the Elk Lodge headquarters and grill in Fort Myers.[723]

In April of 1935, Hendry moved his family back to Jacksonville, Florida.[724] It is believed that was the last time Mr. Hendry was ever in Fort Myers.

The 1940 U.S. Census indicates John Wall Hendry, his wife Gladys and their three children (then 18, 16, and 14) lived in the Needham home at 2344 Forbes Street in Jacksonville, Florida. Mr. Hendry was a Salesman.[725]

Interview with Jake Jacobson, Grandson of John Wall Hendry

Most everything written in this story for the period of 1895 to 1940 is facts that are discoverable through online resources such as the University of Florida Digital Collections, Newspapers.com and Find-A-Grave.com, or by exploring the amazing collection of historical books and memorabilia in the Southwest Florida Historical Society building in Fort Myers, Florida. After completing the initial research for this story, there were several "why" questions the primary sources were unable to answer such as, "Why did John W. Hendry desire to purchase a Florida State League franchise in 1925?" or "Why did Mr. Hendry respond to a reporter's question that way?" Fortunately, there is a living descendent of John Wall Hendry who was kind enough to respond to a letter and to spend time sharing his knowledge of family history and his memories of his mother Elizabeth, and his grandfather John Wall Hendry.

Jake Jacobson is the son of Elizabeth (nee Hendry) Jacobson, daughter of John Wall Hendry. Jake had a successful career in Information Technology, rising to CTO of a Chinese Telecom. Having achieved his career goal, Jake directed his passion to mentoring and teaching people in the information technology field. He picked up tinkering and thriftiness from his grandfather, John Wall Hendry, who raised him.

Jake's Paternal Grandfather was W. C. "Baby Doll" Jacobson, a very talented Major League Baseball player from 1915 to 1927 who missed a season or two while serving in World War I. When his baseball career

Jake Jacobson. Photo by Saisunee Jacobson (2023).

ended, Baby Doll Jacobson bought a farm in Coal Valley, Illinois, and spent his last 50 years working the farm. Jake's great aunt once assembled an exhibit in the Moline - Rock Island, Illinois, area for Baby Doll Jacobson in hopes of drawing attention to his career and building support for the National Baseball Hall of Fame Veterans' Committee to review him as a candidate for induction into the National Baseball Hall of Fame.

Jake was able to pick up the story where the documented history of John Wall Hendry ends with the Hendry family moving from Fort Myers to Jacksonville, Florida.   John and Gladys Hendry spent many years in Jacksonville.

During the 1940s, all three of John Wall Hendry's children served in World War II:

- Eldest son John Wall Hendry Jr., or "Jack" as he was known, was a captain in the U.S. Army and served as a pilot in the Flying Fortress "Hell's Angels."[726] He flew several missions and took fire more than once. He was captured and taken as a prisoner of war for a year; he was awarded the Purple Heart. Jack retired from the U.S. Army as a Captain.
- Daughter Elizabeth Parker Hendry; "Betty" to her friends or "Bette" as her parents called her, served as a WAVE (Women Accepted for Volunteer Emergency Service) for the U.S. Navy in Oklahoma City.[727]
- Son Robert Needham Hendry, a member of Beta Theta Pi Fraternity, also served in the U.S. Army Air Corps. He retired from the U.S. Army Corps of Engineers Reserve with the rank of Captain.[728]

In 1948, John and Gladys Hendry traveled to Flat Rock, North Carolina, for the wedding of their daughter Elizabeth to William T. S. Jacobson of Philadelphia. The reception took place at Mountain Manor in Saluda, North Carolina, the summer home of Mrs. Hendry's brother, Dr. and Mrs. H. M. Needham.[729; 730; 731] The father of the groom was retired Major League Baseball player, W. C. ("Baby Doll') Jacobson of Coal Valley, Illinois. Baby Doll Jacobson did not attend the wedding.

In the early 1950s, John Wall Hendry and wife Gladys purchased Dogwood Shack in Saluda, North Carolina, and renamed it Tall Trees. In the 1950s and 60s, they would travel back and forth often between their home in Jacksonville, Florida, and their cottage in Saluda. These were enjoyable times for the Hendrys. Their three children were grown, and John and Gladys were enjoying a comfortable, simple life together.

Dogwood Shack in Saluda, NC, 1951. Photo courtesy of Jake Jacobson.

Elizabeth (Hendry) and husband Bill Jacobson lived in Pasadena, California with their three teenage children. Mr. Jacobson was on a very successful career trajectory when their fourth child Jake was born in 1963. Tragically, when Jake was just two months old, his father Bill was killed in an automobile accident. Jake has no memory of Bill. Elizabeth moved the four children to Hendersonville, North Carolina, where they would be near her parents.

The simple life that John Wall Hendry and his wife Gladys enjoyed would be a little more exciting now as they helped Elizabeth and her children. The teenagers were self-sufficient, but baby Jake was not. In 1963, John Wall Hendry took on the role of father for his new grandson. The timing was good for Mr. Hendry, he was at a point in life where he was focused on what was most important – his family.

One of the earliest memories Jake Jacobson has of John Wall Hendry is that he would open his sweater to one side and Jake would climb up on his lap and Mr. Hendry would wrap the sweater around him.

Jake recalls taking naps in-between his grandfather John and grandmother Gladys in a huge bed his Needham ancestors brought over from England. As a boy, Jake's grandparents would play hide-and-seek with him. Jake would hide in the matching armoire and his grandparents were unable to find him (or at least they pretended that to be the case). Today, Jake sleeps in that large bed.

After suppers, young Jake and John Wall Hendry would have ice cream together, then they would make a bowl for everyone - so Jake and Mr. Hendry had their second bowl of ice cream with the family.

Other recollections Jake has of his grandfather include:

- John Wall Hendry and his daughter Elizabeth got along well – they were very fond of each other.
- In 1974, Elizabeth went to Europe for 23 days. Jake stayed in Saluda, North Carolina, with John Wall Hendry and went to Saluda School. Jake enjoyed reading *National Geographic* and studying British history.
- Gladys Hendry had four sisters who also lived in Saluda.
- Mr. Hendry once bought a school library in Saluda and converted it into apartments.
- John Wall Hendry was an avid golfer later in life. Jake recalls watching golf on television with his grandfather.
- Mr. Hendry was a member of the Elks Club and Jake remembers his grandfather taking him to the club when he was four years old.
- John Wall Hendry did smoke cigars, but he did not drink.

From 1926: "A shortage of pin boys prevented the fourth round of the Elks' bowling tournament from being held last night…. John Hendry, who offered a prize box of cigars for the highest individual score, rolled in competition last week. He won his own prize when he set a new record of 196. Mr. Hendry has given another box of smokes, and these will be awarded to the leader in this week's results."[732]

Later in life, John Wall Hendry repaired and cleaned coin-counting machines for banks. "He loved to tinker and fix things," Grandson Jake Jacobson recalls.

Photo of John Wall Hendry (1970's) courtesy of Jake Jacobson.

In the photo (above) Mr. Hendry is with a machine he repaired for a local bank. He used to call on the banks and service their machinery. He might charge $75 or $100 depending on the repair [$75 to $100 in 1970, is the equivalent of $550 to $750 in 2023 dollars], but the alternative for the bank was to ship the machine back to the manufacturer – and it could be weeks before the bank received the machine back.

John Wall Hendry always had a cigar in his mouth. Sometimes he broke up a cigar and smoked it through a pipe (he never bought pipe tobacco). Doctors warned him this was dangerous. Mr. Hendry suffered two bouts of throat cancer, but that did not cause him to give up his cigars.

John Wall Hendry was "tough." In 1973, at 78 years old, Mr. Hendry had an aneurysm the size of a grapefruit removed from his chest. As part of his recovery, the doctors encouraged him to take walks. He required two canes to walk. One day he was attacked by two Dobermanns. Mr. Hendry beat them off with his canes and then hobbled back home.

Of John Wall Hendry's three children, Jake recalls his Uncle Jack (John Wall Hendry Jr.) was most like his grandfather. He had a very nice wife, Aunt Gloria, and he loved to have ice cream at night. Jake remembers Jack as being very generous to his parents. Every time Jack and Gloria would visit John and Gladys Hendry, they always brought way more groceries than were needed for their visit. John Wall Hendry instilled in his children to always give generously – and Jack did. When Jake and his (then) future bride Saisunee visited Jack and Gloria in Jacksonville, Jack slipped Saisunee a $100 bill as a wedding gift. Jack suffered from cancer for several years but did not share that information with family until his last year.

John Wall Hendry had a positive attitude in his later years. He never spoke negatively about anything; he never told a story about anything bad. He always talked about the best things. Mr. Hendry taught good breeding. It was proper to speak positive and to say kind things. He did talk about his time in Cuba. He would never say he was away from his wife and children though – he talked about the good work of his teams in the mines.

Jake Jacobson doesn't think of his grandfather in terms of an anecdote or quote, but rather he remembers the influence his grandfather had on him. John Wall Hendry would tell his grandson, "You have the aptitude and the intelligence to do anything you want." It wasn't just what he said, but how he said it with conviction. Mr. Hendry sat Jake down, he looked him in the eye, and he made him believe it. Jake recalls he genuinely felt like his grandfather believed it too.

John Wall Hendry did not talk about the mid 1920s much in his later years – it was clear he was overextended during those times. About a year before his passing, Mr. Hendry sat down with a cassette tape recorder and told the story of his life, including the baseball years. Jake believes he may have a box somewhere that includes those cassette tapes. Jake has moved a couple of times since his grandfather's passing but does not recall ever consciously disposing of the tapes.

After a brief illness, on April 7, 1979, John Wall Hendry passed away in a Hendersonville, North Carolina, hospital. He was 83.[733] His wife Gladys Hendry died in 1996. Mr. and Mrs. Hendry are buried next to each other in the Saluda City Cemetery, Saluda, North Carolina.

Saluda City Cemetery, Saluda, North Carolina. Photo by Ken Breen (2023).

"John Wall Hendry was everything you want a grandfather to be. He was kind, loving and supportive." – Jake Jacobson, grandson of John Wall Hendry.

Curtain Call

Several players in the Florida State League came and went from Terry Park during the Summer of 1926. For many of them, as they left by automobile, bus, train, or boat, they may have never looked back.

The Florida State League's best pitcher in 1926 was Ben Cantwell of the Sanford Celeryfeds. Cantwell was elevated to the major leagues at the end of the 1927 season. He broke in with the New York Giants and played most of the next decade with the Boston Braves.[734] The Giants and Braves played spring training exhibition games against the Philadelphia Athletics at Terry Park during his career, but Cantwell does not appear in a box score as having pitched or played during any of those games, so it is not known whether he ever returned to Fort Myers or not.

Al Lopez, the catcher for the 1926 Tampa Smokers, would return to Terry Park several times during his career. The first game Lopez caught for the Smokers at Terry Park was on May 6, 1926.[735] In 1931, major leaguer Al Lopez caught a spring training game for Brooklyn against the Philadelphia Athletics at Terry Park.[736] After retiring as a player, Lopez managed the Chicago White Sox from 1957 through 1969; his team visited Terry Park for a spring training game against the Pittsburg Pirates each of those years. In 1961, Mr. Lopez appeared in a photo in the *Fort Myers News-Press* with a local insurance man who was his look-alike.[737] In his final year as skipper of the White Sox, Al Lopez managed his team to a 5-1 spring training victory over the Kansas City Royals at Terry Park.[738] Al Lopez was inducted into the National Baseball Hall of Fame as a manager in 1977. Today, his name appears on a banner that hangs at Terry Park, along with the names of several other Hall of Fame inductees who played at the historic ballfield.

As for the 1926 Fort Myers Baseball Club, every effort was made to verify the first name of each person, and to learn more about their story before and after the *Summer of Palms*.

Prospects that did not Report to Fort Myers
for a Pre-season Tryout

Bob Cole

Robert Cole accompanied Manager Buck Conroy on his initial visit from Tampa to Fort Myers in January of 1926. Mr. Cole was a veteran of the Florida State League, he played for Orlando in 1922. On March 15, 1926, the *St. Petersburg Times* reported that Mr. Cole had signed a contract to pitch for the Palms.[739] He said he would report to camp in Fort Myers in early April.[740] There is no evidence that Mr. Cole ever reported to Fort Myers that spring.

Sam Mercer

On March 18, 1926, Palms Manager Buck Conroy announced "Sam Mercer, catcher" as a prospect.[741] There was no mention of where Sam Mercer was from, and there was no further mention of Mr. Mercer related to the Palms after that date. In 1926, there was a Sam Mercer, who was a catcher, for the Twin Cities team in the Eastern Ohio, semi-pro league. Other cities represented in the Eastern Ohio League in 1926 included Coshocton, New Philadelphia, Zanesville, Barnesville, Cambridge, Steubenville, and Newark.[742]

Herbert Young

Shortstop Herbert Young was mentioned as a Palms prospect by Manager Buck Conroy on March 18, 1926.[743] There is no later mention of Mr. Young related to the Palms. The same day, Charlie Allen, manager of the Tampa Smokers, announced he had signed Herbert Young. Mr. Young had been in Tampa trying out for the Washington Senators. Bucky Harris, manager of the Senators, suggested Mr. Young needed some developing and recommended Charlie Allen sign him.[744]

Len Maloney

On April 19, 1926, Manager Buck Conroy, announced he had "obtained Len Maloney, an infielder from Toledo in the American Association. Maloney is highly regarded by Casey Stengel, the new Toledo pilot. He performed credibly in the Southwestern and Mississippi Valley leagues last year and will join the Palms at Sarasota or Bradenton next week."[745] There is nothing to indicate Mr. Maloney met up with the Palms the following week.

Prospects that Tried Out but did not Play for the 1926 Palms

Cody

On March 30, 1926, Palms Manager Buck Conroy announced there were ten prospects already in camp, including Cody, an infielder from Michigan.[746] On April 1, Manager Conroy announced that Cody had been released.[747]

Tanner

On April 1, 1926, Palms Manager Buck Conroy announced that Tanner had been released.[748] This is the first and only mention of Mr. Tanner having tried out for the Palms.

Phil Tanner, a utility infielder, joined the Tampa Smokers on June 10. He came to the Smokers from Spartanburg in the Class B South Atlantic League.[749] It is possible that Phil Tanner is the same person that tried out for the Palms before the start of the season, since Mr. Tanner signed with the Spartanburg club on March 29,[750] which lines up with Buck Conroy's mention of his release on April 1.

Heflin

There is no mention of the arrival of Mr. Heflin. No first name, no indication of where he was from or what position he was trying out for. He was listed as available for the April 6, 1926, game against the Macon club of the South Atlantic League,[751] but he did not play in that game,[752] nor was he a participant in the second game against Macon on April 7.[753] Mr. Heflin was released by Palms Manager Buck Conroy on April 8, 1926.[754]

Harry Kauffman

Palms Manager Buck Conroy was interested in evaluating local players with semi-pro experience. Harry Kauffman was signed for a tryout with the team in March of 1926.[755] There was nothing further documented about Mr. Kauffman in relation to the Palms.

Bill Stanley

On April 8, 1926, Buck Conroy announced the acquisition of Bill Stanley of Kingston, Virginia.[756] Mr. Stanley was a rookie[757] who auditioned for a spot in the outfield.[758] He was released on April 13, 1926.[759]

Robert Mawhor

Robert Mawhor was an infielder with semi-pro experience in Iowa.[760] In March of 1926, he was residing in Fort Myers, and Manager Buck Conroy indicated he would be in camp early and would be able to "get in a little work with Connie Mack's crowd" before the start of Palms' camp on March 27.[761] Mawhor played third base for the Palms during their pre-season exhibition games against Macon on April 6,[762] and April 7, 1926.[763] Mawhor was released on April 13, 1926.[764]

Blankenbaker

Blankenbaker played for the Fort Myers "Regulars" semi-pro team in 1925.[765] He played right field for the Fort Myers Palms in the first pre-season exhibition game against Macon on April 6, 1926, but failed to produce a base hit.[766] Mr. Blankenbaker's name does not appear in association with the Palms after April 9, 1926.

Storey

Storey was an outfield prospect from Lake Okeechobee at Moore Haven, Florida.[767] He was among the first to try out for a spot on the Palms' roster. The release of Mr. Storey was announced by Manager Buck Conroy on April 1, 1926.[768]

Alonzo

Pitcher Alonzo came from Tampa with experience in the Ridge League.[769] He was the starting pitcher against Macon on April 7, 1926.[770] Mr. Alonzo was released on April 8, 1926.[771]

Casendyke

Casendyke, a Ridge League outfielder from St. Petersburg,[772] was one of ten players who reported for tryouts on March 30, 1926. Mr. Casendyke was released on April 8.[773]

In 1926, it was not uncommon for a pre-season prospect's name to be misspelled. A writer might hear a player's name pronounced and spell it phonetically in the newspaper. Over time, the correct spelling would be achieved. If Mr. Alonzo's last name was in fact spelled with an "s," as in Alonso, it is possible that prospects Alonso and Casendyke ended up playing together for the Primo Lord Undertakers in the St. Petersburg City League in 1926.[774]

White

White was an infielder from Columbus, Georgia. He arrived in camp the last week of March, 1926,[775] and was released by Manager Conroy on April 1, 1926.[776]

Tony Thielan

Tony Thielan was a pitcher from Kansas. The Thielan brothers were among the first prospects to report for tryouts in Fort Myers in March of 1926.[777] Announcement of Tony Thielan's release was made by Manager Buck Conroy on April 1.[778]

Larry Thielan

Larry Thielan was a right-handed pitcher from Salina, Kansas, in the Southwestern League.[779] He was impressive in relief against Macon during the Palms pre-season exhibition game on April 7[780] and made an appearance for the Palms on April 15 during the exhibition game against Rollins College.[781] Larry Thielan appeared in the Palms' team photo that was on the front page of the *Fort Myers Tropical News* on April 22, 1926,[782] but never appeared in a regular season game. Mr. Thielan was released by Manager Buck Conroy on May 5,[783] and signed with the Tampa Smokers.[784]

Bob Gibbons

Bob Gibbons was a first baseman from Greensboro, North Carolina, who tried out for the Palms and appeared in the original team photo. "He was recommended for a trial by Connie Mack and Jim Pool, first baseman for the Athletics."[785] Gibbons never appeared in a box score for the Palms and was released by Manager Buck Conroy, along with others on May 5, 1926, to help the Palms achieve the team roster limit. Gibbons signed with Tampa the next day and played for the Smokers against the Palms on May 7, 1926.[786] He was released by Smokers Manager Charlie Allen five days later.[787]

Dexter Morgan

Dexter Morgan arrived in Fort Myers from Philadelphia. Mr. Morgan appeared in the original Palms team photo on April 22, 1926. He is the one player not wearing one of the new team jerseys. Morgan never appeared in a Palms regular season box score. He was released on May 6, and was expected to join the Melbourne Club in the Florida semi-pro Ridge League.[788] By June, he was a "popular catcher" for the Vero Beach team. He returned to Fort Myers on June 16 and following a frantic search to find someone authorized to perform a wedding ceremony, he married Miss Hilda Elizabeth Booth.[789] Miss Booth was from Callahan, Florida, but had been living with relatives in Fort Myers for some time. Mr. Morgan met Miss Booth while he was playing in Fort Myers. The couple planned to make their home in Vero Beach.[790]

Joe Casares

Joe Casares, younger brother of Palms Left Fielder Faustino Casares, arrived at Terry Park on May 20, 1926, for a tryout as a pitcher.[791] Joe and Anthony Downey were scheduled to box ten rounds in the main event at the ballpark in Miami the following night.[792]

In 1927, Joe Casares tried out to be a pitcher for the Tampa Smokers. An article in *The Tampa Daily Times* explained that in addition to being one of the best pitching prospects to try out for the Smokers club, Joe Casares was a professional middle-weight boxer who fought using the name Joe Pino. Tampa Manager Tommy Leach sent Joe Casares to play for his hometown Haines City, Florida, semi-pro team for some additional development.[793] Joe Pino kept on boxing.

Joe Casares died, on December 23, 1939; he was 35. At the time of his passing, in addition to his parents, brother Faustino, and three sisters, Mr. Casares was survived by his wife Eleanor, daughter Vivian and son Richard.[794]

Joe's son Richard attended the University of Florida and was a star football player for the Gators as a quarterback, halfback, and fullback. In 1955, he signed with the Chicago Bears of the National Football League.[795] In 1956, Rick Casares led the NFL in rushing with 1,126 yards including 12 touchdowns on 234 carries. New York Giants' star halfback Frank Gifford finished fifth.[796] Rick Casares passed away on September 13, 2013, he was 82. At the time of his death, Rick was survived by his wife Polly, and was third on the Chicago Bears all-time rushing list behind Walter Payton and Neal Anderson.[797]

Players That Made a Brief Appearance as a Member of the 1926 Palms

Charlie Allen

Allen, who managed the Tampa Smokers from the beginning of the 1926 season until he resigned in June,[798] played his first game as a Palm on July 25 and was released by the team on August 2, 1926.[799] From 1928 through 1932, Charlie coached the Tampa All Stars in the American Legion National Boys' Baseball Tournament. The team won several state titles in a row.[800;801] In 1930, he was appointed coach of the Hillsborough High School Terriers baseball team.[802] In March of 1934, he was hired to coach the Tampa University baseball team.[803] Charlie was involved as an official in football and basketball. Charles Seymour Allen died on January 25, 1947; he was 56. At the time of his death, he was survived by one brother.[804]

McGruger

On May 11, 1926, an article in the *Fort Myers Tropical News* discussing the release of Vincent Macey includes the only mention of McGruger. "A newcomer named McGruger was added to the roster replacing Macey."[805] McGruger made one plate appearance on May 10 when he batted for Pitcher Gene Davenport in the bottom of the ninth inning.[806] There is no record of McGruger's first name and no mention of his release. His name appeared in the Palms season-to-date statistics on May 13,[807] but his single plate appearance was included in the collective "released" tally on May 20.[808]

Rich Porter

Richard G. Porter played outfield for the University of Florida in 1924 and 1925. Mr. Porter was signed by the Lakeland Highlanders in March of 1925. He signed for a tryout with the Palms in May, 1926, and appeared in four games May 13 to 17 but was released May 19. On October 19, 1992, Richard G. Porter passed away in Port St. Joe, Florida; he was 88 years old. Richard Porter's brother, Ned, was a pitcher for the University of Florida Gators in 1924 and 1925. Ned Porter was signed and played for the National League New York Giants in 1926 and 1927.

Tommy Condon

Tommy Condon, an infielder from St. Louis, who was "said to be good enough for the majors" started the 1926 campaign in the Bradenton camp.[809] He was released by the Growers on May 6.[810] Condon was picked up by the Palms during a road trip and played first base on May 15 and right field on May 17. He was released by Manager Buck Conroy on May 20, 1926.[811]

Dutch Bandera

George[812] William[813] "Dutch" Bandera, was a catcher with semi-pro experience in Philadelphia. He reported to camp the last week of March.[814] Dutch is wearing a catcher's chest protector in the Palms' opening day team photo that appeared in the *Fort Myers Tropical News,* on April 22, 1926.[815] Dutch appeared in three games for the Palms from April 23 to April 26. He was released from the team by Manager Joe Johnston on May 28, 1926.[816] Dutch Bandera continued to play semi-pro baseball in Lynn, Massachusetts,[817] and Portland, Maine.

In May of 1932, after completing a series with the Red Sox in Boston, Connie Mack and the Philadelphia Athletics traveled north to play an exhibition game against an "All Maine 9" as part of Portland's Centennial celebration. On May 27, more than 1,000 fans sat through the shivering cold to witness the game. On May 28, a picture in the *Portland Press Herald* captured the moment when Philadelphia Athletics Pitcher Eddie Rommel scored. Catcher Dutch Bandera was perfectly positioned with both feet blocking home plate and would have had to wait three to four steps to tag the approaching Rommel out had the throw to home not sailed high and to the right of Bandera.[818]

In February 1933, a photo of Dutch Bandera appeared in the *Portland Evening Express* with a headline and caption announcing he was being given a tryout by the Brooklyn Dodgers.[819]

In 1938, Dutch Bandera was instrumental in organizing the Dade County League in Miami, Florida. He injured his knee during a game that summer. 400 fans attended the final game of the 1939 Dade County League season and saw the Miami 9 defeat the All Stars 2 to 1. The players refused to accept the gate receipts and directed all of the proceeds to Dutch Bandera to help with the cost of his knee surgery.[820]

Mr. Bandera experienced different jobs over the years from managing a restaurant and bar to selling vacuum cleaners. In 1948, he was a real estate agent with E. J. C. Perkins Realty in Miami. Mr. Bandera planned to sell real estate until 1971 and then retire to Miami Shores.[821] He was a member of the Knights of Columbus in Miami, Florida, and a member of the Miami Real Estate Board.

Dutch Bandera passed away on February 7, 1958; he was 52. At the time of his death, Mr. Bandera was survived by one son, one daughter and two grandchildren.[822]

Hal Fisher

From May 18 through May 26, 1926, (Harold) Hal Fisher played in eight games for the Fort Myers Palms. He was an infielder who was acquired from Ardmore in the Western Association.[823] He played one game in right field and the remainder at first base. Mr. Fisher was released by Manager Johnston on May 28, 1926.[824]

Ed Overstreet

Ed Overstreet was the last player to report to the Palms. Overstreet was the catcher and manager of the pennant winning Arcadia, Florida club in the Ridge League. He arrived at Terry Park, for the final Palms home game and was cleared by the league president, J. B. Asher, to play the final four innings of the game. Mr. Overstreet caught for the Palms in their final five road games of the season.[825]

It is possible that Ed Overstreet was the same Catcher "Overstreet" who played for the Rollins College team in their pre-season exhibition game against the Palms at Terry Park on April 15th. In 1926, Rollins college did not field a regular collegiate team. Their schedule was comprised exclusively of Florida State League and nearby town teams. The brief article in the Rollins College yearbook does not include the full roster of player names but lists a "Moore" as their regular catcher. There is no student with the last name Overstreet in any of the four classes.[826]

Larry Schacht

Larry Schacht, the 21-year-old brother of former Washington Senators Pitcher Al Schact, arrived for a tryout with the Palms on June 9. He came to Fort Myers from New York where he played at New York University and on semi-pro teams.[827] Schacht appeared in two games, one on June 16 and the other on June 23 of 1926. He was released by the Palms and signed by the Bradenton Growers.[828]

In 1927, Schact pitched in the opening game for the Winston-Salem Twins in the Class C Piedmont League.[829] In 1943, he was a pitcher for the U.S. Maritime Training Station team at Sheepshead Bay[830] in Brooklyn, New York.

Howard Johnson

Johnson played for the Lakeland Highlanders in 1925 and started the 1926 season with Jacksonville in the Southeastern League. On June 8, 1926, he pitched just one inning in his only start for the Palms. He gave up two walks, two hits, four runs and was the losing pitcher.[831] Johnson reappeared in 1926 making his debut with the Highlanders on August 28. He pitched a one-hit shutout in the seven-inning, second game of a double-header against the Tampa Smokers.[832] He held the Sarasota Gulls to four hits in a 9 to 2 complete game victory on September 1.[833] Howard

Johnson pitched a five-hit complete game victory over the Palms in the final game played at Terry Park on September 8, 1926.[834]

1926 Fort Myers Baseball Club Team Officials

S. W. Lawler

Watt Lawler was John Wall Hendry's legal representative and vice president of the Fort Myers Baseball Club. In 1925, he represented Hendry in his attempts to acquire the Sanford and Lakeland franchises, and he remained the attorney for the Palms during the 1926 season.[835] Mr. Lawler was the son of a Methodist minister who died in 1924 and is buried in the Fort Myers Cemetery. S. Watt Lawler, Jr., played college football and graduated from Emory and Henry College in Southwest Virginia, then secured a law degree from the University of Florida in 1913. He served in the Navy in World War I. He was a member of the American Legion and the Forty and Eight Society and was a representative in the Florida State Legislature in 1927. Mr. Lawler owned a private law practice in Fort Myers for almost 40 years. In addition, he was the city judge, and he was appointed by Florida Governor Sidney J. Catts as the first state's attorney for the 12th Judicial Circuit. In 1954, Mr. Lawler moved from Fort Myers Beach to Kissimmee, Florida. He had been in poor health for several years. On June 1, 1958, Samuel Watson Lawler, Jr., passed away in Kissimmee; he was 67. At the time of his death, Mr. Lawler was survived by his wife, Mercia and two sisters.[836]

W. H. Merrill

Merrill was the team secretary. He appeared in the original team photo in April 1926, and was often listed as the source when player transactions were announced. Mr. Merrill left the organization in August 1926, to work full-time for Hendry Brothers Realty Company. He would be responsible for a new service department that would bring together people seeking to rent, buy, or sell an apartment or house.[837]

G. E. Hosmer

Mr. Hosmer, served as treasurer of the Palms Baseball Club. He was the publisher of *The Fort Myers Press* and president of the National Editorial Association. George E. Hosmer died on June 27, 1944, at his home in Fort Myers; he was 77. At the time of his passing, Mr. Hosmer was survived by a son and a daughter.[838]

H. B. Mayer

H.B. Mayer was business manager for the Palms. His role was to raise money to support the ongoing operations of the club. After the season, Mr. Mayer volunteered to supervise the City of Fort Myers hurricane cleanup effort.[839] Mayer and his wife Daisy traveled back and forth between Fort Myers and Key West for many years.[840] Mayer worked as a typewriter repairman.[841]

Facsimile of ad appearing in *The Key West Citizen* on January 13, 1938.[842]

During the 1940s, the Mayer's lived in Miami[843] and Fort Myers, Florida.[844] Henry Bernard Mayer passed away on February 13, 1953, in Jacksonville, Florida, at the home of his son-in law and daughter, Frank and Thelma Lowe.[845] Mayer's wife Daisy (nee Hendry) Mayer passed away in 1960.[846] Mayer was a brother-in-law of John Wall Hendry.

Managers of the 1926 Fort Myers Palms

Buck Conroy

William J. "Buck" Conroy[847] demonstrated humility and class when released as manager of the Palms on May 20, 1926. Neither he nor John Wall Hendry spoke to the press about the details of their discussion. Conroy told reporters he would return to his home in Wichita, Kansas, and figure out what he was going to do next.[848]

By August of 1926, Mr. Conroy relocated to Buffalo, New York, where he was employed as a salesperson for Mills Realty Company. Conroy quickly got attention by suggesting a promotion to his new employer, Charles E. Mills, a passionate Buffalo Bisons Minor League Baseball fan. Billy Kelly, first baseman for the Bisons, had 35 home runs with 40 games remaining to be played. The idea was if Kelly achieved 50 home runs by the end of the season, he would receive one of the best lots in one of Mr. Mills real estate developments for free. Mr. Mills loved the idea, and it was featured in an article in *The Buffalo Evening Times*.[849]

In March of 1927, Buck Conroy organized and promoted 32-round International Boxing Tickets in Hagerstown, Maryland, for the benefit of the Hagerstown Baseball Club. [850] By mid-summer, he was scouting for the St. Louis Cardinals.[851]

As a scout for the New York Giants in February of 1928, Conroy ran a training camp for prospects in Bridgeport, Connecticut, and recommended the best prospects to go to Winston-Salem to try out for the Twins.[852] In 1932 he was a member of the Winston-Salem Twins coaching staff.[853]

Joe Johnston

Joe S. Johnston was among the initial group of applicants to report to Terry Park for workouts. He "had minor league experience"[854] [but this could not be verified]. Mr. Johnston played semi-pro baseball for a Tampa Coast Line All-Star team in 1927. Former Palms Pitcher Gene Davenport was on the same team.[855] In October, 1929, Catcher Joe Johnston appears in a box score for a Maas Brothers semi-pro team from Tampa, along with a Casendyke, a Domingo and a Grandio.[856]

Pete Doyle

The professional baseball career of Peter Doyle, Jr., began when he played for the Greenville Spinners of the South Atlantic league in 1919 and 1920. He signed to play with Chattanooga[857] in 1921, but his contract was purchased by Dominic Mullane, manager of the Jacksonville Scouts in the Florida State League.[858] After being named to Joe Tinker's Florida State League All-Star Team at the end of that season,[859] Pete Doyle returned to Tennessee to pitch the final game of the season for the Knoxville All-Stars against the Class A Chattanooga Lookouts.[860]

Mr. Doyle played for the Lakeland Highlanders of the Florida State League in 1924. In 1926, he was a catcher and the manager of the Lake Wales team of the Florida semi-pro Ridge League when John Wall Hendry hired him to manage the Palms.[861] Pete Doyle served as manager of the team for two weeks when a broken finger led to his release.[862]

In 1927, Mr. Doyle managed the Vestal semi-pro team in the Knoxville, Tennessee City League.[863] Returning to Florida in 1928, Doyle spent the summer season with the Fort Lauderdale Tarpons of the Florida State League. His teammates included pitchers Joe Casares and Joe Domingo.[864] Back in Knoxville for the 1929 amateur season, Pete Doyle was referred to as an "old timer in baseball."[865]

Pete Doyle was the brother of Jess Doyle[866] who played Major League Baseball for the Detroit Tigers from 1925 to 1927, and the St. Louis Browns in 1931.[867]

Pat Doran

Doran, a veteran of the South Atlantic League, joined the Palms on May 28, 1926, to play third base.[868] On September 7, he was named the Palms fourth manager of the season.[869] Doran played for the Tampa Smokers in 1927. Just days after the final game of the 1927 season, Doran sustained serious injuries when an automobile he was in skidded off the highway and rolled several times. Doctors did not believe the injuries Doran sustained would prevent him from playing baseball,[870] but there was no mention of him in the 1928 season or thereafter.

The 1926 Fort Myers Palms

Kitty Wickham

Mr. Wickham played 10 years of Minor League Baseball before being signed by the Palms in 1926. He played for the St. Petersburg Saints and Tampa Smokers in 1927, before moving west to play for the Phoenix Senators in 1928 and San Diego Aces in 1929.[871] In 1917, Mr. Wickham served as a Seaman Apprentice in the US Navy during World War I. Rue E. "Kitty" Wickham passed away on April 26, 1975; he was 78.[872]

Joe Domingo

Joe Domingo was a first baseman and pitcher for the Palms in 1926. He began the 1927 Florida State League season with the Miami Hustlers. He was released by the Hustlers in May of 1927 and was signed by the Tampa Smokers a few days later. In March of 1928, he auditioned for the Washington Senators during a spring training workout in Tampa, Florida. Senators Coach Milan let him pitch to 14 batters including major leaguer Bennie Tate and Hall of Famer Sam Rice. Senators President Griffith watched the workout and decided Domingo was not ready to be moved up.[873] Joe never pitched in the major leagues, but he continued to play semi-pro baseball in the Tampa area for several years. On August 29, 1929, he threw a no-hitter for the Port Tampa team over Springhead. The game was played in just 70 minutes.[874] Joe continued to play and manage baseball teams for several years.   Off the field, Joe was a family man and charter member and deacon of Spencer Memorial Baptist Church in Tampa. He spent 20 years working with Tampa Transit Bus Lines. On September 21, 1979, Joseph R. Domingo passed away; he was 74. At the time of his death, Mr. Domingo was survived by his wife Thelma, four children, eight grandchildren, and three great-grandchildren.[875]

Joe Domingo. Photo credit: *The Fort Myers Press* – USA TODAY NETWORK, September 10, 1926.[876]

Mike Bouza

Bouza played for the Palms from opening day through August 1926. He finished the season with Lakeland.[877] In 1927, Bouza played for four of the six Florida State League teams including the Tampa Smokers, Orlando Colts, Miami Hustlers, and the St. Petersburg Saints.[878] Bouza remained in semi-pro baseball for several years. In 1929, he attended the University of Alabama.[879] After playing summer ball in Minnesota, Bouza enrolled in the University of Minnesota in the fall of 1930.[880]

In 1934, Bouza played for the Double-A Baltimore Orioles,[881] and in 1935, he tried out for Mickey Cochrane's Detroit Tigers.[882] He moved from team to team throughout the minor leagues until 1941.[883] In 1945, Bouza consulted with Tom Spicola, president of the new Tampa Smokers' franchise that would begin play in the Florida State League in 1946.[884]

Michael Bouza, Jr., passed away in Tampa on June 19, 1973; he was 65. At the time of his passing Mr. Bouza was survived by his wife Onnolee, one stepson, and one stepdaughter.[885]

Leonard Mayo

(James) Leonard Mayo was signed from Augusta in the Southeastern League. He joined the Palms pitching staff in May. It was announced that Mayo was being returned to Augusta on August 11, 1926.[886]

From 1927 through the first half of 1929, Leonard Mayo played Class B Minor League Baseball in Georgia and Florida in the Southeastern League. He played the second half of 1929 through 1931 in Class C ball moving from Greensboro to High Point to Durham, North Carolina, in the Piedmont League.[887]

Mr. Mayo served in the U.S. Army during World War II. He retired as a maintenance supervisor for Eastern Airlines in 1972. On December 23, 1973, James Leonard Mayo passed away; he was 66. At the time of his death, Mr. Mayo was survived by his wife Gladdice (nee Lindsey) Mayo.[888]

Gene Davenport

E. H. Davenport was a Georgian who had seen action in the South Atlantic League.[889] He came to Fort Myers from Chicago where he played for the Logan Squares, a semi-pro team in the Chicago Twilight League.[890] In 1926, Davenport won 20 games for the Palms. In 1927, Gene Davenport teamed up with his former manager, Joe Johnston, to play semi-pro baseball for the Tampa Coast Line All-Star team.[891]

In the years that followed, Mr. Davenport lived in Tampa, Florida, where he served as a police officer and was employed by the Atlantic Coast Line railroad. On May 13, 1935, Eugene Hunter Davenport passed away; he was 39. At the time of his death, Mr. Davenport was survived by two brothers and three sisters.[892]

Cliff Chancey

Cliff M. Chancey[893] played for the Lafayette Hubs[894] of the Louisiana State League for the first part of the summer of 1920.[895] In February 1921, he was signed by the Daytona Beach Islanders of the Florida State League,[896] but in April, 1921, Daytona Manager Jack Martin sent Chancey to the La Grange team of the Georgia State League.[897]

Chancey first appeared in the Florida State League[898] when he played third base, right field, and catcher during an eight-day stint with the Sanford Celeryfeds in June of 1925.[899] In April of 1926, 23-year-old[900] Cliff Chancey traveled from his home in Gainesville, Florida, to arrive at the Palms' camp.[901] Mr. Chancey would appear one final time in the Florida State League, from the end of May through mid-June of 1928, he played second base for the Orlando Colts.[902]

Vincent Macey

Macey was sent to Fort Myers on option by the Richmond Colts, a Class B Baseball Club in Richmond, Virginia. Macey was with the Palms during the pre-season and played in 13 regular season games. On May 8, 1926, Macey was released back to Richmond.[903]

Earl Daniels

Earl Daniels was recommended to the team by Dr. Baker Whisnant. Mr. Daniels was from Alabama, but Dr. Whisnant located him in Jacksonville, Florida.[904] Mr. Daniels joined the Palms on August 25, 1926, to play first base. He remained with the team through the end of the season.

Jack O'Reilly

Jack O'Reilly came to Fort Myers on an option from the Class B Asheville Tourists.[905] He played in all 125 regular season games for the Palms, primarily as shortstop, occasionally filling in at third base. At the end of the 1926 season, Jack O'Reilly was recalled by Asheville.[906] He spent the 1927 season with the Norfolk Tars of the Virginia League,[907] and the following two seasons with the Asheville Tourists of the South Atlantic League.[908]

During the off-season between 1928 and 1929, Mr. O'Reilly began teaching gym classes and coaching athletic teams at Christian Brothers College High School in St. Louis, Missouri.[909] He reported to camp in Asheville just in time for the 1929 season.[910] After the 1929 season, Jack returned to his teaching position at Christian Brothers.[911] Meanwhile, his baseball contract was traded to Knoxville,[912] but the Knoxville organization dropped out of the South Atlantic League and the players were taken over by their parent organization, the Memphis Chickasaws.

The Charlotte Hornets purchased O'Reilly's contract and he played in Charlotte during the summer of 1930.[913] O'Reilly was released from the Hornets in March of 1931,[914] because he failed to show up in camp by the date demanded by the organization—Jack was continuing to fulfill his obligations to his students at Christian Brother College High.[915] By 1935, Jack O'Reilly was serving as director of the new Sherman Community Center where a group of 300 boys attended the opening class to learn how to handle a basketball.[916]

Cecil McRae

Cecil McRae, the 6-foot 2-inch, 190-pound pitcher who arrived from Asheville,[917] North Carolina, and pitched sterling baseball for the 1926 Palms, was returned to the Asheville Tourists Baseball Club at the end of the season.

On March 21, 1928, a photo of Cecil McRae working out at the Asheville Tourists camp appeared in *The Asheville Times.* The title above the photo read "Old 'Slow Motion'" and the caption beneath the photo indicated McRae had been with the Tourists part of the 1927 season and he hoped to make the team roster in 1928.[918] In March of 1929, Cecil McRae was working out with the Class C High Point, North Carolina, Pointers.[919]

Old "Slow Motion"

Cecil McRae. Photo Credit: *The Asheville Times –*
USA TODAY NETWORK, March 21, 1928.

Philip Grandio

Philip Grandio, of Tampa, Florida, played in all 125 regular season games for the 1926 Fort Myers Palms. "Felipe" Grandio and Margareta Garcia were married in November, 1926.[920] Philip Grandio began the 1927 Florida State League season with the Orlando Colts.[921]

On May 11, 1927, the visiting Miami Hustlers beat Orlando 4 to 3. The two center fielders exchanged words several times during the game.[922] After the game was over, Orlando Center Fielder Philip Grandio and Miami Center Fielder Faustino Casares got into a fistfight in front of the grandstand. They fought until they were both tired out. Both players received $25 fines and indefinite suspensions from league President J. B. Asher, who was at the game.[923] The two team managers, Phil Wells of Orlando and Bill Holloway of Miami, were each fined $25 for allowing the players to fight.[924]

After a game against Sanford on May 26, 1927, Philip Grandio was released from the Orlando Colts.[925] No reason was given for his release. Grandio was signed by Tampa on June 6, 1927,[926] but was released by the Smokers on June 25.[927]

After baseball, Mr. Grandio was a carpenter and a member of Centro Español. He lived in the Tampa Bay area his entire life. Mr. Grandio passed away on September 25, 1987; he was 83. At the time of his passing, Mr. Grandio was survived by his wife Margarita, a son, two grandchildren and two great-grandchildren.[928]

Faustino Casares

Faustino Casares, of Tampa, was one of three players that appeared in all 125 games for the 1926 Fort Myers Palms. He also played left field during the May 3 game that was protested by Orlando and thrown out by Florida State League President J. B. Asher. Faustino was a near permanent fixture in left field, but he pitched for the Palms in two games – the last home game at Terry Park in both the first half and second half of the season (July 3 and September 8 respectively). Faustino began pitching at the age of 12 in Ybor City, Florida. He began to have problems with his pitching arm in 1920, when he was 17, pitching for the Tampa Smokers of the Florida State League.[929]

In 1927, Faustino signed as a member of the new Miami Baseball Club in the Florida State League and played the full season with the Hustlers.[930] When the 1927 season ended, Faustino Casares contract was purchased by the New Orleans Pelicans for $3,000.[931]

A scout for the Washington Senators kept an eye on Faustino while he was a member of the Fairmont Black Diamonds of the Middle Atlantic League from 1929 through 1931. Considered one of the fastest men in baseball, Faustino twice stole "second base while the pitcher stood on the mound with the ball in his hand."

In 1931, a shoulder injury, low minor-league wages, and a desire to get married led Mr. Casares to a job as a cigar maker at Garcia y Vega, where he had met Violet Priede. They were married in 1931.[932] Mr. Casares managed the Intersocial Baseball League in Ybor City in the 1930s and 1940s. He founded and served as president of La Floridana Cigar Company, and later in life, co-founded the Casares and Son Nursery with his son Joe.[933]

On November 9, 1995, Faustino Casares passed away; he was 92. At the time of his death, Mr. Casares was survived by Violeta, his wife of 64 years, two sons, a daughter, seven grandchildren and one great-grandchild.[934]

Cy Williams

When he was assembling the Palms roster in early April 1926, Buck Conroy suggested to John W. Hendry that he purchase Cy Williams from the Augusta Tygers. Gabby Street, a former major leaguer who was now managing at Augusta, had recommended Williams as someone who he was familiar with from his time managing at Muskogee, "where according to the Spalding baseball guide (see page 259) he won 11 games and dropped 5 for a percentage of .688." It is unclear exactly where the misunderstanding occurred, but when Lewis W. "Cy" Williams reported to Fort Myers on April 6, he was not the Cy Williams John W. Hendry and Buck Conroy expected. Williams turned out to be a Cy Williams who had tried out with Augusta but had never played professional baseball.[935] The Cy Williams that Gabby Street had recommended likely pitched for Topeka in 1924 (where he would have faced Street's Muskogee team). He then started 1925 with Augusta before moving to Okmulgee in early June. By the time John Wall Hendry paid Augusta for a Cy Williams in 1926, the Cy Williams Gabby Street was talking about was pitching for Waterloo in the Mississippi Valley League.[936]

Jim Moore

Moore, a veteran of the Muskogee Athletics of the Western Association, pitched his first game for the Palms on August 5, 1926.[937] He completed the 1926 season with the team. In March of 1927, he was one of five pitchers trying out for the Little Rock Travelers who already had eight veteran pitchers on their roster.[938] He failed to make the Travelers' roster and began the 1927 season with the Topeka Jayhawks,[939] of the Western Association. In June, he was traded to the Fort Smith Twins,[940] where he pitched for the remainder of the season – the Twins were Western Association champions.[941] On September 1, 1927, Moore's contract was purchased by the Little Rock Travelers.[942] He pitched shutout baseball in relief for the Travelers in their victory over Nashville on September 14,[943] and on September 18, Moore pitched a complete game for the Travelers in their final game of 1927, a 4-3 win over the Memphis Chicks.[944]

In 1928, Moore again auditioned for the Little Rock Travelers.[945] This time he was successful in making the Travelers' roster.[946] On September 14, he pitched his final game of the season for the Travelers, a 4-3 victory over Chattanooga. He would be moving up to the major leagues after the game; his contract had been purchased by the Cleveland Indians.[947] Jim Moore made his first start as a major leaguer on September 21, 1928, in Cleveland. He limited the Washington Nationals to five hits over nine innings in a 2-1 Cleveland loss.[948] Moore held Goose Gosling (the 1928 American League batting champion)[949] hitless in three at-bats, ending Gosling's 25 consecutive game hitting streak.[950] Moore would move back and forth from Little Rock to Cleveland in 1929, and between Little Rock and the Chicago White Sox in 1930.[951] His first appearance with the White Sox came on September 4, 1930, during a contest against the Indians.[952]

Jim Moore married Vera May Montgomery in Oklahoma City on July 10, 1943.[953] James Stanford Moore died on May 19, 1973; he was 69.[954]

Clarence Spurgeon

"Lefty" Spurgeon, came to Fort Myers with Jim Moore and debuted with the Palms on August 2, 1926.[955] On September 15, Spurgeon relieved Cecil McRae in the fourth inning at Plant Field in Tampa and pitched the final four innings of Palms' franchise history.[956]

Joe Hernandez

After being released by the Palms, Joe Hernandez returned to his native Cuba to play winter ball for the 1926-27 winter season. He was featured on a Cuban baseball card distributed in packs of Aguilitas brand cigarettes.

1926-27 Aguilitas brand cigarette Cheo Hernandez
Baseball Card. Photo by Ken Breen (2024).

Joe began the 1927 Florida State League season with the St. Petersburg Saints, the team he had played for from 1921 to 1925. He pitched and played right field until he was released by the Saints after the first half of the season. He was picked up by Miami in August 1927 and finished the season with the Hustlers.

During the spring of 1939, Mr. Hernandez was one of two umpires in the Key West (Florida) city league.[957] Apparently fed up with animated arguments of calls and insults being yelled at him, Hernandez resigned from his position as an umpire.[958] League officials agreed there needed to be four umpires on the field for the Key West Conchs versus the Roadside Pirates league championship series. By the time the series got underway almost three weeks later, Hernandez had taken the role of pitching coach for the Pirates.[959]

Joe A. "Cheo" Hernandez passed away in Tampa, Florida, on April 7, 1968; he was 74. At the time of his death, Mr. Hernandez was survived by his wife, Margarita, one daughter and one son,[960] two grandchildren and three great-grandchildren.[961]

If this story had been written prior to December 2020, that's where the update about Mr. Hernandez would have ended. To fully appreciate what happened next, we must go back in time and understand the path Joe Hernandez took prior to Buck Conroy signing him to play for the 1926 Fort Myers Palms.

Hernandez was an outstanding baseball player in his native Havana, Cuba. During the 1918-19 Cuban Winter League season, he was a winning pitcher and led the league in hitting with a .588 batting average in 17 games.[962] Hernandez arrived from Cuba for the second half of the 1919 Florida State League season. He got off to a great start with the Tampa Smokers and quickly earned the nickname The Cuban Sphinx.[963] In Tampa, Hernandez went by the name "Jose,"[964] while in Cuba he was known as "Cheo."

When the 1919 Florida State League season ended, Hernandez remained in Tampa and played on an All-Cuban winter team as Cheo Hernandez.[965; 966] By May of 1920, Cheo Hernandez was a member of the Cuban Stars, a team organized in Havana, Cuba, to be a traveling team. The Stars were one of the eight teams that played in the inaugural season of the National Negro League.[967] Cheo Hernandez pitched tirelessly for the Stars. On July 22, 1920, he pitched all 12 innings for the Cuban Stars, and his solo home run in the top of the 12th inning would prove to be the game winner over the Detroit Stars.[968]

Cheo Hernandez played one season for the Cuban Stars. In 1921, he returned to the Florida State League and played for the St. Petersburg Saints. He continued to play winter ball in Havana and summer ball in St. Petersburg each year through 1925. On April 22, 1926, Hernandez was the winning pitcher in the Fort Myers Palms' inaugural game. He pitched nine scoreless innings at Terry Park ensuring the Palms a victory in the first game in franchise history.[969]

100 years after "Cheo" Hernandez pitched for the Cuban Stars, "On December 16, 2020, Major League Baseball announced that Negro League Baseball from 1920 to 1948 would henceforth be considered a Major League."[970] With that proclamation, Joe "Cheo" Hernandez of the 1926 Fort Myers Palms was a Major League Baseball player.

Pictured here as a Miami Hustler in 1927,[971] Joe Hernandez was the winning pitcher in the Palms inaugural game played at Terry Park in Fort Myers, Florida, on April 22, 1926. Photo from *The Miami Herald*. ©1927 McClatchy. All rights reserved. Used under license and used with the permission of Newspapers.com.

1926 Fort Myers Palms Statistics

The process used to compile the statistics for the 1926 Fort Myers Palms started with the individual box score for each game. If the box score in the *Fort Myers Tropical News* was missing, illegible, incomplete, or had information that did not align with the article it was accompanied by, then one or more other newspapers box scores were reviewed including *The Fort Myers Press,* the opposing team's daily newspaper, and Tampa, Florida, newspapers.

The box score for each game was broken apart to create individual player stats that were compiled in individual player spreadsheets. Each player's individual game stats were then totaled. The totals appear on the following pages.

Nothing was inferred. For example, if no available box score confirmed the number of runners left on base for a game, zero was inserted.

A common statistic today is RBI (Runs Batted In). RBIs were not part of the box scores in 1926 and therefore are not part of the statistics compiled here.

A tie game in 1926 was a game that went at least 5 complete innings, and the score was tied when the umpire called the game because of rain or darkness. (Florida State League fields did not have lights in 1926.) Today, a game stopped when the score is tied is "suspended" and resumed later from that point in the game until the final inning (or extra inning) ends with one team leading. In 1926, a game ending in a tie was "over," and the entire game had to be replayed to determine a winner. The box scores for tie games are included in the statistics. Games that were called before five innings were completed are not included.

On May 3, 1926, a complete game between the Fort Myers Palms and the Orlando Colts was protested by Orlando Manager Phil Wells. The protest was upheld by Florida State League President J. B. Asher. The game was thrown out and ordered to be replayed later. The outcome of the May 3 game, and all information in the published box score for that game, is excluded from the statistics.

Team Record						
	W	L	W-L%	TG	PGD	PF
First Half	34	25	0.576	3	1	3rd
Second Half	33	27	0.550	3	0	5th
Full Season	67	52	0.563	6	1	

Average Time of Game: 1 hour 53 minutes.
5/3: Orlando's protest upheld. Game tossed from the records.
5/6: No time of game recorded.
• Seventeen games were rained out. Dozens of other games had delayed starts due to rain, rain delays during the game, or games called early because of rain.
• The Palms won more games in the 1926 season than any other team in the Florida State League.

W - Wins
L - Losses
W-L% - Win-Loss Percent W/(W+L)
TG - Tie Games
PGD - Protested Games Discarded
PF - Place Finished in League Standings

Team Managers								
Manager	GM	W	L	W-L %	TG	PGD	First Game	Last Game
Buck Conroy	24	13	11	0.542	0	1	4/22/1926	5/20/1926
Joe Johnston	81	44	32	0.579	5	0	5/21/1926	8/24/1926
Pete Doyle	14	9	4	0.692	1	0	8/25/1926	9/7/1926
Pat Doran	6	1	5	0.167	0	0	9/8/1926	9/15/1926

GM - Games Managed

W - Games Won

L - Games Lost

W-L% Win-Loss Percent W/(W+L)

TG - Tie Games

PGD - Protested Games Discarded

First Game - Date of First Game Managed

Last Game - Date of Last Game Managed

Team Roster			
NAME	GP	First Game	Last Game
Faustino Casares	125	4/22/1926	9/15/1926
Philip Grandio	125	4/22/1926	9/15/1926
Jack O'Reilly	125	4/22/1926	9/15/1926
Cliff Chancey	124	4/22/1926	9/15/1926
Joe Johnston	104	4/22/1926	8/23/1926
Mike Bouza	99	4/22/1926	8/21/1926
Kitty Wickham	96	5/24/1926	9/15/1926
Pat Doran	84	5/28/1926	9/15/1926
Joe Domingo	80	4/22/1926	9/14/1926
Cecil McRae	48	4/24/1926	9/15/1926
Gene Davenport	42	4/23/1926	9/14/1926
Leonard Mayo	20	5/22/1926	7/29/1926
Earl Daniels	20	8/25/1926	9/15/1926
Joe Hernandez	14	4/22/1926	5/14/1926
Vincent Macey	13	4/22/1926	5/8/1926
Cy Williams	13	4/26/1926	7/22/1926
Pete Doyle	13	8/25/1926	9/6/1926
Clarence Spurgeon	11	7/29/1926	9/15/1926
Jim Moore	10	8/5/1926	9/13/1926
Hal Fisher	8	5/18/1926	5/26/1926
Charlie Allen	7	7/24/1926	7/31/1926
Ed Overstreet	6	9/8/1926	9/15/1926
Richard Porter	4	5/13/1926	5/17/1926
Dutch Bandera	3	4/23/1926	4/26/1926
Tommy Condon	2	5/15/1926	5/17/1926
Larry Schact	2	6/16/1926	6/23/1926
McGruger	1	5/10/1926	5/10/1926
Howard Johnson	1	6/8/1926	6/8/1926

GP - Games Played

First Game - Date of First Game Played

Last Game - Date of Last Game Played

Team Pitching										
CG	SHO	BB	SO	IP	H	R	HR	HB	BK	WP
86	12	398	475	1129.67	1091	489	4	36	2	22

CG - Complete Game

SHO - Complete Game Shutout

BB - Base on Balls/Walks

SO - Strike Outs

IP - Innings Pitched

H - Hits Allowed

R - Runs Allowed

HR - Home Runs Allowed

HB - Hit Batsman

BK - Balks

WP - Wild Pitches

Pitching

NAME	GP	W	L	W-L%	TG	CG	SHO	BB	SO	IP	H	R	HR	HB	BK	WP
Gene Davenport	41	20	13	0.625	1	24	5	85	94	284.33	269	113	1	5	0	1
Cecil McRae	38	17	14	0.581	3	26	3	102	124	276	253	109	1	10	0	7
Joe Domingo	29	16	8	0.625	0	18	3	52	85	198	191	74	1	7	0	2
Leonard Mayo	17	5	7	0.500	0	6	0	29	36	109	106	41	1	3	1	2
Cy Williams	13	3	2	0.333	0	1	0	29	30	55	64	35	0	2	0	2
Jim Moore	10	2	3	0.429	1	4	0	27	36	60.33	47	24	0	1	0	2
Clarence Spurgeon	8	1	3	0.250	0	4	0	19	23	57.33	53	24	0	2	1	3
Joe Hernandez	5	3	1	0.750	0	1	1	18	12	25.67	39	24	0	4	0	1
Larry Schact	2	0	0	0.000	0	1	0	31	30	56	66	39	0	2	0	2
Faustino Casares	2	0	0	0.000	1	1	0	4	5	7	1	2	0	0	0	0
Howard Johnson	1	0	1	0.000	0	0	0	2	0	1	2	4	0	0	0	0

GP - Games Pitched

W - Games Won

L - Games Lost

W-L% Win-Loss Percent W/(W+L)

TG - Tie Game

CG - Complete Game

SHO - Complete Game Shutout

BB - Base on Balls/Walks

SO - Strike Outs

IP - Innings Pitched

H - Hits Allowed

R - Runs Allowed

HR - Home Runs Allowed

HB - Hit Batsman

BK - Balks

WP - Wild Pitches

Team Batting															
AB	R	H	2B	3B	HR	SB	BA	SLG	TB	BB	SO	DP	HBP	SAC	LOB
4018	518	1041	128	73	13	147	0.259	0.337	1354	329	406	81	47	169	851

6/26: Chancey out when hit by a batted ball.
7/1: Doran out when hit by a batted ball.
7/9: Doran out when hit by a batted ball.
7/20: No mention of runners left on base in any newspaper box score for either game of double header.
8/23: Wickham out when hit by a batted ball.

AB - At Bats

R - Runs

H - Hits

2B - Doubles Hit

3B - Triples Hit

HR - Home Run

SB - Stolen Bases

BA - Batting Average (Hits/At Bats)

SLG - Slugging Percentage (Total Bases/At Bats)

TB - Total Bases (Singles + 2 x Doubles + 3 x Triples + 4 x Home Runs)

BB - Base on Balls/Walks

SO - Strike Outs

DP - Double Plays Hit Into

HBP - Hit By Pitch

SAC - Sacrifice Hit, Bunt or Fly

LOB - Runners Left on Base

Batting												
NAME	GP	AB	R	H	2B	3B	HR	SB	BA	SLG	TB	HBP	SAC
Philip Grandio	125	480	65	131	14	8	4	24	0.273	0.360	173	6	22
Jack O'Reilly	125	446	55	105	16	12	1	27	0.235	0.332	148	3	17
Faustino Casares	125	444	72	116	7	13	3	22	0.261	0.356	158	10	19
Cliff Chancey	124	430	53	113	12	1	0	23	0.263	0.295	127	7	22
Mike Bouza	99	368	48	103	16	13	2	7	0.280	0.410	151	3	14
Kitty Wickham	96	360	51	96	14	6	0	20	0.267	0.339	122	4	15
Joe Johnston	104	329	30	74	17	2	0	1	0.225	0.289	95	0	20
Pat Doran	84	291	48	83	7	2	1	10	0.285	0.333	97	3	9
Joe Domingo	80	243	25	73	5	9	0	2	0.300	0.395	96	6	9
Cecil McRae	48	126	15	33	2	2	0	1	0.262	0.310	39	0	5
Gene Davenport	42	109	10	21	4	3	1	1	0.193	0.312	34	0	2
Earl Daniels	20	73	6	19	4	0	0	3	0.260	0.315	23	0	1
Pete Doyle	13	44	4	9	1	0	0	0	0.205	0.227	10	0	0
Leonard Mayo	20	43	4	7	1	0	0	0	0.163	0.186	8	2	1
Vincent Macey	13	42	9	10	1	0	0	5	0.238	0.262	11	0	1
Joe Hernandez	14	39	9	15	2	1	1	1	0.385	0.564	22	1	2
Hal Fisher	8	30	1	2	0	0	0	0	0.067	0.067	2	0	0
Charlie Allen	7	25	5	11	2	0	0	0	0.440	0.520	13	0	2
Cy Williams	13	21	2	8	1	1	0	0	0.381	0.524	11	1	0
Jim Moore	10	21	0	1	0	0	0	0	0.048	0.048	1	0	3
Clarence Spurgeon	11	20	3	6	1	0	0	0	0.300	0.350	7	0	3
Ed Overstreet	6	15	1	1	0	0	0	0	0.067	0.067	1	0	1
Dutch Bandera	3	8	1	2	1	0	0	0	0.250	0.375	3	0	1
Richard Porter	4	7	0	1	0	0	0	0	0.143	0.143	1	1	0
Tommy Condon	2	2	1	1	0	0	0	0	0.500	0.500	1	0	0
Larry Schact	2	1	0	0	0	0	0	0	0.000	0.000	0	0	0
McGruger	1	1	0	0	0	0	0	0	0.000	0.000	0	0	0
Howard Johnson	1	0	0	0	0	0	0	0	0.000	0.000	0	0	0

GP - Games Played

AB - At Bats

R - Runs

H - Hits

2B - Doubles Hit

3B - Triples Hit

HR - Home Run

SB - Stolen Bases

BA - Batting Average (Hits/At Bats)

SLG - Slugging Percentage (Total Bases/At Bats)

TB - Total Bases (Singles + 2 x Doubles + 3 x Triples + 4 x Home Runs)

HBP - Hit By Pitch

SAC - Sacrifice Hit/Bunt or Fly

Team Fielding								
PO	A	E	FLD%	DP	TP	PB	OSB	LOB
3295	1572	268	0.948	85	1	27	132	866

5/18: Triple Play - O'Reilly (SS) to Chancey (2B) to Domingo (1B) to Johnston (C).

7/20: No mention of runners left on base in any newspaper box score for either game of double header.

PO - Putouts

A - Assists

E - Errors Committed

FLD% - Fielding Percentage (Putouts + Assists) / (Putouts + Assists + Errors)

DP - Double Plays Turned

TP - Triple Plays Turned

PB - Passed Balls

OSB - Opponent Stolen Base

LOB - Opponents Runners Left on Base

Fielding - Catcher								
NAME	POS	PO	A	E	FLD%	DP	PB	OSB
Joe Johnston	C	459	135	22	0.964	5	21	113
Cliff Chancey	2B, RF, C	350	332	25	0.965	54	3	7
Pete Doyle	C	40	12	4	0.929	0	1	8
Ed Overstreet	C	24	5	2	0.935	0	2	4

POS - Position(s) Played

PO - Putouts

A - Assists

E - Errors

FLD% - Fielding percentage (Putouts + Assists) / (Putouts + Assists + Errors)

DP - Double Plays Turned

PB - Passed Balls

OSB - Opponent Stolen Bases

<table>
<tr><td colspan="7" align="center">Fielding</td></tr>
<tr><td>NAME</td><td>POS</td><td>PO</td><td>A</td><td>E</td><td>FLD%</td><td>DP</td></tr>
<tr><td>Mike Bouza</td><td>1B, 3B, SS, 2B</td><td>719</td><td>92</td><td>25</td><td>0.970</td><td>52</td></tr>
<tr><td>Faustino Casares</td><td>LF, RHP, 3B, 2B</td><td>302</td><td>29</td><td>16</td><td>0.954</td><td>3</td></tr>
<tr><td>Joe Domingo</td><td>1B, LHP, RF, CF, LF</td><td>280</td><td>51</td><td>16</td><td>0.954</td><td>15</td></tr>
<tr><td>Jack O'Reilly</td><td>SS, 3B</td><td>257</td><td>347</td><td>69</td><td>0.897</td><td>38</td></tr>
<tr><td>Philip Grandio</td><td>CF, RF</td><td>215</td><td>20</td><td>13</td><td>0.948</td><td>1</td></tr>
<tr><td>Earl Daniels</td><td>1B, 3B</td><td>209</td><td>5</td><td>3</td><td>0.986</td><td>9</td></tr>
<tr><td>Kitty Wickham</td><td>RF, 2B, CF, 3B</td><td>177</td><td>59</td><td>12</td><td>0.952</td><td>8</td></tr>
<tr><td>Pat Doran</td><td>3B, CF, 2B</td><td>116</td><td>172</td><td>24</td><td>0.923</td><td>15</td></tr>
<tr><td>Hal Fisher</td><td>1B, RF</td><td>60</td><td>0</td><td>3</td><td>0.952</td><td>4</td></tr>
<tr><td>Vincent Macey</td><td>2B</td><td>27</td><td>24</td><td>8</td><td>0.864</td><td>2</td></tr>
<tr><td>Joe Hernandez</td><td>RHP</td><td>16</td><td>24</td><td>4</td><td>0.909</td><td>2</td></tr>
<tr><td>Cecil McRae</td><td>RHP, RF, CF</td><td>14</td><td>67</td><td>7</td><td>0.920</td><td>1</td></tr>
<tr><td>Tommy Condon</td><td>1B, RF</td><td>11</td><td>0</td><td>0</td><td>1.000</td><td>1</td></tr>
<tr><td>Charlie Allen</td><td>CF</td><td>9</td><td>0</td><td>1</td><td>0.900</td><td>0</td></tr>
<tr><td>Richard Porter</td><td>RF</td><td>4</td><td>0</td><td>0</td><td>1.000</td><td>0</td></tr>
<tr><td>Gene Davenport</td><td>RHP</td><td>2</td><td>86</td><td>7</td><td>0.926</td><td>4</td></tr>
<tr><td>Leonard Mayo</td><td>RHP, LF, RF, CF</td><td>2</td><td>50</td><td>2</td><td>0.963</td><td>1</td></tr>
<tr><td>Clarence Spurgeon</td><td>LHP, RF, LF</td><td>1</td><td>13</td><td>2</td><td>0.875</td><td>0</td></tr>
<tr><td>Dutch Bandera</td><td>RF</td><td>1</td><td>0</td><td>0</td><td>1.000</td><td>0</td></tr>
<tr><td>Jim Moore</td><td>RHP, LF</td><td>0</td><td>24</td><td>2</td><td>0.923</td><td>0</td></tr>
<tr><td>Larry Schact</td><td>RHP</td><td>0</td><td>4</td><td>0</td><td>1.000</td><td>0</td></tr>
<tr><td>Cy Williams</td><td>RHP</td><td>0</td><td>21</td><td>1</td><td>0.955</td><td>0</td></tr>
<tr><td>Howard Johnson</td><td>RHP</td><td>0</td><td>0</td><td>0</td><td>0.000</td><td>0</td></tr>
<tr><td>McGruger</td><td>x</td><td>0</td><td>0</td><td>0</td><td>0.000</td><td>0</td></tr>
</table>

POS - Position(s) Played

PO - Putouts

A - Assists

E - Errors

FLD% - Fielding percentage (Putouts + Assists)/(Putouts + Assists + Errors)

DP - Double Plays Turned

Special Thanks

James L. Gates Jr., Librarian Emeritus, National Baseball Hall of Fame
Glenn Miller, past president, Southwest Florida Historical Society
Jake Jacobson, grandson of John Wall Hendry
Genevieve Bowen, Southwest Florida Historical Society
Nancy Kilmartin, Southwest Florida Historical Society
Leah Lapszynski, Sarasota County History Center
Bob Green, Lee County Parks and Recreation
Melissa Jerome, University of Florida Library
Kym Hudson, Lee County Library System
Florida Digital Newspaper Library
Senator Connie Mack III
Kevin and Jane Leighty
Anthony Shamoun
Newspapers.com
Dr. Michael Hale
David A. Dorsey
Hank Hendry
Michael Zeoli
Tony Nazzaro
John Stallsmith
Ed Pelegrino
Dave Doty
Ken Picking
John Martin
Chris Peters
Judd Loveland
John Vittas
Austin Dutton
Andrew Alfers
Kathleen Kelly
Emily Toborg
Jackson Hicks
Jacqui Heck
Kendall Conti
And to my wife Trudy, thank you for your patience and support.

Addendum

Three ballfields from 1926 still exist. The stadium at historic Terry Park in Fort Myers has been completely rebuilt twice in the last century. City Park in Bradenton has also been rebuilt and is known today as LECOM Park – the spring training home of the Pittsburg Pirates and the home of the Pirates Single-A affiliate, the Bradenton Marauders.

Henley Field in Lakeland, Florida, was built for the Cleveland Indians in 1923. Today, the field is owned by the City of Lakeland and leased to Florida Southern College. There have been extensive renovations to Henley Field, but one part of the original stadium has been preserved – the visitors' clubhouse.

Visitors' locker room at Henley Field, Lakeland, Florida. Photo by Ken Breen

It is very likely that on August 25, 1926, John Wall Hendry stood in the very spot where I snapped this photo and addressed the Fort Myers Palms. That was the day Hendry traveled from Fort Myers to Lakeland to relieve Joe Johnston of his managerial duties, and to introduce new manager Pete Doyle to the Palms.

1 "Prospects Good for Florida's State League," *Fort Myers Press,* (Fort Myers, FL), March 5, 1926, https://newspapers.uflib.ufl.edu/UF00079929/02045/images/4

2 Wikipedia page for "Fort Myers Mighty Mussels," https://en.wikipedia.org/wiki/Fort_Myers_Mighty_Mussels, accessed on January 23, 2023.

3 Miller, Glenn, "Left with only a trace," *Fort Myers News-Press,* (Fort Myers, FL), June 3, 2006, https://www.newspapers.com/image/221118942/

4 Ken Picking, (former *Fort Myers News-Press* sportswriter), in discussion with the author via text messaging, May 30, 2023.

5 Miller, Glenn, "Left with only a trace," *Fort Myers News-Press,* (Fort Myers, FL), June 3, 2006, https://www.newspapers.com/image/221118942/

6 Miller, Glenn, "Left with only a trace," *Fort Myers News-Press,* (Fort Myers, FL), June 3, 2006, https://www.newspapers.com/image/221118942/

7 James L. Gates, Jr., Librarian Emeritus, National Baseball Hall of Fame and Museum, in discussion with the author via email messaging, February 13, 2023.

8 "$1 in 1926 is worth $17.18 today," *CPI Inflation Calculator,* accessed May 2, 2023, https://www.officialdata.org/us/inflation/1925?amount=1

9 Cosgrove, Richard, "Wow! The Average Income in 1924 was just $2,196," *Citizens Voice,* (Wilkes-Barre, PA), May 31, 2020, https://www.citizensvoice.com/lifestyles/community/wow-the-average-income-in-1924-was-just-2-196/article_2ce7a67d-4b0b-55b3-962e-7f1843374e9d.html

10 "History of Minimum Wage Laws," *Law Offices of Timothy Bowles,* Accessed May 2, 2023, https://tbowleslaw.com/history-of-minimum-wage-laws/

11 Stripes Garage, "Gas 25c," *Fort Myers Press,* (Fort Myers, FL), May 19, 1926, https://newspapers.uflib.ufl.edu/UF00079929/00461/images/7

12 "New Filling Station and Auto Laundry," *Fort Myers Press,* (Fort Myers, FL), May 30, 1925, https://newspapers.uflib.ufl.edu/UF00079929/00325/images/6

13 "FREE!," *Fort Myers Tropical News,* (Fort Myers, FL), December 22, 1926, P. 8., Microfilm.

14 "Piggly Wiggly," *Fort Myers Press,* (Fort Myers, FL), April 2, 1926, https://newspapers.uflib.ufl.edu/UF00079929/02069/images/4

15 "Palm Beach Suits," *Fort Myers Press,* (Fort Myers, FL), September 16, 1926, https://newspapers.uflib.ufl.edu/UF00079929/02181/images/6

16 "Swan's," *Fort Myers Press,* (Fort Myers, FL), November 18, 1926, https://newspapers.uflib.ufl.edu/UF00079929/02235/images/5

17 Picking, Ken, "FM Royals play 72 home games," *Fort Myers News-Press,* (Fort Myers, FL), March 10, 1978, https://www.newspapers.com/image/212149920/

18 Picking, Ken, "FM Royals make Terry Park debut vs. KC today," *Fort Myers News-Press,* (Fort Myers, FL), April 6, 1978, https://www.newspapers.com/image/212977183/

19 Picking, Ken, "KC gives FM Royals rough start," *Fort Myers News-Press,* (Fort Myers, FL), April 7, 1978, https://www.newspapers.com/image/212977752/

20 Bowman, Don, "A Royal birth: Fort Myers opens tonight," *Fort Myers News-Press,* (Fort Myers, FL), April 11, 1978, https://www.newspapers.com/image/212979129/

21 Picking, Ken, "FM Royals fizzle; Miami wins 5-3," *Fort Myers News-Press,* (Fort Myers, FL), June 23, 1978, https://www.newspapers.com/image/222297323/

22 Cheshire, Brack, "Read 'em and Weep," *Bradenton Herald,* (Bradenton, FL), July 19, 1926, https://www.newspapers.com/image/682658075/

23 Sports Reference, Baseball Reference, "Fort Myers, Florida Encyclopedia," *Baseball Reference*, Accessed May 22, 2023, https://www.baseball-reference.com/register/team.cgi?city=Fort%20Myers&state=FL&country=US

24 "Baseball," *Fort Myers Daily Press,* (Fort Myers, FL), March 10, 1914, https://newspapers.uflib.ufl.edu/AA00088919/00342/images/1

25 Davis, Hy. "Close Finish for Colonels: Browns Checked in Final Round and Kentuckians are Victors Walker in Stellar Role" *Courier-Journal (1869-1922),* Mar 13, 1914, p. 7. *ProQuest.* Web. 19 Jan. 2024.

26 Baseball Almanac Inc., Baseball Almanac, "Spring Training Sites for All American League Baseball Teams," *Baseball Almanac,* Accessed May 22, 2023, https://www.baseball-almanac.com/teams/springtrainingsites-al.shtml

27 "Connie Mack has his Eyes on this City," *Fort Myers Press,* (Fort Myers, FL), December 24, 1923, https://newspapers.uflib.ufl.edu/UF00079929/01316/images/0

28 "Fort Myers Makes Bid for Big Team," *Fort Myers Press,* (Fort Myers, FL), December 27, 1923, https://newspapers.uflib.ufl.edu/UF00079929/01318/images

29 "Athletics to Train here in Spring of 1925," *Fort Myers Press,* (Fort Myers, FL), January 23, 1924, https://newspapers.uflib.ufl.edu/UF00079929/01339/images

30 "Ball Diamond is Ready for Connie Mack," *Fort Myers Press,* (Fort Myers, FL), July 10, 1924, https://newspapers.uflib.ufl.edu/UF00079929/01485/images

31 "Contract is Let for Grand Stand at Fair Grounds," *Fort Myers Press,* (Fort Myers, FL), December 16, 1924, https://newspapers.uflib.ufl.edu/UF00079929/01619/images

32 "Former Illinois Man Builds Residence," *Fort Myers Press,* (Fort Myers, FL), January 15, 1925, https://newspapers.uflib.ufl.edu/UF00079929/01727/images/4

33 Barrett Manufacturing Company, "Barrett Specification Roofs," *Saturday Evening Post,* 1922.

34 "Connie Mack Pleased with Ball Grounds for Quaker City Team," *Fort Myers Press,* (Fort Myers, FL), January 5, 1925, https://newspapers.uflib.ufl.edu/UF00079929/01718/images/0

35 "Grounds are Ready for Lee County Fair and Connie's Boys," *Fort Myers Press,* (Fort Myers, FL), February 5, 1925, https://newspapers.uflib.ufl.edu/UF00079929/01745/images/0

36 "Quaker City Boys are Given Vacation till First of Week," *Fort Myers Press,* (Fort Myers, FL), February 26, 1926, https://newspapers.uflib.ufl.edu/UF00079929/01763/images

37 Baumgartner, Stan "Athletics Drop the Opening Game to Phillies in Intercity Baseball Battle," *Philadelphia Inquirer,* (Philadelphia, PA), March 13, 1925, https://www.newspapers.com/image/171080953/

38 Nolan, John, J., "5,000 Cheer Ruth During Short Visit to Fort Myers," *Fort Myers Press,* (Fort Myers, FL), March 26, 1925, https://newspapers.uflib.ufl.edu/UF00079929/01702/images/0

39 Baumgartner, Stan, "Mack Signs to Train in Fort Myers for Ten More Years; to Remodel Field," *Philadelphia Inquirer,* (Philadelphia, PA), March 23, 1925, https://www.newspapers.com/image/171075431/

40 Nolan, John, J., "Athletics Looking forward eagerly to Return in 1926," *Fort Myers News,* (Fort Myers, FL), March 28, 1925, https://newspapers.uflib.ufl.edu/UF00079929/01704/images

41 Baumgartner, Stan, "Mack Signs to Train in Fort Myers for Ten More Years; to Remodel Field," *Philadelphia Inquirer,* (Philadelphia, PA), March 23, 1925, https://www.newspapers.com/image/171075431/

42 Ancestry Draft Registration Card database page for "*U.S., World War I Draft registration Cards, 1917-1918 for John Wall Hendry,*" https://www.ancestry.com/discoveryui-content/view/22025784:6482, Accessed May 9, 2023.

43 "John Wall Hendry" *News-Press* (Fort Myers, FL), April 8, 1979. https://www.newspapers.com/image/214174266/.

44 Find a Grave database and images memorial page for "Francis Asbury "Berry" Hendry," Memorial ID 30390556. https://www.findagrave.com/memorial/30390556/francis-asbury-hendry, Accessed April 9, 2023.

45 Hendry County page for History, http://hendrycounty.com/resources/History.html. Access December 28, 2023.

46 "City Mourns Tragic Death of L.A. Hendry," *Fort Myers Press* (Fort Myers, FL), January 2, 1929. https://www.newspapers.com/image/216559981/.

47 "Death of Mrs. Louis Hendry," *Fort Myers Press* (Fort Myers, FL), August 4, 1904. https://newspapers.uflib.ufl.edu/AA00089972/00058/images/0.

48 Jake Jacobson (grandson of John W. Hendry), in discussion with the author, Franklin, North Carolina, March 16, 2023.

49 Jacobson, 2023.

50 Jacobson, 2023.

51 Gwynn High School, 'Junior Class," *The Caloosahatchian,* (Fort Myers, FL: 1914), Southwest Florida Historical Society Archives.

52 Gwynn High School, "Hyacinthian Literary Society," *The Caloosahatchian,* (Fort Myers, FL: 1914), Southwest Florida Historical Society Archives.

53 Gwynn High School, *The Caloosahatchian,* (Fort Myers, FL: 1915), 8, Southwest Florida Historical Society Archives.

54 *The Caloosahatchian,* 1915, 23.

55 *The Caloosahatchian,* 1915, 68.

56 *The Caloosahatchian,* 1915, 71.

57 *The Caloosahatchian,* 1915, 75-76.

58 *The Caloosahatchian,* 1915, 88.

59 "Leave for University" *Fort Myers Press,* (Fort Myers, FL), September 13, 1915, https://newspapers.uflib.ufl.edu/UF00079929/03832/images/0

60 University of Florida, *The Seminole,* (Gainesville, FL: 1916), 70, University of Florida Digital Collections, https://ufdc.ufl.edu/AA00022765/00007/images/75, accessed on April 8, 2023.

61 *The Seminole,* 1916, 146-147.

62 University of Florida, *The Seminole,* (Gainesville, FL: 1918), 60-61, University of Florida Digital Collections, https://ufdc.ufl.edu/AA00022765/00009/zoom/65, accessed on April 8, 2023.

63 *The Seminole,* 1918, 64.

64 Jacobson, 2023.

65 Ancestry database page for *"John Wall Hendry Sr.,"* https://www.ancestry.com/family-tree/person/tree/60627880/person/30061870266//facts, Accessed May 9, 2023.

66 "South Florida Social Notes – Leesburg" *Tampa Tribune,* (Tampa, FL), January 12, 1922, https://www.newspapers.com/image/326100491/.

67 Jacobson, 2023.

68 Jacobson, 2023.

69 Jacobson, 2023.

70 "Plans for Golf Course Mature," *Fort Myers Press,* (Fort Myers, FL), November 20, 1925, https://newspapers.uflib.ufl.edu/UF00079929/01957/images

71 "New Drive is Launched for Seaboard Money," *Fort Myers Press,* (Fort Myers, FL) March 18, 1925, https://newspapers.uflib.ufl.edu/UF00079929/00121/images

72 "About Fort Myers People and Their Visitors," *Fort Myers Tropical News,* (Fort Myers, FL), July 21, 1925, https://newspapers.uflib.ufl.edu/AA00088916/00100/images/2

73 Dean Park Historic District page for "2643 Providence St (1923)," https://deanpark.org/2643-providence-street-1923/, accessed on April 9, 2023.

74 "Obituaries: Robert Needham Hendry," *News and Observer,* (Charlotte, NC), March 9, 2016, https://www.newspapers.com/image/652667625/.

75 Jacobson, 2023.

76 "Public Forum," *Fort Myers Press,* (Fort Myers, FL), April 6, 1925, https://newspapers.uflib.ufl.edu/UF00079929/00137/images/2

77 United States. Department of Commerce. *Fourteenth Census of the United States. State Compendium Florida.* Washington D.C.: U.S. Bureau of the Census, 1920. https://www2.census.gov/prod2/decennial/documents/06229686v8-13ch1.pdf

78 "New Realty Office," *Fort Myers Press,* (Fort Myers, FL) December 6, 1924, https://newspapers.uflib.ufl.edu/UF00079929/01611/images

79 "Hendry Brothers Will Move to New Offices Within One Week," *Fort Myers Press,* (Fort Myers, FL), October 14, 1925, https://newspapers.uflib.ufl.edu/UF00079929/01925/images/6

80 "Real Estate," *Fort Myers Press,* (Fort Myers, FL), August 10, 1025, https://newspapers.uflib.ufl.edu/UF00079929/01869/images/2

81 "Tamiami Estates," *Fort Myers Press,* (Fort Myers, FL), December 15, 1925, https://newspapers.uflib.ufl.edu/UF00079929/01977/images/8

82 "Hendry Brothers Co. Planning New Homes in Fine Subdivision," *Fort Myers Press,* (Fort Myers, FL), February 8, 1926, https://newspapers.uflib.ufl.edu/UF00079929/02024/images/3

83 "Build Fire Safe," *Fort Myers Press,* (Fort Myers, FL), November 5, 1925, https://newspapers.uflib.ufl.edu/UF00079929/01944/images/4

84 "Build Fire Safe," *Fort Myers Press,* (Fort Myers, FL), November 5, 1925, https://newspapers.uflib.ufl.edu/UF00079929/01944/images/4

85 "Sanibel Island is Growing in Favor," *Fort Myers Press,* (Fort Myers, FL), March 30, 1925, https://newspapers.uflib.ufl.edu/UF00079929/00131/images/10

86 "Edison and Ford Visit Sanibel," *Fort Myers Press,* (Fort Myers, FL), February 17, 1925, https://newspapers.uflib.ufl.edu/UF00079929/01755/images/0

87 "Athletics to Visit Sanibel," *Fort Myers Press,* (Fort Myers, FL), March 14, 1925, https://newspapers.uflib.ufl.edu/UF00079929/01692/images

88 "Casa Ybel Sold with 360 Acres to Hendry Bros.," *Fort Myers Press,* (Fort Myers, FL), April 28, 1925, https://newspapers.uflib.ufl.edu/UF00079929/01782/images

89 "Special Offerings for a Few Days," *Fort Myers Press,* (Fort Myers, FL), May 5, 1925, https://newspapers.uflib.ufl.edu/UF00079929/01788/images/5

90 "Realty transfers of Yesterday, June 20, 1925," *Fort Myers Press,* (Fort Myers, FL), June 23, 1925, https://newspapers.uflib.ufl.edu/UF00079929/00343/images/4

91 "$100,000 Paid for 306 Acres on Sanibel Isle," *Fort Myers Press,* (Fort Myers, FL), June 22, 1925, https://newspapers.uflib.ufl.edu/UF00079929/00342/images

92 Morgan, Tom, "Binder Boys invaded City 25 Years Ago," *Fort Myers News*-Press, (Fort Myers, FL), August 20, 1950, https://www.newspapers.com/image/219454829/.

93 Morgan, Tom, "Wild Land Soared in Boomtime," *Fort Myers News-Press,* (Fort Myers, FL), August 23, 1950, https://www.newspapers.com/image/219455016/

94 "Realty Barometer," *Fort Myers Tropical News,* (Fort Myers, FL), February 9, 1926, https://newspapers.uflib.ufl.edu/AA00088916/00138/images/0

95 "John Hendry Gets More Than $150,000 for Naples Tract," *Fort Myers Tropical News,* (Fort Myers, FL), July 21, 1925, https://newspapers.uflib.ufl.edu/AA00088916/00100/images/0

96 "Here We Are," *Fort Myers Tropical News,* (Fort Myers, FL), August 12, 1925, https://newspapers.uflib.ufl.edu/AA00088916/00119/images/2

97 "Jones Skyrocketed with Real Estate Boom," *Fort Myers News-Press,* (Fort Myers, FL), August 22, 1950, https://www.newspapers.com/image/219454980/

98 "We Take Pleasure in Announcing," *Fort Myers Press,* (Fort Myers, FL), August 22, 1925, https://newspapers.uflib.ufl.edu/UF00079929/01880/images/17

99 "John Hendry Pays Half Million for Estero Acreage," *Fort Myers Tropical News,* (Fort Myers, FL), August 22, 1925, https://newspapers.uflib.ufl.edu/AA00088916/00128/zoom/0

100 Morgan, Tom, "Boom Reflected Crazy Country," *Fort Myers News-Press,* (Fort Myers, FL), August 24, 1950, https://www.newspapers.com/image/219455054/

101 Morgan, Tom, "Tom Philips Boom Leader," *Fort Myers News-Press,* (Fort Myers, FL), August 21, 1950, https://www.newspapers.com/image/219454948/

102 Morgan, Tom, "Tom Philips Boom Leader," *Fort Myers News-Press,"* (Fort Myers, FL), August 21, 1950, https://www.newspapers.com/image/219454952/

103 Morgan, Tom, "Boom Reflected Crazy Country," *Fort Myers News-Press,* (Fort Myers, FL), August 24, 1950, https://www.newspapers.com/image/219455071/

104 "Hendry Brothers Will Move to New Offices Within One Week," *Fort Myers Press,* (Fort Myers, FL), October 14, 1925, https://newspapers.uflib.ufl.edu/UF00079929/01925/images/6

105 "We Can Guarantee Delivery of the Following," *Fort Myers Press,* (Fort Myers, FL), October 16, 1925, https://newspapers.uflib.ufl.edu/UF00079929/01927/images/5

106 "Stan Baumgartner Arrives for Winter," *Fort Myers Press,* (Fort Myers, FL), October 13, 1925, https://newspapers.uflib.ufl.edu/UF00079929/01924/images

107 "Ponzi Faces Mail Fraud Charge; Will be Arrested Today," *Fort Myers Press,* (Fort Myers, FL), February 25, 1926, https://newspapers.uflib.ufl.edu/UF00079929/02039/images

108 "Deputies on East Coast Miss Ponzi," *St. Petersburg Times,* (St. Petersburg, FL), February 10, 1926, https://www.newspapers.com/image/314599091/

109 "Athletics Trip Brewers as Babe, in Mack Togs, Fails to Get a Bingle," *Philadelphia Inquirer,* (Philadelphia, PA), March 26, 1925, https://www.newspapers.com/image/171079311/

110 "Mack Signs to Train in Fort Myers for Ten More Years; to Remodel Field," *Philadelphia Inquirer,* (Philadelphia, PA), March 23, 1925, https://www.newspapers.com/image/171075431/

111 "Fans Now Desire Good Local Nine," *Fort Myers Press,* (Fort Myers, FL), March 13, 1925, https://newspapers.uflib.ufl.edu/UF00079929/00063/images/6

112 "Fort Myers Wins First Ball Game in County League," *Fort Myers Press,* (Fort Myers, FL), April 13, 1925, https://newspapers.uflib.ufl.edu/UF00079929/00089/images

113 "Fort Myers' World Series Ball Games to Start Thursday," *Fort Myers Tropical News,* (Fort Myers, FL), July 7, 1925, https://newspapers.uflib.ufl.edu/AA00088916/00088/images/5

114 "Ball Players Dine," *Fort Myers Tropical News,* (Fort Myers, FL), July 7, 1925, https://newspapers.uflib.ufl.edu/AA00088916/00088/images/0

115 "City Championship Baseball Series," *Fort Myers Tropical News,* (Fort Myers, FL), July 9, 1925, https://newspapers.uflib.ufl.edu/AA00088916/00090/images/0

116 "Regulars Take Opening Battle in City Series," *Fort Myers Tropical News,* (Fort Myers, FL), July 10, 1925, https://newspapers.uflib.ufl.edu/AA00088916/00091/images/0

117 "Regulars Again Defeat Palms in Pitcher's Battle," *Fort Myers Tropical News,* (Fort Myers, FL), July 17, 1925, https://newspapers.uflib.ufl.edu/AA00088916/00097/images/0

118 "City Championship Goes to Regulars in 10-Inning Game," *Fort Myers Tropical News,* (Fort Myers, FL), July 24, 1925, https://newspapers.uflib.ufl.edu/AA00088916/00103/images/0

119 The Historical Marker Database, "Citrus to Celery," *HMdb.org*, Accessed August 27, 2023, https://www.hmdb.org/m.asp?m=55378

120 "League Club for Fort Myers," *Fort Myers Tropical News,* (Fort Myers, FL), July 10, 1925, https://newspapers.uflib.ufl.edu/AA00088916/00091/images

121 "Fort Myers' New Baseball Team Loses Two More," *Fort Myers Tropical News,* (Fort Myers, FL), July 11, 1925, https://newspapers.uflib.ufl.edu/AA00088916/00092/images/0

122 "Tampa Players Named Smokers," *Tampa Times,* (Tampa, FL), June 27, 1919, https://www.newspapers.com/image/332754750/

123 Hendry to Fight to get Baseball for Fort Myers," *Fort Myers Tropical News,* (Fort Myers, FL), July 12, 1925, https://newspapers.uflib.ufl.edu/AA00088916/00093/images/0

124 "Hendry Agrees to Arbitrate Baseball Row," *Fort Myers Tropical News,* (Fort Myers, FL), July 14, 1925, https://newspapers.uflib.ufl.edu/AA00088916/00094/images/0

125 "Sanford Franchise to Remain Up-State is Present Outlook," *Fort Myers Press,* (Fort Myers, FL), July 14, 1925, https://newspapers.uflib.ufl.edu/UF00079929/01847/images/4

126 "Lakeland Civic Clubs Asked to Save Ball Team," *Fort Myers Press,* (Fort Myers, FL), July 22, 1925, https://newspapers.uflib.ufl.edu/UF00079929/01854/images/0

127 "South Florida Winter Baseball League Proposed," *Fort Myers Tropical News,* (Fort Myers, FL), July 23, 1925,
https://newspapers.uflib.ufl.edu/AA00088916/00102/zoom/0

128 Jacobson, 2023.

129 "South Florida Winter Baseball League Proposed," *Fort Myers Tropical News,* (Fort Myers, FL), July 23, 1925,
https://newspapers.uflib.ufl.edu/AA00088916/00102/zoom/0

130 "John Hendry Loses Another Chance to Get League Team," *Fort Myers Tropical News,* (Fort Myers, FL), August 2, 1925,
https://newspapers.uflib.ufl.edu/AA00088916/00111/images/0

131 Jacobson, 2023.

132 "Palms Sign Stars When Fort Myers Regulars Disband," *Fort Myers Tropical News,* (Fort Myers, FL), https://newspapers.uflib.ufl.edu/AA00088916/00119/images/2

133 "Fort Myers Team Wins First Game," *Tampa Daily Times,* (Tampa, FL), August 15, 1925, https://www.newspapers.com/image/332732106/

134 Cassie, "Sportively Speaking," *Fort Myers Press,* (Fort Myers, FL), August 17, 1925, https://newspapers.uflib.ufl.edu/UF00079929/01875/images/2

135 "Smokers to play Three Game Series with Fort Myers Nine', *Tampa Daily Times,* (Tampa, FL), September 15, 1925),
https://www.newspapers.com/image/332749496/

136 "Baseball Series Begins Tomorrow," *Fort Myers Press,* (Fort Myers, FL), September 16, 1925, https://newspapers.uflib.ufl.edu/UF00079929/01901/images

137 "Future of Baseball in Fort Myers Depends on Interest Shown in Series," *Fort Myers Press,* (Fort Myers, FL), September 17, 1925,
https://newspapers.uflib.ufl.edu/UF00079929/01902/images/8

138 "Smokers to play Three Game Series with Fort Myers Nine," *Tampa Daily Times,* (Tampa, FL), September 15, 1925),
https://www.newspapers.com/image/332749496/

139 "Smokers Trim Palms, 14 to 0 in First of Series at Fair Grounds," *Fort Myers Press,* (Fort Myers, FL), September 18, 1925,
https://newspapers.uflib.ufl.edu/UF00079929/01903/images

140 "Fort Myers Palms Even Tampa Series By Taking Second Game, 4 to 1," *Fort Myers Press,* (Fort Myers, FL), September 19, 1925,
https://newspapers.uflib.ufl.edu/UF00079929/01904/images/6

141 "Conroy Enters Realty," *Tampa Morning Tribune,* (Tampa, FL), January 7, 1926, https://www.newspapers.com/image/327173473/

142 "Conroy is Named Boss of Ft. Myers 9," *Tampa Morning Tribune,* (Tampa FL), January 22, 1926, https://www.newspapers.com/image/326993034/

143 "Fort Myers has Extra Interest in Ball Games," *Tampa Daily Times,* (Tampa, FL), September 18, 1925, https://www.newspapers.com/image/332750760/

144 Tribune News Service, "Fort Myers Takes Deciding Game from Smokers," *Tampa Sunday Tribune,* (Tampa, FL), September 20, 1925,
https://www.newspapers.com/image/327454431/

145 "Last World Series game Tomorrow," *Fort Myers Press,* (Fort Myers, FL), October 14, 1925, https://newspapers.uflib.ufl.edu/UF00079929/01925/images

146 "City May Have Baseball Team," *Fort Myers Press,* (Fort Myers, FL), November 23, 1925, https://newspapers.uflib.ufl.edu/UF00079929/01959/images

147 "Building Total Nears Million Mark," *Fort Myers Tropical News,* (Fort Myers, FL), April 1, 1926, https://newspapers.uflib.ufl.edu/AA00088916/00182/images/0

148 "15,000 People in Fort Myers," *Fort Myers Tropical News,* (Fort Myers, FL), August 12, 1926, https://newspapers.uflib.ufl.edu/AA00088916/00119/images/0

149 "Number Phones is Doubled 1925 to 1926," *Fort Myers Press,* (Fort Myers, FL), February 16, 1926, https://newspapers.uflib.ufl.edu/UF00079929/02031/images

150 "A Vision Realized…," *Fort Myers Tropical News,* (Fort Myers, FL), January 7, 1927, P.8. Microfilm.

151 "Re-Numbering of Residences Begins Today," *Fort Myers Press,* (Fort Myers, FL), June 21, 1926, https://newspapers.uflib.ufl.edu/UF00079929/00482/images

152 "To Open Soda Water Plant in City Soon," *Fort Myers Press,* (Fort Myers, FL), March 1, 1926, https://newspapers.uflib.ufl.edu/UF00079929/02042/images/3

153 "Image 1 of Sanborn Fire Insurance Map from Fort Myers, Lee County, Florida.," Fort Myers, FL, Sanborn Map Company, January 1930, Retrieved from the Library of Congress, https://www.loc.gov/resource/g3934fm.g3934fm_g012701930/

154 "Al Lang Resigns Post as Leader of Florida State Baseball 'Loop'," *Tampa Tribune,* (Tampa, FL), January 15, 1926, https://www.newspapers.com/image/327184126/

155 "State League May Ask Mike Sexton to Take Leadership of Circuit," *Tampa Tribune,* (Tampa, FL), January 17, 1926, https://www.newspapers.com/image/326989854/

156 "Sexton Re-Elected Baseball President," *Pensacola Journal,* (Pensacola, FL), January 14, 1926, https://newspapers.uflib.ufl.edu/UF00075911/06620/images/5

157 "Baseball Season Will Open Today," *Fort Myers Tropical News,* (Fort Myers, FL), April 22, 1926, https://newspapers.uflib.ufl.edu/AA00088916/00200/images/6

158 "Conroy Is Named Boss of Ft. Myers 9," *Tampa Morning Tribune,* (Tampa, FL), January 22, 1926, https://www.newspapers.com/image/326993034/

159 "Benjamin Arena Ready for Opening Boxing Bout on Friday," *Tampa Daily Times,* (Tampa, FL), November 9, 1925, https://www.newspapers.com/image/332724121/

160 "Well-Known Referee Joins Realty Firm," *Tampa Morning Tribune,* (Tampa, FL), December 31, 1925, https://www.newspapers.com/image/326998687/

161 "Hendry Submits Bid for Local Ball Franchise," *Fort Myers Press,* (Fort Myers, FL), January 22, 1926, https://www.newspapers.com/image/212672220

162 "Manager of Local Ball Team Makes Plans for Team," *Fort Myers Press,* (Fort Myers, FL), January 25, 1926, https://www.newspapers.com/image/212673129/

163 "Sexton Advocates New Florida Loop," *Fort Myers Tropical News,* (Fort Myers, FL), February 11, 1926, https://newspapers.uflib.ufl.edu/AA00088916/00140/images/4

164 "President Shibe of Athletics Due Today Connie and Players to Arrive Sunday," *Fort Myers Tropical News,* (Fort Myers, FL), February 20, 1926, https://newspapers.uflib.ufl.edu/AA00088916/00148/zoom/0

165 "Athletics Take it Easy on Second Day," *Fort Myers Tropical News,* (Fort Myers, FL), February 24, 1926, https://newspapers.uflib.ufl.edu/AA00088916/00151/images/4

166 "Fort Myers Bid for League Berth Up on Wednesday," *Fort Myers Press,* (Fort Myers, FL), February 23, 1926, https://newspapers.uflib.ufl.edu/UF00079929/02037/images/6

167 "Florida Staters Seek Stability in Making Over Loop Tomorrow," *Tampa Morning Tribune,* (Tampa, FL), February 23, 1926, https://www.newspapers.com/image/326625714/

168 "Florida League Will be Formed Next Wednesday," *Fort Myers Press,* (Fort Myers, FL), February 25, 1926, https://newspapers.uflib.ufl.edu/UF00079929/00394/images/0

169 "Bradenton May Have Ball Club in State Loop," *Evening Herald,* (Bradenton, FL), February 24, 1926, https://www.newspapers.com/image/683011578/

170 "St. Petersburg Takes Membership in New League," *St. Petersburg Times,* (St. Petersburg, FL), February 25, 1926, https://www.newspapers.com/image/315727123/

171 "Call Mass Meeting to Assure City of Pro Baseball Club," *The Evening Herald,* (Bradenton, FL), February 25, 1926, https://www.newspapers.com/image/683011748/

172 Isaminger, James C., "Fort Myers Bits," *Philadelphia Inquirer,* (Philadelphia, PA), February 24, 1926, https://www.newspapers.com/image/173393977/

173 Isaminger, James C., "Mack Warns Hurlers to Use Legs; Phillies Work Out," *Philadelphia Inquirer,* (Philadelphia, PA), February 25, 1926, https://www.newspapers.com/image/173397853/

174 "$10,000 Subscribed by Orlando Fans for Baseball Club," *Fort Myers Tropical News,* (Fort Myers, FL), March 4, 1926, https://newspapers.uflib.ufl.edu/AA00088916/00158/images/6

175 Cuffel, Hal, "126 Game Schedule; Split Season Voted," *Orlando Morning Sentinel,* (Orlando, FL), March 4, 1926, https://www.newspapers.com/image/222905957/

176 "Miami Left Out of State League for This Season," *Miami Tribune,* (Miami, FL), March 4, 1926, https://www.newspapers.com/image/616512591/

177 Maginnis, Bob, "Florida State League Increased to Eight-Club Circuit," *Tampa Morning Tribune,* (Tampa, FL), March 4, 1926, https://www.newspapers.com/image/326619028/

178 Rider, Jack, "Pipp Looks good in first Workout; Team Travels to Lakeland," *Orlando Morning Sentinel,* (Orlando, FL), March 10, 1926, https://www.newspapers.com/image/222906364/

179 "Junior Athletics Beat Baltimore 7 to 1," *Fort Myers Tropical News,* (Fort Myers, FL), March 16, 1926, https://newspapers.uflib.ufl.edu/AA00088916/00168/images/6

180 "Bob Cole Signs with Ft. Myers on Mound Staff," *St. Petersburg Times,* (St. Petersburg, FL), March 16, 1926, https://www.newspapers.com/image/314696586/

181 "Occupational Licenses," *Fort Myers Tropical News,* (Fort Myers, FL), November 23, 1925, https://newspapers.uflib.ufl.edu/UF00079929/01959/images/11

182 "Florida Circuit to Meet Friday," *Fort Myers Tropical News,* (Fort Myers, FL), March 18, 1926, https://newspapers.uflib.ufl.edu/AA00088916/00170/images/6

183 "Domingo Will Play State League Ball," *Tampa Tribune,* (Tampa, FL), March 19, 1926, https://www.newspapers.com/image/326637660/

184 "Fort Myers Club to Begin Training in Two Weeks," *Fort Myers Press,* (Fort Myers, FL), March 16, 1926, https://newspapers.uflib.ufl.edu/UF00079929/02054/images/1

185 "Florida Circuit to Meet Friday," *Fort Myers Tropical News,* (Fort Myers, FL), March 18, 1926, https://newspapers.uflib.ufl.edu/AA00088916/00170/images/6

186 "Dr. H. E. Opre to Fight for Opening Day Honors for his Tampa Smokers," *Tampa Sunday Tribune,* (Tampa, FL), March 21, 1926, https://www.newspapers.com/image/326642944/

187 "Macks Trim Phils in Slugging Match 10-8," *Fort Myers Tropical News,* (Fort Myers, FL), March 27, 1926, https://newspapers.uflib.ufl.edu/AA00088916/00178/images/6

188 "Mrs. Connie Mack Loses Bag With $6,000 in Jewels," *Fort Myers Tropical News,* (Fort Myers, FL), March 27, 1926, https://newspapers.uflib.ufl.edu/AA00088916/00178/images/0

189 'Schedule Drafted for State League," *Herald,* (Miami, FL), March 28, 1926, https://www.newspapers.com/image/616535805/

190 "Sanford Club to Join Florida State League," *Palm Beach Post,* (West Palm Beach, FL), March 28, 1926, https://www.newspapers.com/image/133350464/

191 "Landis will Attend Sanford ball Meet," *Tampa Morning Tribune,* (Tampa, FL), March 24, 1926, https://www.newspapers.com/image/326650992/

192 Farry, Charles, F., "Florida State League News," *Evening Reporter-Star*, (Orlando, FL), March 29, 1926, https://www.newspapers.com/image/340853224/

193 "Fort Myers Ball Team to Play Next Week," *Fort Myers Tropical News,* (Fort Myers, FL), April 2, 1926, https://newspapers.uflib.ufl.edu/AA00088916/00183/images/6

194 "Ten Players Arrive in City for Tryouts with Fort Myers Club of Florida State League," *Fort Myers Press,* (Fort Myers, FL), March 30, 1926, https://newspapers.uflib.ufl.edu/UF00079929/02066/images/6

195 "Macks Lost Last game of Florida Series," *Fort Myers Tropical News,* (Fort Myers, FL), March 31, 1926, https://newspapers.uflib.ufl.edu/AA00088916/00181/images/6

196 "Partial Line-Up for Game with Macon Tuesday Given by Conroy," *Fort Myers News,* (Fort Myers, FL), April 1, 1926, https://newspapers.uflib.ufl.edu/UF00079929/02068/images/4

197 "Fort Myers Ball Team to Play Next Week," *Fort Myers Tropical News,* (Fort Myers, FL), April 2, 1926, https://newspapers.uflib.ufl.edu/AA00088916/00183/images/6

198 "Fort Myers Leaguers Play Macon Today," *Fort Myers Tropical News,* (Fort Myers, FL), April 6, 1926, https://newspapers.uflib.ufl.edu/AA00088916/00186/images/8

199 "Landis Authorizes Use of Resin Bag," *Fort Myers Tropical News,* (Fort Myers, FL), April 6, 1926, https://newspapers.uflib.ufl.edu/AA00088916/00186/images/8

200 "Fort Myers Palms Make Bow to Fans With 8 to 7 Victory Over Macon Peaches in Goof Exhibition Game," *Fort Myers Press,* (Fort Myers, FL), April 7, 1926, https://www.newspapers.com/image/212746460/

201 "Fort Myers Team Beats Macon 8 to 7," *Fort Myers Tropical News,* (Fort Myers, FL), April 7, 1926, https://newspapers.uflib.ufl.edu/AA00088916/00187/images/6

202 "Baseball," *Fort Myers Press,* (Fort Myers, FL), April 6, 1926, https://newspapers.uflib.ufl.edu/UF00079929/00425/images/35

203 "Macon Peaches Win Second Game By 10 to 7 Score," *Fort Myers Press,* (Fort Myers, FL), April 8, 1926, https://newspapers.uflib.ufl.edu/UF00079929/00427/images/1

204 Kline, Charley, "Conroy Enthusiastic Over Club Outlook," *Fort Myers Tropical News,* (Fort Myers, FL), April 9, 1926, https://newspapers.uflib.ufl.edu/AA00088916/00189/images/4

205 "Funds Sought to Finance Baseball Club," *Fort Myers Tropical News,* (April 10, 1926), https://newspapers.uflib.ufl.edu/AA00088916/00190/images/4

206 "S. O. S. Call Made by Baseball Club; May Lose Franchise," *Fort Myers Press,* (April 9, 1926), https://newspapers.uflib.ufl.edu/UF00079929/02075/images

207 "Pedrazas Bros. Will Get Baseball Returns During 1926 Season," *Fort Myers Press,* (Fort Myers, FL), April 10, 1926, https://newspapers.uflib.ufl.edu/UF00079929/00429/images/2

208 "Fort Myers Club Placed on Market," *Fort Myers Tropical News,* (Fort Myers, FL), April 11, 1926, https://newspapers.uflib.ufl.edu/AA00088916/00191/images/12

209 Kline, Charlie, "Palms Decked Out in New Uniforms," *Fort Myers Tropical News,* (Fort Myers, FL), April 11, 1926, https://newspapers.uflib.ufl.edu/AA00088916/00191/images/12

210 "Disposal of Club Delayed by Hendry," *Fort Myers Tropical News,* (Fort Myers, FL), April 13, 1926, https://newspapers.uflib.ufl.edu/AA00088916/00192/images/6

211 "Local Fans Watch First Day's Results," *Fort Myers News,* (Fort Myers, FL), April 14, 1926, https://www.newspapers.com/image/212753123/

212 "Palms Ready for Rollins Here Tomorrow," *Fort Myers Press,* (Fort Myers, FL), April 14, 1926, https://newspapers.uflib.ufl.edu/UF00079929/02079/images

213 "McRae Arrives to Join Palms Pitching Staff," *Fort Myers Press,* (Fort Myers, FL), April 15, 1926, https://newspapers.uflib.ufl.edu/UF00079929/00433/images/8

214 "Palms Defeat Rollins Tars Score 10 to 6," *Fort Myers Press,* (Fort Myers, FL), April 16, 1926, https://newspapers.uflib.ufl.edu/UF00079929/02081/images/8

215 "Fort Myers Will Retain Florida League Franchise," *Fort Myers Tropical News,* (Fort Myers, FL), April 18, 1926, https://newspapers.uflib.ufl.edu/AA00088916/00197/images/10

216 "1926 Baseball Schedule for The Florida State League," *Fort Myers Press,* (Fort Myers, FL), April 24, 1926, https://newspapers.uflib.ufl.edu/UF00079929/00441/images/4

217 "Mayor Declares Base Ball Holiday," *Fort Myers Press,* (Fort Myers, FL), April 19, 1926, https://newspapers.uflib.ufl.edu/UF00079929/02083/images/0

218 "Thomas Edison's 43rd Annual Visit to Fort Myers Ends This Afternoon," *Fort Myers Tropical News,* (Fort Myers, FL), April 20, 1926, https://newspapers.uflib.ufl.edu/AA00088916/00198/images/0.

219 "Joe Hernandez named to pitch Season's Opener," *Fort Myers Press,* (Fort Myers, FL), April 21, 1926, https://newspapers.uflib.ufl.edu/UF00079929/02085/images

220 "Fort Myers Ball Team to Play Next Week," *Fort Myers Tropical News,* (Fort Myers, FL), April 2, 1926, https://newspapers.uflib.ufl.edu/AA00088916/00183/images/6

221 "Joe Hernandez Named to Pitch Season's Opener," *Fort Myers Press,* (Fort Myers, FL), April 21, 1926, https://newspapers.uflib.ufl.edu/UF00079929/02085/images

222 "Buck Conroy's Palms in Formal Pose," *Fort Myers Tropical News,* (Fort Myers, FL), April 22, 1926, https://newspapers.uflib.ufl.edu/AA00088916/00200/images

223 "Baseball Season to Open Here Today," *Fort Myers Tropical News,* (Fort Myers, FL), April 22, 1926, https://newspapers.uflib.ufl.edu/AA00088916/00200/images/0

224 "Fort Myers Wins Opening Game, 3 to 0," *Fort Myers Tropical News,* (Fort Myers, FL), April 23, 1926, https://newspapers.uflib.ufl.edu/AA00088916/00201/images/6

225 "Fort Myers Wins Opening Game, 3 to 0," *Fort Myers Tropical News,* (Fort Myers, FL), April 23, 1926, https://newspapers.uflib.ufl.edu/AA00088916/00201/images/6

226 "Saints Lose Season Opener at Fort Myers, 3-0," *St. Petersburg Times,* (St. Petersburg, FL), April 23, 1926, https://www.newspapers.com/image/315103097/

227 Sports Reference, Baseball Reference, "Pedro Dibut," *Baseball Reference*, Accessed May 24, 2023, https://www.baseball-reference.com/players/d/dibutpe01.shtml

228 "Palms to Open Season in Big League Style," *Fort Myers Tropical News,* (Fort Myers, FL), April 20, 1926, https://newspapers.uflib.ufl.edu/AA00088916/00198/images/4

229 "Play by Play Details of Palms' Opening Day Victory Over Saints," *Fort Myers Press,* (Fort Myers, FL), April 23, 1926, https://newspapers.uflib.ufl.edu/UF00079929/00440/images/3

230 "The Weather," *Miami Daily News and Metropolis,"* (Miami, FL), April 23, 1926, https://www.newspapers.com/image/297351955/

231 "Baseball Season to Open Here Today," *Fort Myers Tropical News,* (Fort Myers, FL), April 22, 1926, https://newspapers.uflib.ufl.edu/AA00088916/00200/images/0

232 "Thirsty Baseball Fans Given 1,152 Bottles of NuGrape," *Fort Myers Tropical News,* (Fort Myers, FL), April 23, 1926, https://newspapers.uflib.ufl.edu/AA00088916/00201/images/1

233 Metro Atlanta Chamber of Commerce, "Cool Off," *City Builder,* (Atlanta, GA), July 1926, https://album.atlantahistorycenter.com/digital/collection/ACBuilder/id/8107

234 "The Toggery" *Fort Myers Press,* (Fort Myers, FL), April 6, 1926, https://newspapers.uflib.ufl.edu/UF00079929/00425/images/35

235 "Fort Myers Again Beats St. Pete, 7 to 5," *Fort Myers Tropical News,* (Fort Myers, FL), April 24, 1926, https://newspapers.uflib.ufl.edu/AA00088916/00202/images/4

236 Baumgartner, Stanley, "Athletics Trip Brewers as Babe, in Mack Togs Fails to Get a Bingle," *Philadelphia Inquirer,* (Philadelphia, PA), March 26, 1925, https://www.newspapers.com/image/171079311/

237 "The Weather," *Miami Daily News and Metropolis,* (Miami, FL), April 24, 1926, https://www.newspapers.com/image/297353096/

238 "We're Backing the Palms," *Fort Myers Press,* (Fort Myers, FL), April 23, 1926, https://newspapers.uflib.ufl.edu/UF00079929/00440/images/3

239 "Another Big Day at Baseball Park," *Fort Myers Tropical News,* (Fort Myers, FL), April 24, 1926, https://newspapers.uflib.ufl.edu/AA00088916/00202/images/4

240 "Another Big Day at Baseball Park," *Fort Myers Tropical News,* (Fort Myers, FL), April 24, 1926, https://newspapers.uflib.ufl.edu/AA00088916/00202/images/4

241 "Another Big Day at Baseball Park," *Fort Myers Tropical News,* (Fort Myers, FL), April 24, 1926, https://newspapers.uflib.ufl.edu/AA00088916/00202/images/4

242 "Temperatures," *Fort Myers Tropical News,* (Fort Myers, FL), April 24, 1926, https://newspapers.uflib.ufl.edu/AA00088916/00202/images/6

243 "Venetian Garden Restaurant," *Fort Myers Press,* (Fort Myers, FL), March 18, 1926, https://newspapers.uflib.ufl.edu/UF00079929/02056/images/5

244 "Palms Hold Undisputed League Lead," *Fort Myers Tropical News,* (Fort Myers, FL), April 25, 1926, https://newspapers.uflib.ufl.edu/AA00088916/00203/images/10

245 "Palms Hold Undisputed League Lead," *Fort Myers Tropical News,* (Fort Myers, FL), April 25, 1926, https://newspapers.uflib.ufl.edu/AA00088916/00203/images/10

246 "James E. Hendry Endorses Work of Local Palm Expert," *Fort Myers Press,* (Fort Myers, FL), April 29, 1926, https://newspapers.uflib.ufl.edu/UF00079929/00445/images

247 "Chamber Demands Trail Showdown," *Fort Myers Tropical News,* (Fort Myers, FL), April 23, 1926, https://newspapers.uflib.ufl.edu/AA00088916/00201/images/1

248 "Palms Show Fight in Sarasota Series," *Fort Myers Tropical News,* (Fort Myers, FL), April 29, 1926, https://newspapers.uflib.ufl.edu/AA00088916/00206/images/4

249 "Palms Meet Gulls Again Today After First Defeat of Season," *Fort Myers Press,* (Fort Myers, FL), April 27, 1926, https://newspapers.uflib.ufl.edu/UF00079929/02089/images/3

250 "Tarpon Fielder Is Cut When Fly Ball Breaks His Glasses," *Tampa Morning Tribune,* (Tampa, FL), August 23, 1927, https://www.newspapers.com/image/332340115/

251 Whitner, Cary, "Sarasota Posts Out 10 to 5 Victory Over Ft. Myers," *Sarasota Herald,* (Sarasota, FL), April 27, 1926, https://newspapers.uflib.ufl.edu/AA00088925/00659/images/5

252 "Fort Myers Regains League Leadership," *Fort Myers Tropical News,* (Fort Myers, FL), April 28, 1926, https://newspapers.uflib.ufl.edu/AA00088916/00205/images/4

253 "Fort Myers Team Evens Series by Taking Second Game," *Sarasota Herald,* (Sarasota, FL), April 28, 1926, https://newspapers.uflib.ufl.edu/AA00088925/00660/images/8

254 "Palms Open third Series of Season Today with Bradenton Growers as opponents; McRae Shuts Out Gulls," *Fort Myers Press,* (Fort Myers, FL) April 29, 1926, https://newspapers.uflib.ufl.edu/UF00079929/00445/images/5

255 "Fort Myers Wins from Growers, 9-7," *Fort Myers Tropical News* (Fort Myers, FL), April 30, 1926, https://newspapers.uflib.ufl.edu/AA00088916/00207/images/6

256 "Read 'Em and Weep," *Bradenton Herald,* (Bradenton, FL), April 30, 1926, https://www.newspapers.com/image/682999111/

257 "Eruptions From the Press Coop," *Fort Myers Press,* (Fort Myers, FL), April 30, 1926, https://newspapers.uflib.ufl.edu/UF00079929/02092/images/3

258 "Fort Myers Continues Winning Streak," *Fort Myers Tropical News,* (Fort Myers, FL), May 1, 1926, https://newspapers.uflib.ufl.edu/AA00088916/00208/images/4

259 "Standings of the Baseball Clubs," *Tampa Morning Tribune,* (Tampa, FL), May 1, 1926, https://www.newspapers.com/image/332398521/

260 "Fort Myers Loses Last Game to Bradenton," *Fort Myers Tropical News,* (Fort Myers, FL), May 2, 1926, https://newspapers.uflib.ufl.edu/AA00088916/00209/images/10

261 "Palms to get Royal Greeting tomorrow," *Fort Myers Tropical News,* (Fort Myers, FL), May 2, 1926, https://newspapers.uflib.ufl.edu/AA00088916/00209/images/4

262 Kline, Charlie, "Palms Back Home After First Test of Ability on Road Trip," *Fort Myers Tropical News,* (Fort Myers, FL), May 2, 1926, https://newspapers.uflib.ufl.edu/AA00088916/00209/images/10

263 "Florida State League Teams to Cut Roster," *Fort Lauderdale News,* (Fort Lauderdale, FL), May 3, 1926, https://www.newspapers.com/image/230061035/

264 Parmely, Ray, "State League Team Must Trim Squads to Thirteen Members by Next Thursday," *Tampa Daily Times,* (Tampa, FL), May 3, 1926, https://www.newspapers.com/image/332795169/

265 "Notes of the Game," *Fort Myers Tropical News,* (Fort Myers, FL), May 4, 1926, https://newspapers.uflib.ufl.edu/AA00088916/00210/images/4

266 "The Weather," *Miami Daily News and Metropolis"* (Miami, FL), May 4, 1926, https://www.newspapers.com/image/297336186/

267 "Palms Stage Desperate Eighth Inning Rally to Nose Out Orlando, 4 to 2; Hernandez Slated to Hurl Game Today," *Fort Myers Press,* (Fort Myers, FL), https://newspapers.uflib.ufl.edu/UF00079929/00449/images/3

268 "Colt Heads Seek New Material to Bolster Outfield," *Orlando Morning Sentinel,* (Orlando, FL), May 6, 1926, https://newspapers.uflib.ufl.edu/UF00079944/03624/images/7

269 "Palms Take Opening Game from Orlando," *Fort Myers Tropical News,* (Fort Myers, FL), May 4, 1926, https://newspapers.uflib.ufl.edu/AA00088916/00210/images/4

270 "Support the Palms," *Fort Myers Tropical News,* (Fort Myers, FL), May 4, 1926, https://newspapers.uflib.ufl.edu/AA00088916/00210/images/3

271 "Ladies are Invited to see Palms Play Tampa on Thursday," *Fort Myers Tropical News,* (Fort Myers, FL), May 4, 1926, https://newspapers.uflib.ufl.edu/AA00088916/00210/images/4

272 "The Weather" *Miami Daily News and Metropolis,* (Fort Myers, FL), May 5, 1926, https://www.newspapers.com/image/297337514/

273 "Palms Continue Winning Streak," *Bradenton Herald,* (Bradenton, FL), May 5, 1926, https://www.newspapers.com/image/682636511/

274 "Notes of the Game," *Fort Myers Tropical News,* (Fort Myers, FL), May 6, 1926, https://newspapers.uflib.ufl.edu/AA00088916/00212/images/4

275 "Palms Hold Lead by Scant Margin," *Fort Myers Tropical News,* (Fort Myers, FL), May 6, 1926, https://newspapers.uflib.ufl.edu/AA00088916/00212/images/4

276 "The Weather," *Miami Daily News and Metropolis,* (Miami, FL), May 6, 1926, https://www.newspapers.com/image/297338136/

277 "Loose Fielding Robs Davenport of Well Earned Victory; Palms Use McRae Against Smokers Today," *Fort Myers Press,* (Fort Myers, FL), May 6, 1926, https://newspapers.uflib.ufl.edu/UF00079929/02097/images/1

278 "Notes of the Game," *Fort Myers Tropical News,* (Fort Myers, FL), May 6, 1926, https://newspapers.uflib.ufl.edu/AA00088916/00212/images/4

279 "Palms Want Fans to Help Win Next Two From Tampa," *Fort Myers Tropical News,* (Fort Myers, FL), May 7, 1926, https://newspapers.uflib.ufl.edu/AA00088916/00213/images/6

280 "The Weather," *Miami Daily News and Metropolis,* (Miami, FL), May 7, 1926, https://www.newspapers.com/image/297338636/

281 "Tampa Takes First Game, Score 7 to 4," *Fort Myers Tropical News,* (Fort Myers, FL), May 7, 1926, https://newspapers.uflib.ufl.edu/AA00088916/00213/images/6

282 "Palm Fans Begin to Think Tampa Will Win Again, as Allen's Win Third in Row," *Tampa Morning Tribune,* (Tampa, FL), May 7, 1926, https://www.newspapers.com/image/332403356/

283 "Firemen Increased and Pay Advanced," *Fort Myers Tropical News,* (Fort Myers, FL), May 8, 1926, https://newspapers.uflib.ufl.edu/AA00088916/00214/images/1

284 "Notes of the Game," *Fort Myers Tropical News,* (Fort Myers, FL), May 8, 1926, https://newspapers.uflib.ufl.edu/AA00088916/00214/images/4

285 "The Weather" *Miami Daily News and Metropolis,* (Miami, FL), May 8, 1926, https://www.newspapers.com/image/297339907/

286 "Fort Myers Beats Tampa in Ten Innings," *Fort Myers Tropical News* (Fort Myers, FL), May 8, 1926, https://newspapers.uflib.ufl.edu/AA00088916/00214/images/4

287 "Notes of the Game," *Fort Myers Tropical News,* (Fort Myers, FL), May 8, 1926, https://newspapers.uflib.ufl.edu/AA00088916/00214/images/4

288 "The Weather," *Herald,* (Miami, FL), May 9, 1926,
https://www.newspapers.com/image/616527229/

289 "Boss Allen Chased from Park but Team Takes Finale, 10-9," *Tampa Sunday Tribune,*
(Tampa, FL), May 9, 1926, https://www.newspapers.com/image/332405551/

290 "Lakeland Ties Palms for League Lead," *Fort Myers Tropical News,* (Fort Myers, FL),
May 9, 1926, https://newspapers.uflib.ufl.edu/AA00088916/00215/images/12

291 "Macey Sent Back to Richmond Club," *Fort Myers Tropical News,* (Fort Myers, FL),
May 11, 1926, https://newspapers.uflib.ufl.edu/AA00088916/00216/images/4

292 "Macey Released by Buck Conroy as Team Departs," *Fort Myers Press,* (Fort Myers,
FL), May 10, 1926, https://newspapers.uflib.ufl.edu/UF00079929/02100/images/4

293 "Fort Myers Loses League Lead to Lakeland," *Fort Myers Tropical News,* (Fort Myers,
FL), May 11, 1926, https://newspapers.uflib.ufl.edu/AA00088916/00216/images/4

294 Castleberry, F. M., "Palms Make Fine Showing During First Three Weeks of Season;
Now Out of First Place for First Time," *Fort Myers Press,* (Fort Myers, FL), May 11,
1926, https://newspapers.uflib.ufl.edu/UF00079929/00454/images/7

295 "Eustis Fans Plan Formation of Big Loop Ball Combine," *Orlando Morning Sentinel,*
(Orlando, FL), May 12, 1926, https://www.newspapers.com/image/222628365/

296 "Palms Turn on Lakeland to Tie for Lead," *Fort Myers Tropical News,* (Fort Myers, FL),
May 12, 1926, https://newspapers.uflib.ufl.edu/AA00088916/00217/images/4

297 "Nothing But Praise," *Fort Myers Tropical News,* (Fort Myers, FL), May 12, 1926,
https://newspapers.uflib.ufl.edu/AA00088916/00217/images/3

298 "Palms Dumped to 3rd place by Losing, 5 to 4," *Fort Myers Tropical News,* (Fort
Myers, FL), May 13, 1926,
https://newspapers.uflib.ufl.edu/AA00088916/00218/images/4

299 "Bucky Conroy is Bringing Avenging Crew Form Fort Myers for Smoker Series,"
Tampa Morning Tribune, (Tampa, FL), May 13, 1926,
https://www.newspapers.com/image/332408384/

300 Castleberry, F. M., "Fort Myers Club Votes Against Any Increase in Player Limit or
Salary Rule; Tampa Also casts Negative Vote," *Fort Myers Press,* (Fort Myers, FL) May
14, 1926, https://newspapers.uflib.ufl.edu/UF00079929/02104/images/4

301 "Smoker Rally in Ninth Beats Palms, 5 to 4," *Tampa Morning Tribune*, (Tampa, FL),
May 14, 1926, https://www.newspapers.com/image/332409019/

302 Castleberry, F. M. "Fort Myers Club Will Open Monday in Sanford After Completing
Series This Afternoon with Tampa Smokers," *Fort Myers Press,* (Fort Myers, FL), May
15, 1926, https://newspapers.uflib.ufl.edu/UF00079929/02105/images/10

303 "Fort Myers Defeated by Smokers, 8 to 5," *Fort Myers Tropical News,* (Fort Myers,
FL), May 15, 1926, https://newspapers.uflib.ufl.edu/AA00088916/00220/images/6

304 "Smokers Cop Second Straight Game from Palms," *Tampa Morning Tribune,* (Tampa,
FL), May 15, 1926, https://www.newspapers.com/image/332409648/

305 "Martinez Will Get Real Test in Rice Bout Tonight," *Tampa Daily Times,* (Tampa, FL),
May 14, 1926, https://www.newspapers.com/image/332798217/

306 "Domingo Shuts Out Tampa, Score 3 to 0," *Fort Myers Tropical News,* (Fort Myers,
FL), May 16, 1926, https://newspapers.uflib.ufl.edu/AA00088916/00221/images/12

307 "Bradenton Team Begins Practice Tuesday, April 5," *Fort Myers Press,* (Fort Myers,
FL), April 2, 1926, https://www.newspapers.com/image/212740040/

308 "Base-Bawls," *Orlando Morning Sentinel,* (Orlando, FL), May 16, 1926,
https://newspapers.uflib.ufl.edu/UF00079944/03634/images/9

309 "Joe Domingo Blanks Tampa," *Bradenton Herald,* (Bradenton, FL), May 16, 1926,
https://www.newspapers.com/image/682639949/

310 Associated Press, "Asher Allows Protest," *Miami Herald,* (Miami, FL), May 18, 1926,
https://www.newspapers.com/image/616534306/

311 "Prexy J. B. Asher Awards Orlando Colts Protest Over Fort Myers," *Orlando Morning
Sentinel,* (Orlando, FL), May 18, 1926,
https://newspapers.uflib.ufl.edu/UF00079944/03636/images/8

312 Mac, "The Morning After," *Tampa Tribune,* (Tampa, FL), May 18, 1926,
https://www.newspapers.com/image/332411624/

313 "Asher Allows Protest Made at Fort Myers," St. *Peterburg Times,* (St. Petersburg, FL),
May 18, 1926, https://www.newspapers.com/image/314686006/

314 Sports Reference, Baseball Reference, "Dixie Parker," *Baseball Reference,* Accessed
May 21, 2023, https://www.baseball-reference.com/players/p/parkedi01.shtml

315 "Grower Boss Quits Post; Parker Named," *Tampa Morning Tribune,* (Tampa, FL), May
18, 1926, https://www.newspapers.com/image/332411645/

316 "Fort Myers Gains Triple Tie for First," *Fort Myers Tropical News,* (Fort Myers, FL),
May 18, 1926, https://newspapers.uflib.ufl.edu/AA00088916/00222/images/4

317 Kline, Charley, "Palms Back Home: Meet Gulls Today," *Fort Myers Tropical News,*
(Fort Myers, FL), May 20, 1926,
https://newspapers.uflib.ufl.edu/AA00088916/00224/images/6

318 Castleberry, F. M., "Palms will Return to Home Soil Tomorrow," *Fort Myers Press,*
(Fort Myers, FL), May 19, 1926,
https://newspapers.uflib.ufl.edu/UF00079929/02108/images/7

319 Sports Reference, Baseball Reference, "Ben Cantwell," *Baseball Reference*, Accessed
May 21, 2023, https://www.baseball-reference.com/players/c/cantwbe01.shtml

320 Castleberry, F. M., "Palms Arrive Near Daylight From Sanford," *Fort Myers Press,* (Fort
Myers, FL), May 20, 1926,
https://newspapers.uflib.ufl.edu/UF00079929/00462/images/5

321 "Fort Myers Blanked for First Time, 8 to 0," *Fort Myers Tropical News,* (Fort Myers,
FL), May 19, 1926, https://newspapers.uflib.ufl.edu/AA00088916/00223/images/4

322 Kline, Charlie, "Palms Back Home; Meet Bulls Today," *Fort Myers Tropical News,* (Fort
Myers, FL), May 20, 1926,
https://newspapers.uflib.ufl.edu/AA00088916/00224/images/6

323 Sports Reference, Baseball Reference, "John Wilson," *Baseball Reference*, Accessed
May 21, 2023, https://www.baseball-
reference.com/register/player.fcgi?id=wilson020joh

324 "Domingo Defeated in Second Start," *Fort Myers Tropical News,* (Fort Myers, FL),
May 20, 1926, https://newspapers.uflib.ufl.edu/AA00088916/00224/images/6

325 Castleberry, F. M., "Palms will Return to Home Soil Tomorrow," *Fort Myers Press,*
(Fort Myers, FL), May 19, 1926,
https://newspapers.uflib.ufl.edu/UF00079929/02108/images/7

326 Castleberry, F. M., "Palms Arrive Near Daylight from Sanford," *Fort Myers Press,* (Fort
Myers, FL), May 20, 1926,
https://newspapers.uflib.ufl.edu/UF00079929/00462/images/5

327 "Palms Secure New Pitchers," *Fort Myers Press,* (Fort Myers, FL), May 20, 1926, https://newspapers.uflib.ufl.edu/UF00079929/00462/images/0

328 "Olson Hits Umps; Both are Pinched," *Fort Myers Tropical News,* (Fort Myers, FL), May 20, 1926, https://newspapers.uflib.ufl.edu/AA00088916/00224/images/6

329 Castleberry, F. M., "Palms Arrive Near Daylight from Sanford," *Fort Myers Press,* (Fort Myers, FL), May 20, 1926, https://newspapers.uflib.ufl.edu/UF00079929/00462/images/5

330 "Notes of the Game," *Fort Myers Tropical News,* (Fort Myers, FL), May 21, 1926, https://newspapers.uflib.ufl.edu/AA00088916/00225/images/6

331 "Notes of the Game," *Fort Myers Tropical News,* (Fort Myers, FL), May 21, 1926, https://newspapers.uflib.ufl.edu/AA00088916/00225/images/6

332 "Castleberry, F. M., "Sarasota Gulls Score Run in Tenth to Nose Out Palms, 4 to 3; Visitors Hit Timely to Take First of Series," *Fort Myers Press,* (Fort Myers, FL), May 21, 1926, https://newspapers.uflib.ufl.edu/UF00079929/02110/images/5

333 "Conroy Leaves City Following Release," *Fort Myers Press,* (Fort Myers, FL), May 21, 1926, https://newspapers.uflib.ufl.edu/UF00079929/02110/images/0

334 "Conroy Released as Pilot of Palms," *Fort Myers Tropical News,* (Fort Myers, FL), May 21, 1926, https://newspapers.uflib.ufl.edu/AA00088916/00225/images/0

335 "Conroy Released as Pilot of Palms," *Fort Myers Tropical News,* (Fort Myers, FL), May 21, 1926, https://newspapers.uflib.ufl.edu/AA00088916/00225/images/0

336 "Notes of the Game," *Fort Myers Tropical News,* (Fort Myers, FL), May 22, 1926, https://newspapers.uflib.ufl.edu/AA00088916/00226/images/4

337 "Conroy Released as Palms Pilot," *Fort Myers Tropical News,* (Fort Myers, FL), May 21, 1926, https://newspapers.uflib.ufl.edu/AA00088916/00225/images/1

338 "Davenport Pitches Sensational Game," *Fort Myers Tropical News,* (Fort Myers, FL), May 22, 1926, https://newspapers.uflib.ufl.edu/AA00088916/00226/images/4

339 Sports Reference, Baseball Reference, "Jumbo Brown," *Baseball Reference*, Accessed May 24, 2023, https://www.baseball-reference.com/players/b/brownju01.shtml

340 "Sarasota Manager is Also Released," *Fort Myers Tropical News,* (Fort Myers, FL), May 22, 1926, https://newspapers.uflib.ufl.edu/AA00088916/00226/images/4

341 "Four Managers in State League Dropped in Week," Castleberry, F. M., *Fort Myers Press,* (Fort Myers, FL), May 25, 1926, https://newspapers.uflib.ufl.edu/UF00079929/02113/images/4

342 Sports Reference, Baseball Reference, "James Black," *Baseball Reference*, Accessed May 12, 2023, https://www.baseball-reference.com/register/player.fcgi?id=black-002jam

343 "Notes of the Game," *Fort Myers Tropical News,* (Fort Myers, FL), May 23, 1926, https://newspapers.uflib.ufl.edu/AA00088916/00227/images/12

344 "Notes of the Game," *Fort Myers Tropical News,* (Fort Myers, FL), May 23, 1926, https://newspapers.uflib.ufl.edu/AA00088916/00227/images/12

345 Castleberry, F. M., "McRae Is likely To Open Against St. Pete Today," *Fort Myers Press,* (Fort Myers, FL), May 24, 1926, https://newspapers.uflib.ufl.edu/UF00079929/00465/images/4

346 "Improvements At Ballpark," *Fort Myers Press,* (Fort Myers, FL), May 24, 1926, https://www.newspapers.com/image/212777443/

347 "Negros Will Have Special Bleachers," *Fort Myers Tropical News,* (Fort Myers, FL), May 25, 1926, https://newspapers.uflib.ufl.edu/AA00088916/00228/images/4

348 "Setting an Example for His Men," *St. Petersburg Times,* (St. Petersburg, FL), May 26, 1926, https://www.newspapers.com/image/314764847/

349 "Hewitt's Pitching Mystifies Palms," *Fort Myers Tropical News,* (Fort Myers, FL), May 25, 1926, https://newspapers.uflib.ufl.edu/AA00088916/00228/images/4

350 "Palms Return Home Tomorrow," *Fort Myers Press,* (Fort Myers, FL), May 26, 1926, https://newspapers.uflib.ufl.edu/UF00079929/02114/images

351 "Palms Rained Out at St. Petersburg," *Fort Myers Tropical News,* (Fort Myers, FL), May 26, 1926, https://newspapers.uflib.ufl.edu/AA00088916/00229/images/4

352 "League Standing Shaken Up by President," *Bradenton Herald,* (Bradenton, FL), May 27, 1926, https://www.newspapers.com/image/682643984/

353 Johns, Keith, "Saints Engage Palms in Twin Program Today," *St. Petersburg Times,* (St. Petersburg, FL), May 26, 1926, https://www.newspapers.com/image/314764847/

354 Associated Press, "Saints Divide with Palms," *Bradenton Herald,* (Bradenton, FL), May 27, 1926, https://www.newspapers.com/image/682643984/

355 "Growers File Protest Against Sanford Team," *Tampa Morning Tribune,* (Tampa, FL), May 28, 1926, https://www.newspapers.com/image/332419010/

356 Kline, Charlie, "League Ruling Sends Sanford to Top Place," *Fort Myers Tropical News,* (Fort Myers, FL), May 27, 1926, https://newspapers.uflib.ufl.edu/AA00088916/00230/images/4

357 "The Weather," *Miami Daily News and Metropolis,* (Miami, FL), May 28, 1926, https://www.newspapers.com/image/298511034/

358 Kline, Charley, "Rain Halts Palms – Double Bill Saturday," *Fort Myers Tropical News,* (Fort Myers, FL), May 28, 1926, https://newspapers.uflib.ufl.edu/AA00088916/00231/images/4

359 "Merchant Days for Ball Club," *Fort Myers Press,* (Fort Myers, FL), May 28, 1926, https://newspapers.uflib.ufl.edu/UF00079929/02116/images

360 "Double Header is Scheduled Today," *Fort Myers Tropical News,* (Fort Myers, FL), May 29, 1926, https://newspapers.uflib.ufl.edu/AA00088916/00232/images/6

361 "The Weather," *Miami Daily News and Metropolis,* (Miami, FL), May 29, 1926, https://www.newspapers.com/image/298511052/

362 "Palms Pound Ball to Beat Sanford, 13 to 4," *Fort Myers Tropical News,* (Fort Myers, FL), May 29, 1926, https://newspapers.uflib.ufl.edu/AA00088916/00232/images/6

363 "Fans to Aid Club in Raising Funds," *Fort Myers Tropical News,* (Fort Myers, FL), May 30, 1926, https://newspapers.uflib.ufl.edu/AA00088916/00233/images/12

364 "The Weather," *Miami Herald,* (Miami, FL), May 30, 1926, https://www.newspapers.com/image/616576770/

365 "Bunts Beat Palms in Final with Sanford," *Fort Myers Tropical News,* (Fort Myers, FL), May 30, 1926, https://newspapers.uflib.ufl.edu/AA00088916/00233/images/12

366 "Pedrazas Brothers Entertain Players," *Fort Myers Press,* (Fort Myers, FL), May 31, 1926, https://newspapers.uflib.ufl.edu/UF00079929/02118/images/2

367 "The Weather," *Miami Daily News and Metropolis,* (Miami, FL), June 1, 1926, https://www.newspapers.com/image/298511140/

368 "Palms Capture Opening Game with Growers," *Fort Myers Press,* (Fort Myers, FL), June 1, 1926, https://newspapers.uflib.ufl.edu/UF00079929/02119/images/13

369 "Series to Open This Afternoon at Terry Park," *Fort Myers Press,* (Fort Myers, FL), May 31, 1926, https://newspapers.uflib.ufl.edu/UF00079929/02118/images/7

370 "Standings" *St. Petersburg Times,* (St. Petersburg, FL), June 1, 1926, https://www.newspapers.com/image/314765793/

371 "The Weather," *Miami Daily News and Metropolis,* (Miami, FL), June 2, 1926, https://www.newspapers.com/image/298511166/

372 "Palms Make it 2 Straight from Growers," *Fort Myers Tropical News,* (Fort Myers, FL), June 2, 1926, https://newspapers.uflib.ufl.edu/AA00088916/00235/images/6

373 "Olson Out," *Bradenton Herald,* (Bradenton, FL), June 2, 1926, https://www.newspapers.com/image/682645856/

374 "The Weather," *Miami Herald,* (Miami, FL), June 3, 1926, https://www.newspapers.com/image/616576922/

375 Castleberry, F. M., "Palms Gather 16 Hits and Win Third Straight," *Fort Myers Press,* (Fort Myers, FL), June 3, 1926, https://newspapers.uflib.ufl.edu/UF00079929/00471/images/5

376 "Palms Banqueted After 3rd Victory," *Fort Myers Tropical News,* (Fort Myers, FL), June 3, 1926, https://newspapers.uflib.ufl.edu/AA00088916/00236/images/4

377 "Baseball Players Guests at Dinner," *Fort Myers Press,* (Fort Myers, FL), June 3, 1926, https://newspapers.uflib.ufl.edu/UF00079929/00471/images/5

378 "Palms Win Opening Game at Orlando, 3 to 1," *Fort Myers Tropical News,* (Fort Myers, FL) June 4, 1926, https://newspapers.uflib.ufl.edu/AA00088916/00237/images/6

379 "Brother of Al Schacht Signed by Local Club," *Fort Myers Press,* (Fort Myers, FL), June 5, 1926, https://newspapers.uflib.ufl.edu/UF00079929/02123/images/5

380 "Palms Beaten by Orlando, Score 5 to 2," *Fort Myers Tropical News,* (Fort Myers, FL), June 5, 1926, https://newspapers.uflib.ufl.edu/AA00088916/00238/images/6

381 Kline, Charley, "Passes Recalled By Baseball Club," *Fort Myers Tropical News,* (Fort Myers, FL), June 6, 1926, https://newspapers.uflib.ufl.edu/AA00088916/00239/images/10

382 "Pitcher Breaks Up Extra Inning Game," *Fort Myers Tropical News,* (Fort Myers, FL), June 6, 1926, https://newspapers.uflib.ufl.edu/AA00088916/00239/images/10

383 "Palms to Meet Highlanders in 3-Game Series," *Fort Myers Press,* (Fort Myers, FL), June 7, 1926, https://newspapers.uflib.ufl.edu/UF00079929/02124/images/7

384 "Rotarians Hear Officials Tell of Public Work," *Fort Myers Press,* (Fort Myers, FL), June 8, 1926, https://newspapers.uflib.ufl.edu/UF00079929/00475/images

385 "Davenport Allows Only Five Hits and Palms Win Opening Clash of Crucial Series with Lakeland, Score 4 to 1," *Fort Myers Press,* (Fort Myers, FL), June 8, 1926, https://newspapers.uflib.ufl.edu/UF00079929/00475/images/7

386 "The Weather," *Miami Daily News and Metropolis,* (Miami, FL), June 8, 1926, https://www.newspapers.com/image/298511328/

387 "Davenport Allows Only Five Hits and Palms Win Opening Clash of Crucial Series with Lakeland, Score 4 to 1," *Fort Myers Press,* (Fort Myers, FL), June 8, 1926, https://newspapers.uflib.ufl.edu/UF00079929/00475/images/7

388 Kline, Charley, "Palms Win Opening Game from Lakeland," *Fort Myers Tropical News,* (Fort Myers, FL), June 8, 1926, https://newspapers.uflib.ufl.edu/AA00088916/00240/images/4

389 "Davenport Allows Only Five Hits and Palms Win Opening Clash of Crucial Series with Lakeland, Score 4 to 1," *Fort Myers Press,* (Fort Myers, FL), June 8, 1926, https://www.newspapers.com/image/212640479/

390 Kline, Charley, "Palms Win Opening Game from Lakeland," *Fort Myers Tropical News,* (Fort Myers, FL), June 8, 1926, https://newspapers.uflib.ufl.edu/AA00088916/00240/images/4

391 "The Weather," *Miami Daily News and Metropolis,* (Miami, FL), June 9, 1926, https://www.newspapers.com/image/298511352/

392 Kline, Charley, "Fort Myers Blanked by Lakeland, 4 to 0," *Fort Myers Tropical News,* (Fort Myers, FL), June 9, 1926, https://newspapers.uflib.ufl.edu/AA00088916/00241/images/4

393 "The Weather," *Miami Daily News and Metropolis,* (Miami, FL), June 10, 1926, https://www.newspapers.com/image/298511363/

394 "Rain Stops Last Lakeland Contest," *Fort Myers Tropical News,* (Fort Myers, FL), June 10, 1926, https://newspapers.uflib.ufl.edu/AA00088916/00242/images/4

395 "The Weather," *Miami Daily News and Metropolis,* (Miami, FL), June 11, 1926, https://www.newspapers.com/image/298511397/

396 Castleberry, F. M. "Palms and Gulls Battle Eleven Innings to Draw," *Fort Myers Press,* (Fort Myers, FL), June 11, 1926, https://newspapers.uflib.ufl.edu/UF00079929/02128/images/6

397 Kline, Charley, "Palms and Sarasota Play 11 Innings to Tie," *Fort Myers Tropical News,* (Fort Myers, FL), June 11, 1926, https://newspapers.uflib.ufl.edu/AA00088916/00243/images/6

398 "The Weather," *Miami Daily News and Metropolis,* (Miami, FL), June 11, 1926, https://www.newspapers.com/image/298511434/

399 Kline, Charley, "Palms to Play 2 Games with Gulls Today," *Fort Myers Tropical News,* (Fort Myers, FL), June 12, 1926, https://newspapers.uflib.ufl.edu/AA00088916/00244/images/6

400 "The Weather," *Miami Daily News and Metropolis,* (Miami, FL), June 12, 1926, https://www.newspapers.com/image/298511434/

401 Kline, Charley, "Palms to Play 2 Games with Gulls Today," *Fort Myers Tropical News,* (Fort Myers, FL), June 12, 1926, https://newspapers.uflib.ufl.edu/AA00088916/00244/images/6

402 "Seventh Inning Rally Scores 5 Runs, Palms Win," *Fort Myers Press,* (Fort Myers, FL), June 12, 1926, https://www.newspapers.com/image/212641447/

403 Kline, Charlie, "Palms Split Even in 2 Games with Gulls," *Fort Myers Tropical News,* (Fort Myers, FL), June 13, 1926, https://newspapers.uflib.ufl.edu/AA00088916/00245/images/10

404 "Palms Open Three Game Series at Sarasota," *Fort Myers Press,* (Fort Myers, FL), June 14, 1926, https://newspapers.uflib.ufl.edu/UF00079929/00479/images/7

405 "Palms Take Second Place in League Race," *Fort Myers Tropical News,* (Fort Myers, FL), June 15, 1925, https://newspapers.uflib.ufl.edu/AA00088916/00246/images/4

406 "Battle Royale for Club Tonight," *Fort Myers Tropical News,* (Fort Myers, FL), https://newspapers.uflib.ufl.edu/AA00088916/00247/images/4

407 "Fort Myers Trims Sarasota, 4 to 2," *Fort Myers Tropical News,* (Fort Myers, FL), June 16, 1926, https://newspapers.uflib.ufl.edu/AA00088916/00247/images/4

408 "Palms Drop Final Game to Sarasota, 5 to 2," *Fort Myers Tropical News,* (Fort Myers, FL), June 17, 1926, https://newspapers.uflib.ufl.edu/AA00088916/00248/images/4

409 "Palms at Home to Meet Colts in Four Games," *Fort Myers Press,* (Fort Myers, FL), June 17, 1926, https://newspapers.uflib.ufl.edu/UF00079929/02132/images/7

410 "Boxing Fans Enjoy Battle Royal for Ball Club Benefit," *Fort Myers Tropical News,* (Fort Myers, FL), June 17, 1926, https://newspapers.uflib.ufl.edu/AA00088916/00248/images/4

411 "Orlando Will Play Two Games With fort Myers Today," *Fort Myers Tropical News,* (Fort Myers, FL), June 17, 1926, https://newspapers.uflib.ufl.edu/AA00088916/00248/images/4

412 "The Weather," *Miami Daily News and Metropolis,* (Miami, FL), June 18, 1926, https://www.newspapers.com/image/298511592/

413 "Palms Win Both Ends of Double Bill Yesterday," *Fort Myers Press,* (Fort Myers, FL), June 18, 1926, https://newspapers.uflib.ufl.edu/UF00079929/02133/images/6

414 Kline, Charley, "Notes of the Game," *Fort Myers Tropical News,* (Fort Myers, FL), June 18, 1926, https://newspapers.uflib.ufl.edu/AA00088916/00249/images/6

415 "Palms Giving Orlando Colts Big Trimming," *Fort Myers Press,* (Fort Myers, FL), June 17, 1926, https://www.newspapers.com/image/212642331/

416 Kline, Charley, "Notes of the Game," *Fort Myers Tropical News,* (Fort Myers, FL), June 19, 1926, https://newspapers.uflib.ufl.edu/AA00088916/00250/images/4

417 "The Weather," *Miami Daily News and Metropolis,* (Miami, FL), June 19, 1926, https://www.newspapers.com/image/298511604/19

418 "Orlando Loses Third Straight to Fort Myers Palms," *Orlando Morning Sentinel,* (Orlando, FL), June 19, 1926, https://newspapers.uflib.ufl.edu/UF00079944/03667/images/7

419 "The Weather," *Herald,* (Miami, FL), June 20, 1926, https://www.newspapers.com/image/616572316/

420 "Palms Lose Final Game to Orlando, 3 to 2, *Fort Myers Tropical News,* (Fort Myers, FL), June 20, 1926, https://newspapers.uflib.ufl.edu/AA00088916/00251/images/18

421 "The Weather," *Herald,* (Miami, FL) June 22, 1926, https://www.newspapers.com/image/616573095/

422 "Special Service on Sanford Games," "*Fort Myers Tropical News,* (Fort Myers, FL), June 22, 1926, https://newspapers.uflib.ufl.edu/AA00088916/00252/images/4

423 "Second Boxing Show Thursday Night at Park," *Fort Myers Press,* (Fort Myers, FL), June 22, 1926, https://newspapers.uflib.ufl.edu/UF00079929/02136/images/7

424 Associated Press, "Celeryfeds and Palms Play Five-Inning Tie," *Tampa Morning Tribune,* (Tampa, FL), June 23, 1926, https://www.newspapers.com/image/332413030/

425 "Another Double Bill Scheduled This Afternoon," *Fort Myers Press,* (Fort Myers, FL), June 23, 1926, https://newspapers.uflib.ufl.edu/UF00079929/00484/images/9

426 "Palms Divide Twin Bill with Sanford," *Fort Myers Tropical News,* (Fort Myers, FL), June 24, 1926, https://newspapers.uflib.ufl.edu/AA00088916/00254/images/4

427 "Baseball Club to Quit League After July 3rd," *Fort Myers Tropical News,* (Fort Myers, FL), June 24, 1926, https://newspapers.uflib.ufl.edu/AA00088916/00254/images/0

428 "Baseball Benefit Bouts to be Held at Park Tonight," *Fort Myers Tropical News,* (Fort Myers, FL), June 24, 1926, https://newspapers.uflib.ufl.edu/AA00088916/00254/images/4

429 Fort Myers Baseball Club, "Oh Boys!" Advertisement. *Fort Myers Press,* (Fort Myers, FL), June 23, 1926, P.7. https://newspapers.uflib.ufl.edu/UF00079929/00484/images/4

430 "Lions Start Move to Keep Ball Club in City of Palms," *Fort Myers Press,* (Fort Myers, FL), June 24, 1926, https://newspapers.uflib.ufl.edu/UF00079929/02138/images

431 "Palms Shut Out Orlando in Five Inning Contest," *Fort Myers Press,* (Fort Myers, FL), June 25, 1926, https://newspapers.uflib.ufl.edu/UF00079929/02139/images/3

432 "Leach is Named to Manage Tampa Club in League," *Fort Myers Press,* (Fort Myers, FL), June 25, 1926, https://newspapers.uflib.ufl.edu/UF00079929/02139/images/3

433 Sports Reference, Baseball Reference, "Tommy Leach," *Baseball Reference*, Accessed May 17, 2023, https://www.baseball-reference.com/players/l/leachto01.shtml

434 "Ball Club Fate to be Settled This Evening," *Fort Myers Press,* (Fort Myers, FL), June 25, 1926, https://newspapers.uflib.ufl.edu/UF00079929/02139/images/0

435 "Lions Start Move to Keep Ball Club in City of Palms," *Fort Myers Press,* (Fort Myers, FL), June 24, 1925, https://newspapers.uflib.ufl.edu/UF00079929/02138/images

436 "Two New Faces in Colt Lineup," *Orlando Morning Sentinel,* (Orlando, FL), June 26, 1926, https://newspapers.uflib.ufl.edu/UF00079944/03674/images/22

437 Sports Reference, Baseball Reference, "Bob Vines," *Baseball Reference*, Accessed May 24, 2023, https://www.baseball-reference.com/players/v/vinesbo01.shtml

438 "Palms Lose to Orlando, Score 6 to 5," *Fort Myers Tropical News,* (Fort Myers, FL), June 26, 1926, https://newspapers.uflib.ufl.edu/AA00088916/00256/zoom/4

439 "Drive to Save Ball Club Will be Launched Today," *Fort Myers Tropical News,* (Fort Myers, FL), June 26, 1926, https://newspapers.uflib.ufl.edu/AA00088916/00256/images/0

440 "Committees Plan Ball Club Rescue," *Fort Myers Tropical News,* (Fort Myers, FL), June 25, 1926, https://newspapers.uflib.ufl.edu/AA00088916/00255/images/0

441 "Drive to Save Ball Club Will be Launched Today," *Fort Myers Tropical News,* (Fort Myers, FL), June 26, 1926, https://newspapers.uflib.ufl.edu/AA00088916/00256/images/0

442 "One-third of Needed Fund Collected for Ball Club," Fort *Myers Tropical News,* (Fort Myers, FL), June 27, 1926, https://newspapers.uflib.ufl.edu/AA00088916/00257/images/4

443 "$25 in 1926 is worth $431.77 today," *CPI Inflation Calculator,* accessed August 27, 2023, https://www.officialdata.org/us/inflation/1926?amount=25

444 "Palms Beat Colts in Last Game of Series," *Fort Myers Tropical News,* (Fort Myers, FL), June 27, 1926, https://newspapers.uflib.ufl.edu/AA00088916/00257/images/12

445 "Yesterday's Donors to Baseball Fund', *Fort Myers Tropical News,* (Fort Myers, FL), June 27, 1926, https://newspapers.uflib.ufl.edu/AA00088916/00257/images/12

446 "Funds Sought for Ball Club," *Fort Myers Press,* (Fort Myers, FL), June 28, 1926, https://newspapers.uflib.ufl.edu/UF00079929/00487/images/0

447 "Club Presidents to Hold Meeting at Tampa, 11 A. M.," *Fort Myers Press,* (Fort Myers, FL), June 28, 1926, https://newspapers.uflib.ufl.edu/UF00079929/00487/images/4

448 "The Weather," *Miami Daily News and Metropolis,* (Miami, FL), June 29, 1926, https://www.newspapers.com/image/297515930/

449 "Palms Capture First Game of St. Pete Series," *Fort Myers Press,* (Fort Myers, FL), June 29, 1926, https://newspapers.uflib.ufl.edu/UF00079929/00488/images/4

450 "Yesterday's Donors to Baseball Fund," *Fort Myers Tropical News,* (Fort Myers, FL), https://newspapers.uflib.ufl.edu/AA00088916/00258/images/4

451 "Free Bus Will Carry Ball Fans," *Fort Myers Press,* (Fort Myers, FL), June 29, 1926, https://newspapers.uflib.ufl.edu/UF00079929/00488/images/0

452 Google, "First St & Jackson St, Fort Myers to Terry Park," *Google Maps,* accessed May 18, 2023, https://bit.ly/3OmmZFj

453 Sanborn Map Company, "Fort Myers, Lee County, Florida," *Maps: Sanborn Fire Insurance Maps of Florida,* https://ufdc.ufl.edu/UF00074170/00002/images/0

454 Associated Press, "6 Wins Taken from Sanford; Palms Pruned of 3 Defeats," *Fort Myers Tropical News,* (Fort Myers, FL), June 30, 1926, https://newspapers.uflib.ufl.edu/AA00088916/00259/images/4

455 "The Weather," *Miami Daily News and Metropolis,* (Miami, FL), June 30, 1926, https://www.newspapers.com/image/297516366/

456 "St. Pete Beats Fort Myers in Twelfth," *Fort Myers Tropical News,* (Fort Myers, FL), June 30, 1926, https://newspapers.uflib.ufl.edu/AA00088916/00259/images/4

457 "Notes of the Game," *Fort Myers Tropical News,* (Fort Myers, FL), June 30, 1926, https://newspapers.uflib.ufl.edu/AA00088916/00259/images/4

458 "Baseball Club Gets Another Day of Grace," *Fort Myers Tropical News,* (Fort Myers, FL), June 30, 1926, https://newspapers.uflib.ufl.edu/AA00088916/00259/images/0

459 "Yesterday's Donors to Baseball Fund," *Fort Myers Tropical News,* (Fort Myers, FL), June 30, 1926, https://newspapers.uflib.ufl.edu/AA00088916/00259/images/1

460 "The Weather," *Miami Daily News and Metropolis,* (Miami, FL), July 1, 1926, https://www.newspapers.com/image/297517028/

461 "Notes of the Game," *Fort Myers Tropical News,* (Fort Myers, FL), July 2, 1926, https://newspapers.uflib.ufl.edu/AA00088916/00261/images/6

462 "Hendry Decides to Keep Team in Fort Myers," *Fort Myers Tropical News,* (Fort Myers, FL), July 1, 1926, https://newspapers.uflib.ufl.edu/AA00088916/00260/images/0

463 "Statistics of the Diamond" *Tampa Daily Times,* (Tampa, FL), July 1, 1926, https://www.newspapers.com/image/332820723/

464 "Lions are Praised for Raising Funds to Aid Ball Club," *Fort Myers Tropical News,* (Fort Myers, FL), July 2, 1926, https://newspapers.uflib.ufl.edu/AA00088916/00288/images/5

465 "Palms Must Win Entire Series," *Fort Myers Press,* (Fort Myers, FL), July 1, 1926, https://newspapers.uflib.ufl.edu/UF00079929/00490/images/5

466 "The Weather," *Miami Daily News and Metropolis,* (Miami, FL), July 2, 1926, https://www.newspapers.com/image/297519818/

467 "Palms Lose Last Chance to Lead League," *Fort Myers Tropical News,* (Fort Myers, FL), July 2, 1926, https://newspapers.uflib.ufl.edu/AA00088916/00288/images/6

468 "Notes of the Game," *Fort Myers Tropical News,* (Fort Myers, FL), July 2, 1926, https://newspapers.uflib.ufl.edu/AA00088916/00288/images/6

[469] "Sarasota Seeks Fund to Remain in League," *Tampa Morning Tribune,* (Tampa, FL), July 3, 1926, https://www.newspapers.com/image/332201841/

[470] "The Weather," *Miami Daily News and Metropolis,* (Fort Myers, FL), July 3, 1926, https://www.newspapers.com/image/297520107/

[471] "Palms Even Series With 6 to 3 Victory," *Fort Myers Tropical News,* (Fort Myers, FL), July 3, 1926, https://newspapers.uflib.ufl.edu/AA00088916/00262/images/4

[472] "The Weather," *Herald,* (Miami, FL), July 4, 1926, https://www.newspapers.com/image/616575417/

[473] "Palms Finish First Half in Third Place," *Fort Myers Tropical News,* (Fort Myers, FL), July 4, 1926, https://newspapers.uflib.ufl.edu/AA00088916/00263/images/10

[474] "Club Standings" *Fort Myers Tropical News,* (Fort Myers, FL), July 4, 1926, https://newspapers.uflib.ufl.edu/AA00088916/00263/images/10

[475] "Palms and Lakeland Split Holiday Bill," *Fort Myers Tropical News,* (Fort Myers, FL), July 6, 1926, https://newspapers.uflib.ufl.edu/AA00088916/00291/images/4

[476] Sports Reference, Baseball Reference, "Roy Ellam," *Baseball Reference*, Accessed May 19, 2023, https://www.baseball-reference.com/register/player.fcgi?id=ellam-001roy

[477] "Palms Score 3 to 1 Victory at Lakeland," *Fort Myers Tropical News,* (Fort Myers, FL), July 7, 1926, https://newspapers.uflib.ufl.edu/AA00088916/00292/images/4

[478] "Rally by Kiwanis in Final Inning Beats Lions Club," *Fort Myers Tropical News,* (Fort Myers, FL), July 9, 1926, https://newspapers.uflib.ufl.edu/AA00088916/00294/images/6

[479] "Lions and Kiwanis Clubs Will Clash on Diamond Today," *Fort Myers Tropical News,* (Fort Myers, FL), July 8, 1926, https://newspapers.uflib.ufl.edu/AA00088916/00266/images/4

[480] "Bradenton Wins First of Series," *Fort Myers Press,* (Fort Myers, FL), July 9, 1926, https://newspapers.uflib.ufl.edu/UF00079929/00495/images/7

[481] "Fort Myers Loses to Bradenton, 5 to 2," *Fort Myers Tropical News,* (Fort Myers, FL), July 9, 1926, https://newspapers.uflib.ufl.edu/AA00088916/00294/images/6

[482] "Baseball Passes," *Fort Myers Press,* (Fort Myers, FL), July 9, 1926, https://newspapers.uflib.ufl.edu/UF00079929/00495/images/0

[483] "Fort Myers Defeats Bradenton, 7 to 3," *Fort Myers Tropical News,* (Fort Myers, FL), July 10, 1926, https://newspapers.uflib.ufl.edu/AA00088916/00268/images/4

[484] "Mike Kelly's String of Victories Broken," *Tampa Morning Tribune,* (Tampa, FL), July 10, 1926, https://www.newspapers.com/image/332202441/

[485] "Three New Players Sign with Bradenton Growers," *Tampa Sunday Tribune,* (Tampa, FL), July 11, 1926, https://www.newspapers.com/image/332202599/

[486] "Richardson's Homer Defeats Fort Myers, 3 to 1," *Bradenton Herald,* (Bradenton, FL), July 11, 1926, https://www.newspapers.com/image/682656224/

[487] "The Weather," *Miami Daily News and Metropolis,* (Miami, FL), July 13, 1926, https://www.newspapers.com/image/297538340/

[488] "Tampa Blanked to Open Fort Myers Series, 1-0," *Tampa Morning Tribune,* (Tampa, FL), July 13, 1926, https://www.newspapers.com/image/332202946/

[489] "The Weather," *Miami Daily News and Metropolis,* (Miami, FL), July 14, 1926, https://www.newspapers.com/image/297539617/

490 Sports Reference, Baseball Reference, "Buck Stanton," *Baseball Reference*, Accessed May 24, 2023, https://www.baseball-reference.com/players/s/stantbu01.shtml

491 "Head of Moving Picture Company to be Honored," *Fort Myers Press,* (Fort Myers, FL), February 9, 1926, https://newspapers.uflib.ufl.edu/UF00079929/02025/images/2

492 "Notes of the Game," *Fort Myers Tropical News,* (Fort Myers, FL), July 14, 1926, https://newspapers.uflib.ufl.edu/AA00088916/00298/images/6

493 "Palms Again Victors 3 to 1," *Fort Myers Press,* (Fort Myers, FL), July 14, 1926, https://newspapers.uflib.ufl.edu/UF00079929/00497/images/0

494 "Tampa Drops Hurling Duel to Fort Myers, 3-1," *Tampa Morning Tribune* (Tampa, FL), July 14, 1926, https://www.newspapers.com/image/332203048/

495 "Sarasota Club Fails in Drive for Funds to Finance Baseball," *Tampa Tribune* (Tampa, FL), July 15, 1926, https://www.newspapers.com/image/332203150/

496 "The Weather," *Miami Daily News and Metropolis,* (Miami, FL), July 15, 1926, https://www.newspapers.com/image/297540755/

497 "Palms Make it 3 Straight from Tampa," *Fort Myers Tropical News,* (Fort Myers, FL), July 15, 1926, https://newspapers.uflib.ufl.edu/AA00088916/00272/images/4

498 "Sarasota to Stay in State League," *Fort Myers Tropical News,* (Fort Myers, FL), July 15, 1926, https://newspapers.uflib.ufl.edu/AA00088916/00300/images/4

499 "Ball Club End is Near," *Bradenton Herald,* (Bradenton, FL), July 16, 1926, https://www.newspapers.com/image/682657271/

500 "The Weather," *Miami Daily News and Metropolis,* (Miami, FL), July 16, 1926, https://www.newspapers.com/image/297542589/

501 "Diamond Dust," *Fort Myers Press,* (Fort Myers, FL), July 16, 1926, https://newspapers.uflib.ufl.edu/UF00079929/00499/images/4

502 "Palms Take First of Bradenton Series," *Fort Myers Tropical News,* (Fort Myers, FL), July 16, 1926, https://newspapers.uflib.ufl.edu/AA00088916/00300/images/4

503 "The Weather," *Miami Daily News and Metropolis,* (Miami, FL), July 17, 1926, https://www.newspapers.com/image/297542803/

504 "Mike Kelly is Sold to Philadelphia Nationals," *Bradenton Herald,* (Bradenton, FL) September 1, 1926, https://www.newspapers.com/image/682754035/

505 "Palms and Bradenton Play 10 Inning Tie," *Fort Myers Tropical News,* (Fort Myers, FL), July 17, 1926, https://newspapers.uflib.ufl.edu/AA00088916/00274/images/4

506 "Notes of the Game," *Fort Myers Tropical News,* (Fort Myers, FL), July 17, 1926, https://newspapers.uflib.ufl.edu/AA00088916/00274/images/9

507 "Umpire Gives Sanford Game as Gulls Stall," *Tampa Tribune* (Tampa, FL), July 18, 1926, https://www.newspapers.com/image/332203517/

508 "Notes of the Game," *Fort Myers Tropical News,* (Fort Myers, FL), July 18, 1926, https://newspapers.uflib.ufl.edu/AA00088916/00302/images/10

509 "The Weather," *Herald,* (Miami, FL), July 18, 1926, https://www.newspapers.com/image/616516228/

510 Sports Reference, Baseball Reference, "Gene Elliott," *Baseball Reference*, Accessed May 21, 2023, https://www.baseball-reference.com/players/e/ellioge01.shtml

511 "Palms Take Last from Bradenton, 6 to 2," *Fort Myers Tropical News,* (Fort Myers, FL), July 18, 1926, https://newspapers.uflib.ufl.edu/AA00088916/00302/images/10

[512] Cheshire, Brack, "Read 'em and Weep," *Bradenton Herald,* (Bradenton, FL), July 19, 1926, https://www.newspapers.com/image/682658075/

[513] "Growers' Fate Now Hanging in Balance," *Tampa Tribune,* (Tampa, FL), July 21, 1926, https://www.newspapers.com/image/332204014/

[514] "Leach's Smokers Face Palms in Double Bill Today," *Tampa Daily Times,* (Tampa, FL), July 20, 1926, https://www.newspapers.com/image/332830107/

[515] "New Boxing Club Program Tonight," *Fort Myers Tropical News,* (Fort Myers, FL), July 20, 1926, https://newspapers.uflib.ufl.edu/AA00088916/00276/images/4

[516] "League Leading Palms Who Meet Smokers Here Today at Plant Field," *Tampa Times*, (Tampa, FL), July 20, 1926. https://www.newspapers.com/image/332830107/

[517] "Fort Myers Loses Two Games to Tampa," *Fort Myers Tropical News,* (Fort Myers, FL) July 20, 1926, https://newspapers.uflib.ufl.edu/AA00088916/00304/images/4

[518] "Timely Rallies Net Smokers Two Wins Over Palms," *Tampa Daily Times,* (Tampa, FL) July 21, 1926, https://www.newspapers.com/image/332830450/

[519] "Del Pino Scores Knockout Victory Over Slim Chino," *Fort Myers Tropical News,* (Fort Myers, FL), July 21, 1926, https://newspapers.uflib.ufl.edu/AA00088916/00304/images/4

[520] "Grandio's Hitting Defeats Tampa, 2 to 1," *Fort Myers Tropical News,* (Fort Myers, FL), July 22, 1926, https://newspapers.uflib.ufl.edu/AA00088916/00305/images/4

[521] "Palms protest Games with Smokers, Charging Tampa Has Too Many 'Class' Men," *Tampa Morning Tribune,* (Tampa, FL), July 22, 1926, https://www.newspapers.com/image/332204090/

[522] "Locals Drop Final Game as Palms Protest Entire Series Amid Hot Dispute," *The Tampa Daily Times,* (Tampa, FL), July 22, 1926, https://www.newspapers.com/image/332830724/

[523] "President Lifts Suspension of Gulls' Manager," *St. Petersburg Times,* (St. Petersburg, FL), July 22, 1926, https://www.newspapers.com/image/314609195/

[524] "Grandio Hits Homer and Triple at St. Pete," *Fort Myers Tropical News,* (Fort Myers, FL), July 23, 1926, https://newspapers.uflib.ufl.edu/AA00088916/00306/images/4

[525] "Second Tilt is Snatched by Sanford," *Bradenton Herald,* (Bradenton, FL), July 25, 1926, https://www.newspapers.com/image/682659256/

[526] "Timely Hitting Wins for Palms, 3 to 1," *Fort Myers Tropical News,* (Fort Myers, FL), July 24, 1926, https://newspapers.uflib.ufl.edu/AA00088916/00307/images/4

[527] "Bradenton Club Financed Will Finish Out Season," *Tampa Sunday Tribune,* (Tampa, FL), July 25, 1926, https://www.newspapers.com/image/332334285/

[528] "Defeat at St. Pete Drops Palms to Fourth," *Fort Myers Tropical News,* (Fort Myers, FL), July 25, 1926, https://newspapers.uflib.ufl.edu/AA00088916/00281/images/12

[529] Kline, Charley, "Notes of the Game," *Fort Myers Tropical News,* (Fort Myers, FL), July 27, 1926, https://newspapers.uflib.ufl.edu/AA00088916/00309/images/4

[530] "Fort Myers Files protest of Games Won by Smokers," *Fort Myers Tropical News,* (Fort Myers, FL), July 27, 1926, https://newspapers.uflib.ufl.edu/AA00088916/00282/images/4

[531] "The Weather," *Miami Daily News and Metropolis,"* (Miami, FL), July 27, 1926, https://www.newspapers.com/image/297342983/

[532] "Palms Mowed Down by Lakeland, 8 to 6," *Fort Myers Tropical News,* (Fort Myers, FL), July 27, 1926, https://newspapers.uflib.ufl.edu/AA00088916/00309/images/4

533 "Palms Drop Series Opener to Highlanders by 6 to 8 Score in Large Swat Fest," *Fort Myers Press,* (Fort Myers, FL), July 27, 1926, https://newspapers.uflib.ufl.edu/UF00079929/00507/images/4

534 "Fort Myers Escapes as Tropical Storm Sweeps Northward," *Fort Myers Tropical News,* (Fort Myers, FL), July 28, 1926, https://newspapers.uflib.ufl.edu/AA00088916/00283/images/0

535 "Notes of the Game," *Fort Myers Tropical News,* (Fort Myers, FL), July 28, 1926, https://newspapers.uflib.ufl.edu/AA00088916/00283/images/6

536 "The Weather," *Miami Daily News and Metropolis,"* (Miami, FL), July 28, 1926, https://www.newspapers.com/image/297344354/

537 Kline, Charley, "Chancey Steals Home with Winning Run," *Fort Myers Tropical News,* (Fort Myers, FL), July 28, 1926, https://newspapers.uflib.ufl.edu/AA00088916/00283/images/6

538 "Diamond Dust," *Fort Myers Press*, (Fort Myers, FL), July 29, 1926, https://newspapers.uflib.ufl.edu/UF00079929/00509/images/4

539 "The Weather," *Miami Daily News and Metropolis,"* (Miami, FL), July 29, 1926, https://www.newspapers.com/image/297344354/

540 "Palms Mount to Second in League Race," *Fort Myers Tropical News,* (Fort Myers, FL), July 29, 1926, https://newspapers.uflib.ufl.edu/AA00088916/00311/images/3

541 "New Faces Appear in Palms' Line-up," *Tampa Morning Tribune,* (Tampa, FL), July 30, 1926, https://www.newspapers.com/image/332336880/

542 "Palms will Test 2 New Hurlers," *Fort Myers Tropical News,* (Fort Myers, FL), July 29, 1926, https://newspapers.uflib.ufl.edu/UF00079929/00509/images/4

543 "Palms Beaten by Sarasota, 5 to 1," *Fort Myers Tropical News,* (Fort Myers, FL), July 30, 1926, https://newspapers.uflib.ufl.edu/AA00088916/00285/images/4

544 "Palms Down Sarasota and Lead League," *Fort Myers Tropical News,* (Fort Myers, FL), July 31, 1926, https://newspapers.uflib.ufl.edu/AA00088916/00313/images/4

545 "Protested Wins Stand as League Head Finds no Cause for Penalty," *Tampa Morning Tribune,* (Tampa, FL), July 31, 1926, https://www.newspapers.com/image/332337294/

546 "Dinner to Fete Palms Sunday," *Fort Myers Press,* (Fort Myers, FL), July 31, 1926, https://newspapers.uflib.ufl.edu/UF00079929/00511/images/0

547 "Palms Win and Take Series from Gulls," *Fort Myers Tropical News,* (Fort Myers, FL), August 1, 1926, https://newspapers.uflib.ufl.edu/AA00088916/00314/images/10

548 Kline, Charley, "First Place Palms Return to Battle Sarasota Here," (Fort Myers, FL), August 1, 1926, https://newspapers.uflib.ufl.edu/AA00088916/00314/images/10

549 "Club Standings," *Orlando Morning Sentinel,* (Orlando, FL), August 1, 1926, https://www.newspapers.com/image/223024245/

550 "The Weather," *Miami Daily News and Metropolis,* (Miami, FL), August 3, 1926, https://www.newspapers.com/image/297348484/

551 "Diamond Dust," *Fort Myers Press,* (Fort Myers, FL), August 3, 1926, https://newspapers.uflib.ufl.edu/UF00079929/00513/images/4

552 "Fans Rush Umpire as Rain Halts Game," *Fort Myers Tropical News,* (Fort Myers, FL), August 3, 1926, https://newspapers.uflib.ufl.edu/AA00088916/00315/images/3

553 "Notes of the Game," *Fort Myers Tropical News,* (Fort Myers, FL), August 4, 1926, https://newspapers.uflib.ufl.edu/AA00088916/00316/images/4

554 "The Weather," *Miami Tribune*, (Miami, FL), August 4, 1926,
     https://www.newspapers.com/image/616370765/

555 "Palms Split with Gulls; Lose First Place," *Fort Myers Tropical News*, (Fort Myers, FL),
     August 4, 1926, https://newspapers.uflib.ufl.edu/AA00088916/00316/images/3

556 "Kiwanis to Attend Punta Gorda Show," *Fort Myers Tropical News*, (Fort Myers, FL),
     August 5, 1926, https://newspapers.uflib.ufl.edu/AA00088916/00317/images/1

557 "Notes of the Game," *Fort Myers Tropical News*, (Fort Myers, FL), August 5, 1926,
     https://newspapers.uflib.ufl.edu/AA00088916/00317/images/4

558 "The Weather," *Miami Tribune*, (Miami, FL), August 5, 1926,
     https://www.newspapers.com/image/616370776/

559 "Diamond Dust," *Fort Myers Press*, (Fort Myers, FL), August 5, 1926,
     https://newspapers.uflib.ufl.edu/UF00079929/02145/images/9

560 "Palms Win Rubber Game of Gull Series," *Fort Myers Tropical News*, (Fort Myers, FL),
     August 5, 1926, https://newspapers.uflib.ufl.edu/AA00088916/00317/images/4

561 Kline, Charley, "Notes of the Game," *Fort Myers Tropical News*, (Fort Myers, FL),
     August 6, 1926, https://newspapers.uflib.ufl.edu/AA00088916/00318/images/4

562 "The Weather," *Miami Daily News and Metropolis*, (Miami, FL), August 6, 1926,
     https://www.newspapers.com/image/297350566/

563 "Palms Assume League Lead as Moore Humbles Orlando," *Fort Myers Tropical News*,
     (Fort Myers, FL), August 6, 1926, https://www.newspapers.com/image/212860487/

564 "Diamond Dust," *Fort Myers Press*, (Fort Myers, FL), August 6, 1926,
     https://newspapers.uflib.ufl.edu/UF00079929/00516/images/4

565 "Notes of the Game," *Fort Myers Tropical News*, (Fort Myers, FL), August 7, 1926,
     https://newspapers.uflib.ufl.edu/AA00088916/00319/images/4

566 "The Weather," *Miami Daily News and Metropolis*, (Miami, FL), August 7, 1926,
     https://www.newspapers.com/image/297351634/

567 "Palms Make it Two Straight Over Colts," *Fort Myers Tropical News*, (Fort Myers, FL),
     August 7, 1926, https://newspapers.uflib.ufl.edu/AA00088916/00319/images/4

568 "Diamond Dust," *Fort Myers Press*, (Fort Myers, FL), August 7, 1926,
     https://newspapers.uflib.ufl.edu/UF00079929/02147/images/6

569 "Kane Draws Crowds to Theater Benefit for Baseball Club," *Fort Myers Tropical News*,
     (Fort Myers, FL), August 7, 1926,
     https://newspapers.uflib.ufl.edu/AA00088916/00319/images/4

570 "The Weather," *Herald*, (Miami, FL), August 8, 1926,
     https://www.newspapers.com/image/616654713/

571 "Notes of the Game," *Fort Myers Tropical News*, (Fort Myers, FL), August 8, 1926,
     https://newspapers.uflib.ufl.edu/AA00088916/00320/images/12

572 "Palms Crush Colts and Sweep Series," *Fort Myers Tropical News*, (Fort Myers, FL),
     August 8, 1926, https://newspapers.uflib.ufl.edu/AA00088916/00320/images/12

573 "Notes of the Game," *Fort Myers Tropical News*, (Fort Myers, FL), August 8, 1926,
     https://newspapers.uflib.ufl.edu/AA00088916/00320/images/12

574 "Diamond Dust," *Fort Myers Press*, (Fort Myers, FL), August 9, 1926,
     https://newspapers.uflib.ufl.edu/UF00079929/02148/images/3

575 "Palms Go 11 Innings to Draw at Sanford," *Fort Myers Tropical News*, (Fort Myers,
     FL), August 10, 1926,
     https://newspapers.uflib.ufl.edu/AA00088916/00321/images/2

576 "Boxing Show Here on Thursday Night for Baseball Club," *Fort Myers Tropical News,* (Fort Myers, FL), August 10, 1926, https://newspapers.uflib.ufl.edu/AA00088916/00321/images/2

577 "Palms Turn Back Mayo to Augusta," *Fort Myers Tropical News,* (Fort Myers, FL), August 12, 1926, https://newspapers.uflib.ufl.edu/AA00088916/00323/images/2

578 "Palms Split Double Header at Sanford," *Fort Myers Tropical News,* (Fort Myers, FL), August 11, 1926, https://newspapers.uflib.ufl.edu/AA00088916/00322/images/2

579 "Sanford Divides Bill with Palms," *Orlando Morning Sentinel,* (Orlando, FL), August 11, 1926, https://newspapers.uflib.ufl.edu/UF00079944/03716/images/4

580 "Palms Lose Final Game with Sanford," *Fort Myers Tropical News,* (Fort Myers, FL), August 12, 1926, https://newspapers.uflib.ufl.edu/AA00088916/00323/images/2

581 "Base Bawls," *Orlando Morning Sentinel,* (Orlando, FL), August 13, 1926, https://newspapers.uflib.ufl.edu/UF00079944/03718/images/5

582 "Palms Capture Opening Game at Orlando," *Fort Myers Tropical News,* (Fort Myers, FL), August 13, 1926, https://newspapers.uflib.ufl.edu/AA00088916/00324/images/4

583 "Louis and Earns Battle to Draw," *Fort Myers Press,* (Fort Myers, FL), August 13, 1926, https://newspapers.uflib.ufl.edu/UF00079929/00521/images/5

584 "Colts Win and Even Series with Palms," *Fort Myers Tropical News,* (Fort Myers, FL), August 14, 1926, https://newspapers.uflib.ufl.edu/AA00088916/00325/images/4

585 "Smokers Pound Out Another Win Over Celeryfeds," *Tampa Daily Times,* (Tampa, FL), August 14, 1926, https://www.newspapers.com/image/332837012/

586 "Team Returns Sunday for Week's Stay," *Fort Myers Press,* (Fort Myers, FL), August 14, 1926, https://newspapers.uflib.ufl.edu/UF00079929/02153/images/5

587 "Palms Beaten in Final Game at Orlando," *Fort Myers Tropical News,* (Fort Myers, FL), August 15, 1926, https://newspapers.uflib.ufl.edu/AA00088916/00326/images/10

588 "Double Bill On Tap This Afternoon; Rain Halts First of St. Pete Series," *Fort Myers Press,* (Fort Myers, FL), August 17, 1926, https://newspapers.uflib.ufl.edu/UF00079929/02155/images/5

589 "Basebawls," *Orlando Morning Sentinel,* (Orlando, FL), August 15, 1926, https://newspapers.uflib.ufl.edu/UF00079944/03720/images/6

590 "Palms Open Week's Home Stay with Game Today at Terry Park," *Fort Myers Press,* (Fort Myers, FL), August 16, 1926, https://newspapers.uflib.ufl.edu/UF00079929/00523/images

591 "The Weather," *Miami Daily News and Metropolis,* (Miami, FL), August 17, 1926, https://www.newspapers.com/image/297338483/

592 "Palms Rained Out, Two Games Today," *Fort Myers Tropical News,* (Fort Myers, FL), August 17, 1926, https://newspapers.uflib.ufl.edu/AA00088916/00327/images/1

593 "The Weather," *Miami Daily News and Metropolis,* (Miami, FL), August 18, 1926, https://www.newspapers.com/image/297338549/

594 "Palms Divide Twin Bill With Saint Pete," *Fort Myers Tropical News,* (Fort Myers, FL), August 18, 1926, https://newspapers.uflib.ufl.edu/AA00088916/00328/images/3

595 "Palms Divide Double Header with St. Pete," *Fort Myers Press,* (Fort Myers, FL), August 18, 1926, https://newspapers.uflib.ufl.edu/UF00079929/00525/images/7

596 "Palms Divide Twin Bill with Saint Pete," *Fort Myers Tropical News,* (Fort Myers, FL), August 18, 1926, https://newspapers.uflib.ufl.edu/AA00088916/00328/images/3

597 "The Weather," *Miami Daily News and Metropolis,* (Miami, FL), August 19, 1926, https://www.newspapers.com/image/297339409/

598 "Fort Myers Takes Series from Saint Pete," *Fort Myers Tropical News,* (Fort Myers, FL), August 19, 1926, https://newspapers.uflib.ufl.edu/AA00088916/00329/images/3

599 "Palms Triumph in Third Game of Saint Series," *Fort Myers Press,* (Fort Myers, FL), August 19, 1926, https://newspapers.uflib.ufl.edu/UF00079929/02157/images/4

600 "Notes of the Game," *Fort Myers Tropical News,* (Fort Myers, FL), August 19, 1926, https://newspapers.uflib.ufl.edu/AA00088916/00329/images/3

601 "The Weather," *Miami Daily News and Metropolis,* (Miami, FL), August 20, 1926, https://www.newspapers.com/image/297340029/

602 Kline, Charley, "Palms Rained Out; Double Header Today," *Fort Myers Tropical News,* (Fort Myers, FL), August 20, 1926, https://newspapers.uflib.ufl.edu/AA00088916/00330/images/4

603 "Sanford Manager Picks Star Talent to Oppose Palms," *Fort Myers Tropical News,* (Fort Myers, FL), August 20, 1926, https://newspapers.uflib.ufl.edu/AA00088916/00330/images/4

604 "Palms Entertained at Chicken Dinner," *Fort Myers Tropical News,* (Fort Myers, FL), August 20, 1926, https://newspapers.uflib.ufl.edu/AA00088916/00330/images/4

605 "The Weather," *Miami Daily News and Metropolis,* (Miami, FL), August 21, 1926, https://www.newspapers.com/image/297340684/

606 Kline, Charley, "Rain Again Stops Palms; Twin Bill Today," *Fort Myers Tropical News,* (Fort Myers, FL), August 21, 1926, https://newspapers.uflib.ufl.edu/AA00088916/00331/images/2

607 "The Weather," *Herald,* (Miami, FL), August 22, 1926, https://www.newspapers.com/image/616655485/

608 "Palms Lose Two; Drop to Third Place," *Fort Myers Tropical News,* (Fort Myers, FL), August 22, 1926, https://newspapers.uflib.ufl.edu/AA00088916/00332/images/10

609 "Leachmen Rained Out at Bradenton as Palms Lose Two," *Tampa Sunday Tribune,* (Fort Myers, FL), August 22, 1926, https://www.newspapers.com/image/332373747/

610 Associated Press, "Colts are Awarded Forfeit Over Gulls," *Tampa Sunday Tribune,* (Fort Myers, FL), August 22, 1926, https://www.newspapers.com/image/332373747/

611 "Orlando Burlesques Gulls Out of Final," *Orlando Morning Sentinel,* (Orlando, FL), August 22, 1926, https://newspapers.uflib.ufl.edu/UF00079944/03726/images/4

612 "Palms Leave on Road Trop to Meet Lakeland, Bradenton," *Fort Myers Press,* (Fort Myers, FL), August 23, 1926, https://newspapers.uflib.ufl.edu/UF00079929/00529/images/7

613 "Rain Halts Palms in Game at Lakeland," *Fort Myers Tropical News,* (Fort Myers, FL), August 25, 1926, https://newspapers.uflib.ufl.edu/AA00088916/00334/images/3

614 "Hendry Bros. Get Detailed Returns from Palms Games," *Fort Myers Press,* (Fort Myers, FL), August 23, 1926, https://newspapers.uflib.ufl.edu/UF00079929/00529/images/0

615 "Palms Lost First Game at Lakeland, 5-2," *Fort Myers Tropical News,* (Fort Myers, FL), August 24, 1926, https://newspapers.uflib.ufl.edu/AA00088916/00333/images/4

616 Parmely, Ray, "Smokers Fail in Opening Game at St. Petersburg," *Tampa Daily Times,* (Tampa, FL), August 24, 1926, https://www.newspapers.com/image/332840708/

617 "Palms Rained Out for the Fourth Time in Eight Days," *Fort Myers Press,* (Fort Myers, FL), August 25, 1926, https://newspapers.uflib.ufl.edu/UF00079929/02162/images/7

618 "Double Header on Card Today," *Fort Myers Press,* (Fort Myers, FL), August 25, 1926, https://newspapers.uflib.ufl.edu/UF00079929/02162/images/7

619 "Passes Recalled by Baseball Club," *Fort Myers Press,* (Fort Myers, FL), August 25, 1926, https://newspapers.uflib.ufl.edu/UF00079929/02162/images/7

620 "Doyle Displaces Joe S. Johnston as Palms' Boss," *Fort Myers Press,* (Fort Myers, FL), August 25, 1926, https://newspapers.uflib.ufl.edu/UF00079929/02162/images/0

621 "Fort Myers Takes Deciding Game from Smokers," *Tampa Sunday Tribune,* (Tampa, FL), September 20, 1925, https://www.newspapers.com/image/327454431/

622 "New Manager to Make Bow," *Fort Myers Press,* (Fort Myers, FL), August 30, 1926, https://newspapers.uflib.ufl.edu/UF00079929/00533/images/5

623 "Doyle Displaces Joe S. Johnston as Palms' Boss," *Fort Myers Press,* (Fort Myers, FL), August 25, 1926, https://newspapers.uflib.ufl.edu/UF00079929/00530/images

624 "Palms Under New Pilot Beat Lakeland, 6-1," *Fort Myers Tropical News,* (Fort Myers, FL), August 26, 1926, https://newspapers.uflib.ufl.edu/AA00088916/00335/images/3

625 "Fort Myers Swamps Bradenton, 13 to 1," *Fort Myers Tropical News,* (Fort Myers, FL), August 27, 1926, https://newspapers.uflib.ufl.edu/AA00088916/00336/images/5

626 "Baseball," *Bradenton Herald,* (Bradenton, FL), August 25, 1926, https://www.newspapers.com/image/682752634/

627 "Palms Win Second Straight from Growers," *Fort Myers Tropical News,* (Fort Myers, FL), August 28, 1926, https://newspapers.uflib.ufl.edu/AA00088916/00337/images/4

628 "Palms Emerge Winners, 5-4," *Fort Myers Press,* (Fort Myers, FL), August 28, 1926, https://newspapers.uflib.ufl.edu/UF00079929/02165/images/5

629 "Palms Sweep Series and Lead League," *Fort Myers Tropical News,* (Fort Myers, FL), August 29, 1926, https://newspapers.uflib.ufl.edu/AA00088916/00338/images/10

630 "Prexy Asher Shifts Colt Series with Bradenton [to] Tinker Field," *Orlando Morning Sentinel,* (Orlando, FL), August 29, 1926, https://www.newspapers.com/image/223041631/

631 "Growers Transfer Colt Series to Orlando," *Bradenton Herald,* (Bradenton, FL), August 29, 1926, https://www.newspapers.com/image/682753398/

632 "Leads League Southpaws," *Fort Myers Tropical News,* (Fort Myers, FL), August 29, 1926, https://www.newspapers.com/image/332381633/

633 "Mike Bouza Released; Signs with Lakeland," *Fort Myers Tropical News,* (Fort Myers, FL), August 31, 1926, https://newspapers.uflib.ufl.edu/AA00088916/00339/images/4

634 "The Weather," *Miami Daily News and Metropolis,* (Miami, FL), August 31, 1926, https://www.newspapers.com/image/297347672/

635 "Salvatz Leads Tampa to 3-1 Win in First," *Tampa Morning Tribune,* (Tampa, FL), August 31, 1926, https://www.newspapers.com/image/332383503/

636 "Palms Nosed Out by Smokers, Score 3-1," *Fort Myers Tropical News,* (Fort Myers, FL), August 31, 1926, https://newspapers.uflib.ufl.edu/AA00088916/00339/images/4

637 "The Weather," *Miami Daily News and Metropolis,* (Miami, FL), September 1, 1926, https://www.newspapers.com/image/297348715/

638 "Florida State League Race Becomes Free-For-All Affair," *Fort Myers Press,* (Fort Myers, FL), September 1, 1926, https://newspapers.uflib.ufl.edu/UF00079929/02168/images/4

639 "Palms Drop Another to Smokers, 5 to 2," *Fort Myers Tropical News,* (Fort Myers, FL), September 1, 1926, https://newspapers.uflib.ufl.edu/AA00088916/00340/zoom/3

640 "Standings," *Fort Myers Press,* (Fort Myers, FL), September 1, 1926, https://newspapers.uflib.ufl.edu/UF00079929/02168/images/4

641 "J. B. Asher, State League Prexy, Here Today for Short Conference," *Fort Myers Press,* (Fort Myers, FL), September 1, 1926, https://newspapers.uflib.ufl.edu/UF00079929/02168/images/0

642 "Palms to Open Grower Series with Twin Bill," *Fort Myers Press,* (Fort Myers, FL), September 1, 1926, https://www.newspapers.com/image/212861508/

643 "Walter O. Sheppard Dies in Motor Crash South of Dade City," *Fort Myers Press,* (Fort Myers, FL), August 30, 1926, https://newspapers.uflib.ufl.edu/UF00079929/00533/images

644 "The Weather," *Miami Daily News and Metropolis,* (Miami, FL), September 2, 1926, https://www.newspapers.com/image/297349809/

645 "Palms Capture Final from Smokers, 7 to 3," *Fort Myers Tropical News,* (Fort Myers, FL), September 2, 1926, https://newspapers.uflib.ufl.edu/AA00088916/00341/images/3

646 "Colts Annex Double Bill from Growers," *Orlando Morning Sentinel,* (Orlando, FL), September 2, 1926, https://newspapers.uflib.ufl.edu/UF00079944/03737/images/4

647 "The Weather," *Miami Daily News and Metropolis,* (Miami, FL), September 3, 1926, https://www.newspapers.com/image/297350343/

648 "Palms Advance on Colts, Feds," *Fort Myers Press,* (Fort Myers, FL), September 3, 1926, https://newspapers.uflib.ufl.edu/UF00079929/02170/images/5

649 "Palms Fight to Stanzas and Win 7-6," *Bradenton Herald,* (Bradenton, FL), September 3, 1926, https://www.newspapers.com/image/682754429/

650 "Palms Nose Out Growers, 7 to 6," *Fort Myers Press,* (Fort Myers, FL), September 3, 1926, https://newspapers.uflib.ufl.edu/UF00079929/02170/images/5

651 "Palms Climb to Second Place in Race," *Fort Myers Tropical News,* (Fort Myers, FL), September 3, 1926, https://newspapers.uflib.ufl.edu/AA00088916/00342/images/4

652 "The Weather," *Miami Daily News and Metropolis,* (Miami, FL), September 4, 1926, https://www.newspapers.com/image/297350870/

653 "Fort Myers Regains Lead in League Race," *Fort Myers Tropical News,* (Fort Myers, FL), September 4, 1926, https://newspapers.uflib.ufl.edu/AA00088916/00343/zoom/5

654 "Notes of the Game," *Fort Myers Tropical News,* (Fort Myers, FL), September 5, 1926, *https://newspapers.uflib.ufl.edu/AA00088916/00344/images/10*

655 "The Weather," *Herald,* (Miami, FL), September 5, 1926, https://www.newspapers.com/image/616533028/

656 Kline, Charley, "Palms Win Fourth Straight from Growers," *Fort Myers Tropical News,* (Fort Myers, FL), September 5, 1926, https://newspapers.uflib.ufl.edu/AA00088916/00344/images/10

657 "The Weather," *Miami Daily News and Metropolis,* (Miami, FL), September 7, 1926, https://www.newspapers.com/image/297352850/

658 "Moore Saves Palms in 2nd," *Fort Myers Press,* (Fort Myers, FL), September 7, 1926, https://newspapers.uflib.ufl.edu/UF00079929/00540/images/1

659 "Palms Close Season Here with Lakeland," *Fort Myers Tropical News,* (Fort Myers, FL), September 7, 1926, https://newspapers.uflib.ufl.edu/AA00088916/00345/images/3

660 "Palms Change Managers for Fourth Time," *Fort Myers Tropical News,* (Fort Myers, FL), September 8, 1926, https://newspapers.uflib.ufl.edu/AA00088916/00346/images/0

661 "McRae and O'Reilly to Go to Asheville," *Fort Myers Tropical News,* (Fort Myers, FL), September 8, 1926, https://newspapers.uflib.ufl.edu/AA00088916/00346/images/5

662 "The Weather," *Miami Daily News and Metropolis,* (Miami, FL), September 8, 1926, https://www.newspapers.com/image/297353393/

663 "Palms Change Managers for Fourth Time," *Fort Myers Tropical News,* (Fort Myers, FL), September 8, 1926, https://newspapers.uflib.ufl.edu/AA00088916/00346/images/0

664 "Doran is Named as Palms' Boss," *Fort Myers Press,* (Fort Myers, FL), September 8, 1926, https://newspapers.uflib.ufl.edu/UF00079929/02174/images/7

665 "Palms Play Last Schedule Game of Year here Tomorrow," *Fort Myers Press,* (Fort Myers, FL), September 8, 1926, https://newspapers.uflib.ufl.edu/UF00079929/02173/images/1

666 "Palms Lose Third Straight; Drop in Race," *Fort Myers Tropical News,* (Fort Myers, FL), September 9, 1926, https://newspapers.uflib.ufl.edu/AA00088916/00347/images/3

667 "Play-by-Play of St. Pete Series for Ball Fans Here," *Fort Myers Tropical News,* (Fort Myers, FL), September 9, 1926, https://newspapers.uflib.ufl.edu/AA00088916/00347/images/3

668 "Palms Win First Game at St. Pete, 3 to 2," *Fort Myers Tropical News,* (Fort Myers, FL), September 10, 1926, https://newspapers.uflib.ufl.edu/AA00088916/00348/images/5

669 "Palms Lose Third Straight; Drop in Race," *Fort Myers Tropical News,* (Fort Myers, FL), September 11, 1926, https://newspapers.uflib.ufl.edu/AA00088916/00347/images/3

670 "Standings," *Fort Myers Press,* (Fort Myers, FL), September 11, 1926, https://newspapers.uflib.ufl.edu/UF00079929/00544/images/4

671 "Palms Rained Out; Pennant Chance Remains," *Fort Myers Tropical News,* (Fort Myers, FL), September 12, 1926, https://newspapers.uflib.ufl.edu/AA00088916/00350/images/10

672 "Announces Series," *Palm Beach Post,* (Palm Beach, FL), September 13, 1926, https://www.newspapers.com/image/133337076/

673 "Tinker Plans Little World Series Games," *St. Petersburg Times,* (St. Petersburg, FL), September 13, 1926, https://www.newspapers.com/image/314696635/

674 "State League Race is in Doubt on Last Day of Season," *Fort Myers Press,* (Fort Myers, FL), September 15, 1926,
https://newspapers.uflib.ufl.edu/UF00079929/00546/images/5

675 "Second Straight Won by Smokers," *Fort Myers Press,* (Fort Myers, FL), September 15, 1926, https://newspapers.uflib.ufl.edu/UF00079929/00546/images/5

676 "Smokers Blank Palms in Final," *Fort Myers Press,* (Fort Myers, FL), September 16, 1926, https://newspapers.uflib.ufl.edu/UF00079929/02181/images/7

677 "Club Standings," *Fort Myers Tropical News,* (Fort Myers, FL) September 16, 1926,
https://newspapers.uflib.ufl.edu/AA00088916/00353/images/3

678 McCarthy, Marvin, "Doc. Opre Won't Seek to Have Celeryfeds Complete Schedule," *Tampa Tribune,* (Tampa, FL), September 16, 1926.
https://www.newspapers.com/image/332391915/

679 "Palms at Home to Sign Payroll," *Fort Myers Press,* (Fort Myers, FL), September 16, 1926, https://newspapers.uflib.ufl.edu/UF00079929/02181/images/7

680 "Wind, Rain, Storm Takes Heavy Toll," *Fort Myers Press,* (Fort Myers, FL), September 18, 1926, https://newspapers.uflib.ufl.edu/UF00079929/02183/images

681 "Sanibel and Captiva Flooded," *Fort Myers Press,* (Fort Myers, FL), September 20, 1926, https://newspapers.uflib.ufl.edu/UF00079929/00550/images

682 "Devastation in Miami from the 1926 Hurricane," [Place of Publication Not Identified: Publisher Not Identified, 1926-09-19]. Retrieved from the Library of Congress, www.loc.gov/item/2021670726/

683 "H. B. Mayer to Take Charge of Cleanup Campaign in City," *Fort Myers Press,* (Fort Myers, FL), October 8, 1926,
https://newspapers.uflib.ufl.edu/UF00079929/02200/images

684 "Trucks Needed in Clean-Up," *Fort Myers Press,* (Fort Myers, FL), October 12, 1926, https://newspapers.uflib.ufl.edu/UF00079929/02203/images

685 "Cleanup Dictator Turns over Work to City's Forces," *Fort Myers Press,* (Fort Myers, FL), October 17, 1926,
https://newspapers.uflib.ufl.edu/AA00088916/00380/images/4

686 "Hendry Bros. Moving Offices," *Fort Myers Press,* (Fort Myers, FL), November 8, 1926, https://newspapers.uflib.ufl.edu/UF00079929/02226/images

687 "United Markets Open Near Jan. 10," *Fort Myers Press,* (Fort Myers, FL), December 6, 1926, https://newspapers.uflib.ufl.edu/UF00079929/02249/zoom/0

688 "Sarasota Berth Yet Uncertain," *Bradenton Herald,* (Bradenton, FL), December 5, 1926, https://www.newspapers.com/image/682618250/

689 Mac, The Morning after, "Baseball Took Strides and "Doc" Opre," *Tampa Morning Tribune,* (Tampa, FL), December 30, 1926,
https://www.newspapers.com/image/332209493/

690 "Date for Meeting of State League Set by President," *St. Petersburg Times,* (St. Petersburg, FL), January 16, 1927,
https://www.newspapers.com/image/314690131/

691 Tribune News Service, "Shake-Up Looms in State League Ranks," *Tampa Morning Tribune,* (Tampa, FL), January 19, 1927,
https://www.newspapers.com/image/332404141/

692 "League Officials Praise Celeryfeds on Finance Plan," *Orlando Morning Sentinel,* (Orlando, FL), January 17, 1927, https://www.newspapers.com/image/222842158/

693 "Miami and West Palm Beach Seek State League Places," *Fort Myers Tropical News,* (Fort Myers, FL), January 19, 1927, P. 3. Microfilm.

694 Kline, Charley, "Fort Myers Fans Move to get Baseball," *Fort Myers Tropical News,* (Fort Myers, FL), February 10, 1927, P. 6., Microfilm.

695 "Baseball to be Settled Monday," *Fort Myers Press,* (Fort Myers, FL), February 11, 1927, https://newspapers.uflib.ufl.edu/UF00079929/02305/images

696 "Fans Told Fort Myers Can Have Ball Club," *Fort Myers Tropical News,* (Fort Myers, FL), February 11, 1927, Section 2, P. 1., Microfilm.

697 "Plans for Baseball Fail to Materialize," *Fort Myers Tropical News,* (Fort Myers, FL), February 15, 1926, P. 3., Microfilm.

698 "Club Organized to Back League Baseball Here," *Fort Myers Tropical News,* (Fort Myers, FL), February 22, 1927, P.1., Microfilm.

699 "Baseball Backers Will Meet Today," *Fort Myers Tropical News,* (Fort Myers, FL), March 2, 1927, Section 2, P. 1., Microfilm.

700 "Ball Club Waits Action by League," *Fort Myers Tropical News,* (Fort Myers, FL), March 3, 1927, Section 2, P. 1., Microfilm.

701 Associated Press, "State League to be Formed During Week," *Pensacola Journal,* (Pensacola, FL), March 20, 1927, https://www.newspapers.com/image/352978106/

702 "Fort Myers Abandons Bid for Baseball," *Fort Myers Tropical News,* (Fort Myers, FL), March 20, 1927, Section 2, P. 1., Microfilm.

703 Associated Press, "Florida State League Cut to 6 Club Loop this Year," *Fort Myers Tropical News,* (Fort Myers, FL), March 22, 1927, P. 3., Microfilm.

704 Associated Press, "Fort Myers Likely to be Sixth Entry in Florida League," *Tampa Morning Tribune,* (Tampa, FL), March 29, 1926), https://www.newspapers.com/image/332547249/

705 "Fort Myers Not After Franchise in League," *Herald,* (Miami, FL), March 29, 1927, https://www.newspapers.com/image/616566384/

706 "State League Still Shy Sixth Member," *Fort Myers Tropical News,* (Fort Myers, FL), April 6, 1927, p.6, Microfilm.

707 "Miami Offered Baseball Team," *Herald, (*Miami, FL), April 7, 1927, https://www.newspapers.com/image/616567005/

708 "Asher Reported Seeking East Coast State Loop Team," *Tampa Daily Times,* (Tampa, FL), April 7, 1927, https://www.newspapers.com/image/333238485/

709 "Asher Offers Fort Myers and W. Palm Beach Teams; Miami Accepts Franchise," *Tampa Daily Times,* (Tampa, FL), April 12, 1927, https://www.newspapers.com/image/333239610/

710 Carver, Lawton, "Plans are Revived for Eight Club State League," *Tampa Morning Tribune,* (Tampa, FL), April 13, 1927, https://www.newspapers.com/image/332554292/

711 "Fifty Players Seeking Berths in Miami Team," *Miami Daily News and Metropolis,* (Miami, FL), April 13, 1927, https://www.newspapers.com/image/301944370/

712 "Florida State League Opens Season Today," *Fort Myers Press,* (Fort Myers, FL), April 21, 1927, https://newspapers.uflib.ufl.edu/UF00079929/02364/images/7

713 "Connie Mack may Arrive Here Today," *Fort Myers Tropical News,* (Fort Myers, FL), February 17, 1927, P. 3, Microfilm.

714 "Connie Mack Shops for New Straw Lid," *Fort Myers Tropical News,* (Fort Myers, FL), February 19, 1927, Section 2, P. 1, Microfilm.

715 "Elks Form Bowling League with Four Active Teams," *Fort Myers Press,* (Fort Myers, FL), January 4, 1927, https://newspapers.uflib.ufl.edu/UF00079929/02273/images/0

716 Dean Park Historic District, page for "2643 Providence St (1923)," https://deanpark.org/2643-providence-street-1923/, accessed on April 9, 2023.

717 "Personal Mention," *Fort Myers Press,* (Fort Myers, FL), October 10, 1928, https://www.newspapers.com/image/216967041/.

718 "Fort Myers Man is Shot by Nephew on Hunting Trip," *Tampa Times,* (Tampa, FL), January 2, 1929, https://www.newspapers.com/image/332355918/.

719 "Personals," *Fort Myers Press,* (Fort Myers, FL), May 10, 1929, https://www.newspapers.com/image/216571380/.

720 Jake Jacobson, (grandson of John W. Hendry), in discussion with the author, Franklin, North Carolina, March 16, 2023.

721 Jacobson, 2023.

722 "Mr. and Mrs. John Hendry," *Fort Myers Press,* (Fort Myers, FL), May 9, 1934, https://www.newspapers.com/image/220289787/

723 "Vivian Lee Named Elks Lodge Ruler," *Fort Myers Press,* (Fort Myers, FL), December 13, 1934, https://www.newspapers.com/image/220320421/.

724 "About Fort Myers People and their Visitors," *Fort Myers Press,* (Fort Myers, FL), April 21, 1935. https://www.newspapers.com/image/219747077/

725 Ancestry.com, "John W. Hendry," *1940 United States Federal Census,* accessed May 18, 2023, https://bit.ly/45fWyag

726 "Hell's Angels' Shells," *Fort Worth Star-Telegram,* (Fort Worth, TX), October 12, 1943, https://www.newspapers.com/image/636521195/

727 Wilson, Madelaine, "It Isn't Navy, but it's Swell, WAVES Wear Formals, Dance," *Daily Oklahoman,* (Oklahoma City, OK), December 3, 1944, https://www.newspapers.com/image/449546258/

728 "Robert Needham Hendry," *News and Observer,* (Raleigh, NC), March 9, 2016, https://www.newspapers.com/image/652667625/

729 "To Wed Orion Man," *Daily Dispatch,* (Moline, IL), August 18, 1948, https://www.newspapers.com/image/340392850/

730 "William T.S. Jacobson, Former Rock Islander, Weds in North Carolina," *Rock Island Argus,* (Rock Island, IL), August 23, 1948, https://www.newspapers.com/image/568472912/

731 Bartleson, Geraldine, "Elizabeth Hendry Becomes Bride of William Jacobson," *Fort Myers News-Press,* (Fort Myers, FL), August 26, 1948, https://www.newspapers.com/image/221879022/

732 "Visitor Rolls 254 to Set New Record on Bowling Alleys," *Fort Myers Tropical News,* (Fort Myers, FL), February 9, 1926, https://newspapers.uflib.ufl.edu/AA00088916/00138/images/4

733 "Western North Carolina Deaths, Funerals," *Asheville Citizen-Times,* (Asheville, NC), Sunday, April 8, 1979, https://www.newspapers.com/image/944677819/

734 Sports Reference, Baseball Reference, "Ben Cantwell," *Baseball Reference,* Accessed April 29, 2023, https://www.baseball-reference.com/players/c/cantwbe01.shtml

735 "Tampa Smokers Show Class in 7 to 4 Victory Over Palms Thursday; League Champs Hit in a Pinch to Win Contest," *Fort Myers Press,* (Fort Myers, FL), May 7, 1926, https://www.newspapers.com/image/212768849/

736 Isaminger, James C., "Uncle Wilbert Uses 23 Men to Assemble 17 Sizzling Slashes," *Philadelphia Inquirer,* (Philadelphia, PA), March 20, 1931, https://www.newspapers.com/image/173195257/

737 "Look Alikes?," *Fort Myers News-Press,* (Fort Myers, FL), March 23, 1961, https://www.newspapers.com/image/212238798/

738 Dozer, Richard, "Peters, John Throw Blanks as Sox Defeat Royals, 5-1," *Chicago Tribune,* (Chicago, IL), March 20, 1969, https://www.newspapers.com/image/376640433/

739 "Bob Cole Signs with Ft. Myers On Mound Staff," *St. Petersburg Times,* (Fort Myers, FL), March 16, 1926, https://www.newspapers.com/image/314696586/

740 "Bob Cole to Sign with Ft. Myers 9," *Tampa Morning Tribune,* (Tampa, FL), March 17, 1926, https://www.newspapers.com/image/326634246/

741 "Domingo Will Play State League Ball," *Tampa Morning Tribune,* (Tampa, FL), March 19, 1926, https://www.newspapers.com/image/326637660/

742 "Regulars to Meet Twin Cities Today," *Coshocton Tribune,* (Coshocton, OH), April 25, 1926, https://www.newspapers.com/image/321714413/

743 "Domingo Will Play State League Ball," *Tampa Morning Tribune,* (Tampa, FL), March 19, 1926, https://www.newspapers.com/image/326637660/

744 "Smokers Get Nats' Tryout," *St. Petersburg Times,* (St. Petersburg, FL), March 19, 1926, https://www.newspapers.com/image/314696918/

745 "Palms to Open Season in Big League Style," *Fort Myers Tropical News,* (Fort Myers, FL), April 20, 1926, https://newspapers.uflib.ufl.edu/AA00088916/00198/images/4

746 "Ten Players Arrive in City for Tryouts with Fort Myers Club of Florida State League," *Fort Myers Press,* (Fort Myers, FL), March 30, 1926, https://www.newspapers.com/image/212736373/

747 "Partial Line-Up for Game with Macon Tuesday Given by Conroy," *Fort Myers Press,* (Fort Myers, FL), April 1, 1926, https://www.newspapers.com/image/212737702/

748 "Partial Line-Up for Game with Macon Tuesday Given by Conroy," *Fort Myers Press,* (Fort Myers, FL), April 1, 1926, https://www.newspapers.com/image/212737702/

749 "Tanner Makes Debut as Tampa Keystoner," *Tampa Morning Tribune,* (Tampa, FL), June 11, 1926, https://www.newspapers.com/image/332406887/

750 "Five More Join Mike's Outfit," *Knoxville Journal,* (Knoxville, TN), March 30, 1926, https://www.newspapers.com/image/586312269/

751 "Fort Myers Leaguers Play Macon Today," *Fort Myers Tropical News,* (Fort Myers, FL), April 6, 1926, https://newspapers.uflib.ufl.edu/AA00088916/00186/images/8

752 "Fort Myers Team Beats Macon 8 to 7," *Fort Myers Tropical News,* (Fort Myers, FL), April 7, 1926, https://newspapers.uflib.ufl.edu/AA00088916/00187/images/6

753 "Palms Fall Short in 9th Inning Rally," *Fort Myers Tropical News,* (Fort Myers, FL), April 8, 1926, https://newspapers.uflib.ufl.edu/AA00088916/00188/images/4

754 "Conroy Enthusiastic Over Club Outlook," *Fort Myers Tropical News,* (Fort Myers, FL), April 9, 1926, https://newspapers.uflib.ufl.edu/AA00088916/00189/images/4

755 "Florida Circuit to Meet Friday," *Fort Myers Tropical News,* (Fort Myers, FL), March 18, 1926, https://newspapers.uflib.ufl.edu/AA00088916/00170/images/6

756 Kline, Charley, "Conroy Enthusiastic Over Club Outlook," *Fort Myers Tropical News,* (Fort Myers, FL), April 9, 1926, https://newspapers.uflib.ufl.edu/AA00088916/00189/images/4

757 "Palms Ready for Rollins Here Tomorrow," *Fort Myers Press,* (Fort Myers, FL), April 14, 1926, https://www.newspapers.com/image/212753123/

758 "Funds Sought to Finance Baseball Club," *Fort Myers Tropical News,* (Fort Myers, FL), April 10, 1926, https://newspapers.uflib.ufl.edu/AA00088916/00190/images/4

759 "Conroy Cuts Loose Two More Players," *Fort Myers Tropical News,* (Fort Myers, FL), April 14, 1926, https://newspapers.uflib.ufl.edu/AA00088916/00193/images/6

760 "Fort Myers Ball Team to Play Next Week," *Fort Myers Tropical News,* (Fort Myers, FL), April 2, 1926, https://newspapers.uflib.ufl.edu/AA00088916/00183/images/6

761 "Florida Circuit to Meet Friday," *Fort Myers Tropical News,* (Fort Myers, FL), March 19, 1926, https://newspapers.uflib.ufl.edu/AA00088916/00170/images/6

762 "The Box Score," *Fort Myers Tropical News,* (Fort Myers, FL), April 7, 1926, https://newspapers.uflib.ufl.edu/AA00088916/00187/images/6

763 "The Box Score," *Fort Myers Tropical News,* (Fort Myers, FL), April 8, 1926, https://newspapers.uflib.ufl.edu/AA00088916/00188/images/4

764 "Conroy Cuts Loose Two More Players," *Fort Myers Tropical News,* (Fort Myers, FL), April 14, 1926, https://newspapers.uflib.ufl.edu/AA00088916/00193/images/6

765 "City Championship Baseball Series Will Start Today," *Fort Myers Tropical News,* (Fort Myers, FL), July 9, 1925, https://newspapers.uflib.ufl.edu/AA00088916/00090/images/0

766 "Fort Myers Team Beats Macon 8 to 7," *Fort Myers Tropical News,* (Fort Myers, FL), April 7, 1926, https://newspapers.uflib.ufl.edu/AA00088916/00187/images/6

767 "Ten Players Arrive in City for Tryouts with Fort Myers Club of Florida State League," *Fort Myers Press,* (Fort Myers, FL), March 30, 1926, https://www.newspapers.com/image/212736373/

768 "Partial Line-up for Game with Macon Tuesday Given by Conroy," *Fort Myers Press,* (Fort Myers, FL), April 1, 1926, https://www.newspapers.com/image/212737702/

769 "Fort Myers Ball Team to Play Next Week," *Fort Myers Tropical News,* (Fort Myers, FL), April 2, 1926, https://newspapers.uflib.ufl.edu/AA00088916/00183/images/6

770 "Palms Fall Short in 9th Inning Rally," *Fort Myers Tropical News,* (Fort Myers, FL), April 8, 1926, https://newspapers.uflib.ufl.edu/AA00088916/00188/images/4

771 "Conroy Enthusiastic Over Club Outlook," *Fort Myers Tropical News,* (Fort Myers, FL), April 9, 1926, https://newspapers.uflib.ufl.edu/AA00088916/00189/images/4

772 "Ten Players Arrive in City for Tryouts with Fort Myers Club of Florida State League," *Fort Myers Tropical News,* (Fort Myers, FL), March 30, 1926, https://www.newspapers.com/image/212736373/

773 "Conroy Enthusiastic Over Club Outlook," *Fort Myers Tropical News,* (Fort Myers, FL), April 9, 1926, https://newspapers.uflib.ufl.edu/AA00088916/00189/images/4

774 "Undertakers Defeat St. Petersburg Nine," *Tampa Morning Tribune,* (Tampa, FL), August 23, 1926, https://www.newspapers.com/image/332376364/

775 "Ten Players Arrive in City for Tryouts with Fort Myers Club of Florida State League," *Fort Myers Press,* (Fort Meres, FL), March 30, 1926, https://www.newspapers.com/image/212736373/

776 "Partial Line-Up for Game with Macon Tuesday Given by Conroy," *Fort Myers Press,* (Fort Myers, FL), April 1, 1926, https://www.newspapers.com/image/212737702/

777 "Ten Players Arrive in City for Tryouts with Fort Myers Club of Florida State League," *Fort Myers Press,* (Fort Myers, FL), March 30, 1926, https://www.newspapers.com/image/212736373/

778 "Partial Line-Up for Game with Macon Tuesday Given by Conroy," *Fort Myers Press,* (Fort Myers, FL), April 1, 1926, https://www.newspapers.com/image/212737702/

779 "Fort Myers Ball Team to Play Next Week," *Fort Myers Tropical News,* (Fort Myers, FL), April 2, 1926, https://newspapers.uflib.ufl.edu/AA00088916/00183/images/6

780 "Macon Peaches Win Second Game By 10 to 7 Score," *Fort Myers Press,* (Fort Myers, FL), April 8, 1926, https://www.newspapers.com/image/212747285/

781 "Fort Myers Palms Trim Rollins Nine," *Tampa Morning Tribune,* (Tampa, FL), April 16, 1926, https://www.newspapers.com/image/326710506/

782 "Buck Conroy's Boys in Formal Pose," *Fort Myers Tropical News,* (Fort Myers, FL), April 22, 1926, https://newspapers.uflib.ufl.edu/AA00088916/00200/images

783 "Notes of the Game," *Fort Myers Tropical News,* (Fort Myers, FL), May 6, 1926, https://newspapers.uflib.ufl.edu/AA00088916/00212/images/4

784 "Growers Nose Out Tampa smokers in Ninth, 8-7," *Tampa Morning Tribune,* (Tampa, FL), May 11, 1926, https://www.newspapers.com/image/332406937/

785 "Fort Myers Leaguers Play Macon Today," *Fort Myers Tropical News,* (Fort Myers, FL), April 6, 1926, https://newspapers.uflib.ufl.edu/AA00088916/00186/images/8

786 "Fort Myers Wins in Tenth on Bouza's Sacrifice Fly; Palms Leave Tomorrow to be Away Until Thursday, May 20," *Fort Myers Press,* (Fort Myers, FL) May 8, 1926, https://www.newspapers.com/image/212769009/

787 "Bucky Conroy is Bringing Avenging Crew from Fort Myers for Smoker Series," *Tampa Morning Tribune,* (Tampa, FL), May 13, 1926, https://www.newspapers.com/image/332408384/

788 "Notes of the Game," *Fort Myers Tropical News,* (Fort Myers, FL), May 6, 1926, https://newspapers.uflib.ufl.edu/AA00088916/00212/images/4

789 "Vero Beach Baseball Player Weds Here," *Fort Myers Tropical News,* (Fort Myers, FL), June 17, 1926, https://newspapers.uflib.ufl.edu/AA00088916/00248/images/4

790 "Made a Hit in Fort Myers and a Home Run Here," *Vero Beach Press,* (Vero Beach, FL), June 14, 1926, https://www.newspapers.com/image/887188862/

791 "Notes of the Game," *Fort Myers Tropical News,* (Fort Myers, FL), May 21, 1926, https://newspapers.uflib.ufl.edu/AA00088916/00225/images/6

792 "Middleweights in Principal Battle," *Herald,* (Miami, FL), May 21, 1926, https://www.newspapers.com/image/616536065/

793 "Local Middleweight Boxer is Smoker Rookie Pitcher," *Tampa Daily Times,* (Tampa, FL), April 25, 1927, https://www.newspapers.com/image/333242966/

794 "Officer Kills Tampan During Tussle for Gun," *Tampa Morning Tribune,* (Tampa, FL), December 23, 1939, https://www.newspapers.com/image/332791916/

795 "Bears Sign Casares; 1952 Star Back Due Out of Army," *Chicago Daily Tribune,* (Chicago, IL), January 24, 1955, https://www.newspapers.com/image/372482794/

796 "Rick Casares NFL's Best Ball Carrier," *Morning Call,* (Allentown, PA), January 31, 1957, https://www.newspapers.com/image/280148122/

797 Johnston, Joey, "Casares left his mark at Jefferson, UF," *Tampa Tribune,* (Tampa, FL), September 15, 2013, https://www.newspapers.com/image/343257184/

798 "Allen Resigns as Manager of Tampa Club," *Tampa Daily Times,* (Tampa, FL), June 24, 1926, https://www.newspapers.com/image/332813827/

799 "Palms and Sarasota Open Series at Terry Park Today," *Fort Myers Press,* (Fort Myers, FL), August 2, 1926, https://www.newspapers.com/image/212860284/

800 "Tampa All-Stars Seek American Legion Junior Title," *Tampa Morning Tribune,* (Tampa, FL), July 21, 1928, https://www.newspapers.com/image/332307716/

801 "Legion Juniors Win Their Fifth State Championship," *Tampa Daily Times*, (Tampa, FL), August 6, 1932, https://www.newspapers.com/image/130511024/

802 "Allen, Ex-Smoker, Named Terrier Baseball Coach," *Tampa Daily Times,* (Tampa, FL), February 12, 1930, https://www.newspapers.com/image/333272523/

803 "Prospects for Winning Baseball Team at Tampa University are Bright," *Tampa Tribune,* (Tampa, FL), March 5, 1934, https://www.newspapers.com/image/333532251/

804 "Charles Allen, Sports Figure in Tampa, Dies," *Tampa Morning Tribune* (Tampa, FL), January 25, 1947. https://www.newspapers.com/image/327654629/

805 "Macey Sent Back to Richmond Club," *Fort Myers Tropical News,* (Fort Myers, FL), May 11, 1926, https://newspapers.uflib.ufl.edu/AA00088916/00216/images/4

806 "Fort Myers Loses League Lead to Lakeland," *Fort Myers Tropical News,* (Fort Myers, FL), May 11, 1926, https://newspapers.uflib.ufl.edu/AA00088916/00216/images/4

807 "With the Palms," *Fort Myers Press,* (Fort Myers, FL), May 13, 1926, https://www.newspapers.com/image/212771991/

808 "With the Palms," *Fort Myers Press,* (Fort Myers, FL), May 20, 1926, https://www.newspapers.com/image/212775416/

809 "Growers to Open Regular Training Sessions Monday," *Evening Herald,* (Bradenton, FL), April 3, 1926, https://www.newspapers.com/image/682995490/

810 "More Than Score of Players Tested as Bosses Seek Rag Taking Clan," *Bradenton Herald,* (Bradenton, FL), July 4, 1926, https://www.newspapers.com/image/682654414/

811 "Palms Secure New Pitchers," *Fort Myers Press,* (Fort Myers, FL), May 20, 1926, https://www.newspapers.com/image/212775173/

812 "Eight Players are Decorated with Tinware," *Daily Evening Item,* (Lynn, MA), April 29, 1929, https://www.newspapers.com/image/946226685/

813 Sports Reference, Baseball Reference, "George Bandera," *Baseball Reference*, Accessed July 1, 2023, https://www.baseball-reference.com/register/player.fcgi?id=bander001geo

814 "Fort Myers Ball Team to Play Next Week," *Fort Myers Tropical News,* (Fort Myers, FL), April 2, 1926, https://newspapers.uflib.ufl.edu/AA00088916/00183/images/6

815 "Buck Conroy's Palms in Formal Pose," *Fort Myers Tropical News,* (Fort Myers, FL), April 22, 1926, https://newspapers.uflib.ufl.edu/AA00088916/00200/images/0

816 "Merchant Days for Ball Club," *Fort Myers Press,* (Fort Myers, FL), May 28, 1926, https://www.newspapers.com/image/212779244/

817 "Twelve Players Reserved for Worcester Club," *Daily Evening Item,* (Lynn, MA), September 14, 1928, https://www.newspapers.com/image/947009664/

818 Cornish, Bud, "Philadelphia Athletics Romp Over All-Maine Nine in Exhibition Game, 10 to 1," *Portland Press Herald,* (Portland, ME), May 28, 1932, https://www.newspapers.com/image/847499597/

819 "Dutch Bandera Will Work Out with Dodgers in Spring Camp," *Portland Evening Express,* (Portland, ME), February 18, 1933, https://www.newspapers.com/image/852260885/

820 "Mr. Baseball Sings Swan Song as Miami Humbles All Stars, 2 to 1," *Herald,* (Miami, FL), October 16, 1939, https://www.newspapers.com/image/618418608/

821 "Bandera Now with Perkins Realty," *Miami Daily News,* (Miami, FL), February 29, 1948, https://www.newspapers.com/image/298500082/

822 "Gesu Rites for Broker Wednesday," *Miami Herald,* (Miami, FL), February 9, 1958, https://www.newspapers.com/image/619660399/

823 Sports Reference, Baseball Reference, "Hal Fisher," *Baseball Reference*, Accessed July 1, 2023, https://www.baseball-reference.com/register/player.fcgi?id=fisher005har

824 "Merchant Days for Ball Club," *Fort Myers Press,* (Fort Myers, FL), May 28, 1926, https://www.newspapers.com/image/212779244/

825 "Palms Lose Third Straight; Drop in Race," *Fort Myers Tropical News,* (Fort Myers, FL), September 9, 1926, https://newspapers.uflib.ufl.edu/AA00088916/00347/images/3

826 Rollins College Students, "The Tomokan Yearbook, 1926," *The Tomokan.* 9. https://scholarship.rollins.edu/tomokan/9

827 "Larry Schacht Arrives in City to Join Palms," *Fort Myers Press,* (Fort Myers, FL), June 10, 1926, https://www.newspapers.com/image/212640971/

828 "Wimbles' Sacrifice in Seventh Beats Tampa, 2-1," *Bradenton Herald,* (Bradenton, FL), July 2, 1926, https://www.newspapers.com/image/682653968/

829 "Salisbury Beats Winston-Salem in Opening Game of Season," *Winston-Salem Journal,* (Winston-Salem, NC), April 21, 1927, https://www.newspapers.com/image/931998604/

830 "Roundup," *Brooklyn Eagle,* (Brooklyn, NY), June 26, 1943, https://www.newspapers.com/image/53665706/

831 "Fort Myers Blanked by Lakeland, 4 to 0," *Fort Myers Tropical News,* (Fort Myers, FL), June 9, 1926, https://newspapers.uflib.ufl.edu/AA00088916/00241/images/4

832 "Highlanders Deal Smokers Twin Blow," *Tampa Sunday Tribune*, (Tampa, FL), August 29, 1926, https://www.newspapers.com/image/332381592/

833 "Gulls, 2; Lakeland, 9," *St. Petersburg Times,* (St. Petersburg, FL), September 2, 1926, https://www.newspapers.com/image/314693710/

834 "Palms Lose Third Straight; Drop in Race," *Fort Myers Tropical News,* (Fort Myers, FL), September 9, 1926, https://newspapers.uflib.ufl.edu/AA00088916/00347/images/3

835 "Lakeland Civic Clubs Asked to Save Ball Team," *Fort Myers Press,* (Fort Myers, FL), July 22, 1925, https://www.newspapers.com/image/212620028/

836 "Watt Lawler Dies; Lawyer, Legislator," *Fort Myers News-Press,* (Fort Myers, FL), June 3, 1958, https://www.newspapers.com/image/212145286/

837 "Announcement," *Fort Myers Tropical News,* (Fort Myers, FL), August 26, 1926, https://newspapers.uflib.ufl.edu/AA00088916/00335/images/4

838 "G. E. Hosmer Dies in Florida," *Atlanta Constitution,* (Atlanta, GA), June 29, 1944, https://www.newspapers.com/image/384689506/

839 "H. B. Mayer to Take Charge of Cleanup Campaign in City," *Fort Myers Press,* (Fort Myers, FL), October 8, 1926, https://www.newspapers.com/image/212862941/

840 "Arrived Here," *Key West Citizen,* (Key West, FL), October 3, 1938, https://www.newspapers.com/image/842158589/

841 The Citizen Office, "Announcing the presence of H.B. Mayer," *Key West Citizen,* (Key West, FL), January 13, 1938, https://www.newspapers.com/image/842131635/

842 "H. B. Mayer, Expert Typewriter Repairman," *Key West Citizen,* (Key West, FL), January 13, 1938, https://www.newspapers.com/image/842131635/

843 McLeod, Ellen, "Everglades," *Fort Myers News-Press,* (Fort Myers, FL), April 29, 1946, https://www.newspapers.com/image/221451181/

844 Butler, Lucille, "Everglades," *Fort Myers News-Press,* (Fort Myers, FL), August 9, 1947, https://www.newspapers.com/image/221510586/

845 "Bernard Mayer Dies," *Fort Myers News-Press,* (Fort Myers, FL), February 25, 1953, https://www.newspapers.com/image/213651882/

846 "Funerals," *Fort Myers News-Press,* (Fort Myers, FL), August 15, 1960, https://www.newspapers.com/image/219303507/

847 "Well-Known Referee Joins Realty Firm," *Tampa Morning Tribune,* (Tampa, FL), December 31, 1925, https://www.newspapers.com/image/326998687/

848 "Conroy Released as Pilot of Palms," *Fort Myers Tropical News,* (Fort Myers, FL), May 21, 1926, https://newspapers.uflib.ufl.edu/AA00088916/00225/images/0

849 "Sheridan Drive Lot for Kelly if he Makes Fifty Home Runs," *Buffalo Evening Times,* (Buffalo, NY), August 16, 1926, https://www.newspapers.com/image/891981624/

850 "Matchmaker Conroy is Working on Another All-Star Boxing Show for City," *Morning Herald,* (Hagerstown, MD), March 12, 1927, https://www.newspapers.com/image/20752159/

851 "From the Crow's Nest," *Public Opinion,* (Chambersburg, PA), July 5, 1927, https://www.newspapers.com/image/450473392/

852 "Wayne County Plans Basketball Tourney," *News and Record,* (Greensboro, NC), February 26. 1932, https://www.newspapers.com/image/937185655/

853 "Twins Get Real Workout Preparatory to Game Tomorrow," *Twin City Sentinel,* (Winston-Salem, NC), April 7, 1932, https://www.newspapers.com/image/932327062/

854 "Fort Myers Ball Team to Play Next Week," *Fort Myers Tropical News,* (Fort Myers, FL), April 2, 1926, https://newspapers.uflib.ufl.edu/AA00088916/00183/images/6

855 "Tampa All-Star Team Meets Growers Here Thursday," *Bradenton Herald,* (Bradenton, FL), June 12, 1927, https://www.newspapers.com/image/682595664/

856 "Maas Brothers' Team Blanks Seminoles," *Bradenton Herald,* (Bradenton, FL), October 7, 1929, https://www.newspapers.com/image/682617822/

857 "Pete Doyle Signed by Chattanooga Team," *Sunday Record,* (Columbia, SC), February 13, 1921, https://www.newspapers.com/image/744322885/

858 "Jacksonville Gets Two," *Miami Metropolis,* (Miami, FL), March 26, 1921, https://www.newspapers.com/image/298244307/

859 "Tinker Selects All Star Cast," *Tampa Morning Tribune,* (Tampa, FL), September 1, 1921, https://www.newspapers.com/image/326084022/

860 "Pete Doyle to Hurl Last Game," *Knoxville Sentinel,* (Knoxville, TN), September 27, 1921, https://www.newspapers.com/image/586684392/

861 "Palms Make Another Change of Managers," *Fort Myers Tropical News,* (Fort Myers, FL), August 26, 1926,
https://newspapers.uflib.ufl.edu/AA00088916/00335/images/3

862 "Palms Change Managers for Fourth Time," *Fort Myers Tropical News,* (Fort Myers, FL), September 8, 1926,
https://newspapers.uflib.ufl.edu/AA00088916/00346/zoom/0

863 "City League Organized; Ebb Doyle Elected President," *Knoxville News-Sentinel,* (Knoxville, TN), February 17, 1927,
https://www.newspapers.com/image/772707551/

864 "Hawkins will Twirl Opening Contest Here," *St. Petersburg Times,* (St. Petersburg, FL), May 24, 1928, https://www.newspapers.com/image/314695858/

865 "Six News-Sentinel Loops Start Play," *Knoxville News-Sentinel,* (Knoxville, TN), April 14, 1929, https://www.newspapers.com/image/772142182/

866 "Knoxville Ball Tossers Leave," *Knoxville Sentinel,* (Knoxville, TN), March 11, 1921, https://www.newspapers.com/image/586674097/

867 Sports Reference, Baseball Reference, "Dess Doyle" *Baseball Reference*, Accessed July 2, 2023, https://www.baseball-reference.com/register/player.fcgi?id=doyle-001jes

868 "Merchant Days for Ball Club," *Fort Myers Press,* (Fort Myers, FL), May 28, 1926, https://www.newspapers.com/image/212779244/

869 "Doran is Named as Palms' Boss," *Fort Myers Press,* (Fort Myers, FL), September 8, 1926, https://www.newspapers.com/image/212861836/

870 "Tampa Ball Player Hurt in Car Wreck," *Tampa Morning Tribune,* (Tampa, FL), September 10, 1927, https://www.newspapers.com/image/332349465/

871 Sports Reference, Baseball Reference, "Kitty Wickham" *Baseball Reference*, Accessed April 29, 2023, https://www.baseball-reference.com/register/player.fcgi?id=wickha001r--

872 "Rue E Wickham," *Find A Grave,* Accessed July 4, 2023, https://www.findagrave.com/memorial/3764245/rue-e-wickham

873 "Domingo Has First Chance to Show His Wares to Senators," *Tampa Tribune,* (Tampa, FL), March 2, 1928, https://www.newspapers.com/image/332417423/

874 "Joe Domingo Hurls No-Hit Victory 3-0," *Tampa Tribune* (Tampa, FL), August 29, 1929, https://www.newspapers.com/image/332542471/

875 "Funeral Notices," *Tampa Tribune,* (Tampa, FL), September 23, 1979, https://www.newspapers.com/image/335284050/

876 "Palms Southpaw Certain of Brilliant Record With 1926 Season Near Close," *Fort Myers Press,* (Fort Myers, FL), September 10, 1926, https://www.newspapers.com/image/212861908/

877 "Three for Lakeland" *Tampa Morning Tribune*, (Tampa, FL), September 2, 1926, https://www.newspapers.com/image/332384544/

878 Sports Reference, Baseball Reference, "Mike Bouza," *Baseball Reference,* accessed April 19, 2023, https://www.baseball-reference.com/register/player.fcgi?id=bouza-001mig

879 "Who's Here and There," *Tampa Morning Tribune,* (Tampa, FL) December 21, 1929, https://www.newspapers.com/image/332480128/

880 "Personals," *Tampa Daily Times,* (Tampa, FL), October 2, 1930,
https://www.newspapers.com/image/333510578/

881 Sports Reference, Baseball Reference, "Mike Bouza," *Baseball Reference,* accessed
April 19, 2023, https://www.baseball-reference.com/register/player.fcgi?id=bouza-
001mig

882 Newton, Red, "The Morning After," *Tampa Morning Tribune* (Tampa, FL), March 13,
1935, https://www.newspapers.com/image/332762568/

883 Sports Reference, Baseball Reference, "Mike Bouza," *Baseball Reference,* accessed
April 19, 2023, https://www.baseball-reference.com/register/player.fcgi?id=bouza-
001mig

884 Kinley, Wilbur, "Spicola, Partner to Attend Meet," *Tampa Daily Times,* (Tampa, FL)
November 22, 1945, https://www.newspapers.com/image/332856271/

885 "Death Notices," *Tampa Times,* (Tampa, FL), June 20, 1973,
https://www.newspapers.com/image/328048191/

886 "Palms Turn Back Mayo to Augusta," *Fort Myers Tropical News,* (Fort Myers, FL),
August 12, 1926, https://newspapers.uflib.ufl.edu/AA00088916/00323/images/2

887 Sports Reference, Baseball Reference, "James Mayo," *Baseball Reference*, Accessed
July 1, 2023, https://www.baseball-reference.com/register/player.fcgi?id=mayo--
001j--

888 "James 'Len' Mayo, 66, Ex-Cracker Pitcher," *Atlanta Journal and Constitution,*
(Atlanta, GA), December 30, 1973,
https://www.newspapers.com/image/398824764/

889 "Ten Players arrive in City for Tryouts with Fort Myers Club of Florida State League,"
Fort Myers Press, (Fort Myers, FL), March 30, 1926,
https://www.newspapers.com/image/212736373/

890 "Fort Myers Ball Team to Play Next Week," *Fort Myers Tropical News,* (Fort Myers,
FL), April 2, 1926, https://newspapers.uflib.ufl.edu/AA00088916/00183/images/6

891 "Tampa All-Star Team Meets Growers Here Thursday," *Bradenton Herald,*
(Bradenton, FL), June 12, 1927, https://www.newspapers.com/image/682595664/

892 "Obituaries," *Orlando Morning Sentinel,* (Orlando, FL), May 16, 1935,
https://www.newspapers.com/image/313710436/

893 "Pedrazas Brothers Entertain Players," *Fort Myers Press,* (Fort Myers, FL), May 31,
1926, https://www.newspapers.com/image/212780374/

894 "Chancey Coming Says Telegram," *Daily Advertiser,* (Lafayette, LA), March 25, 1920,
https://www.newspapers.com/image/261726129/

895 "Chancey is Given Release," *Daily Advertiser,* (Lafayette, LA), June 8, 1920,
https://www.newspapers.com/image/261649109/

896 Utellum, "Baseball View," *St. Petersburg Times,* (St. Petersburg, FL), February 26,
1921, https://www.newspapers.com/image/314880012/

897 "Martin Sends Gortner to Another League—Others Go," *Plainfield Courier-News,*
April 13, 1921, https://www.newspapers.com/image/220661283/

898 "Lakeland Swamps Celeryfeds 17-2," *Tampa Morning Tribune,* (Tampa, FL), June 5,
1925, https://www.newspapers.com/image/326535784/

899 "Saints Swamp Celeryfeds in Second Contest," *St. Petersburg Times,* (St. Petersburg,
FL), June 13, 1925, https://www.newspapers.com/image/314862855/

900 "Funds Sought to Finance Baseball Club," *Fort Myers Tropical News,* (Tampa, FL), April 10, 1026, https://newspapers.uflib.ufl.edu/AA00088916/00190/images/4

901 "Fort Myers Ball Team to Play Next Week," *Fort Myers Tropical News,* (Fort Myers, FL), April 2, 1926, https://newspapers.uflib.ufl.edu/AA00088916/00183/images/6

902 "Colts Tighten Grip on Lead with 17 to 2 Victory," *Orlando Morning Sentinel,* (Orlando, FL), May 31, 1928, https://www.newspapers.com/image/223032688/

903 "Macey Sent Back to Richmond Club," *Fort Myers Topical News,* (Fort Myers, FL), May 11, 1926, https://newspapers.uflib.ufl.edu/AA00088916/00216/images/4

904 "Blockmen Gives Colts Setback," *Fort Myers Press,* (Fort Myers, FL), August 27, 1926, https://www.newspapers.com/image/212861352/

905 "Funds Sought to Finance Baseball Club," *Fort Myers Tropical News,* (Fort Myers, FL), April 10, 1926, https://newspapers.uflib.ufl.edu/AA00088916/00190/images/4

906 "McRae and O'Reilly to Go to Asheville," *Fort Myers Tropical News,* (Fort Myers, FL), September 8, 1926, https://newspapers.uflib.ufl.edu/AA00088916/00346/images/5

907 "Tars and Truckers Split Holiday Bill," *Norfolk Ledger-Dispatch,* (Norfolk, VA), May 31, 1927, https://www.newspapers.com/image/950992162/

908 "Tourist Batterymen Report Week from Tomorrow," *Sunday Citizen,* (Asheville, NC), March 11, 1928, https://www.newspapers.com/image/198549998/

909 "O'Reilly Makes Good as Mentor of Prep Teams," *Asheville Times,* (Asheville, NC), March 7, 1929, https://www.newspapers.com/image/942819966/

910 "Denies O'Reilly Hold-out; Baylin or Shaney to Pitch," *Sunday Citizen,* (Asheville, NC), April 14, 1929, https://www.newspapers.com/image/195454916/

911 Herr, Robert W., "Maplewood Gains Its Fourth Victory in County League; McBride and Soldan Victors," *St. Louis Post-Dispatch,* (St. Louis, MO), https://www.newspapers.com/image/139694852/

912 "Eight Smokies Have Been Sold by Sally Champions," *Sunday Record,* (Columbia, SC), January 30, 1930, https://www.newspapers.com/image/744586840/

913 "Jack O'Reilly to Play for Hornets During 1930 Drive," *Sunday Citizen,* (Asheville, NC), April 13, 1930, https://www.newspapers.com/image/195484954/

914 "Schacht, O'Reilly Are Released by Bees," *Charlotte News,* (Charlotte, NC), March 24, 1931, https://www.newspapers.com/image/617202021/

915 "Western Will Oppose Soldan Nine Saturday," *St. Louis Post-Dispatch,* (St. Louis, MO), March 26, 1931, https://www.newspapers.com/image/139513140/

916 "Eager Youngsters Gather for Opening of Junior Basketball School," *St. Louis Star-Times,* (St. Louis, MO), January 26, 1935, https://www.newspapers.com/image/205417580/

917 "Palms ready for Rollins Here Tomorrow," *Fort Myers Press,* (Fort Myers, FL), April 14, 1926, https://www.newspapers.com/image/212753123/

918 "Old 'Slow Motion'," *Asheville Times,* (Asheville, NC), March 21, 1928, https://www.newspapers.com/image/942642431/

919 "Champs in Fine Shape for the Battle," *Asheville Times,* (Asheville, NC), April 1, 1929, https://www.newspapers.com/image/942620173/

920 "Marriage Licenses," *Tampa Tribune,* (Tampa, FL), November 21, 1926, https://www.newspapers.com/image/332337009/

921 "Grandio Cavorts in Colt Uniform for First Time," *Orlando Morning Sentinel,* (Orlando, FL), April 15, 1927, https://www.newspapers.com/image/224397754/

922 "Casares and Grandio Battle After Game" *Tampa Morning Tribune,* (Tampa, FL), May 12, 1927, https://www.newspapers.com/image/332342118/

923 "State Loop Players Fight Before Asher," *St. Petersburg Times,* (St. Petersburg, FL), May 12, 1927, https://www.newspapers.com/image/315114904/

924 "Miami Hustlers Nose Out Orlando 4 to 3," *Orlando Morning Sentinel,* (Orlando, FL), Ma 12, 1927, https://www.newspapers.com/image/224398919/

925 "Orlando Colts Hit Timely to Defeat Feds in Last of Series," *Orlando Morning Sentinel,* (Orlando, FL), May 29, 1927, https://www.newspapers.com/image/223158039/

926 "Smokers Drop Series Opener to Feds by 4-3 Score," *Tampa Morning Tribune,* (Tampa, FL), June 7, 1927, https://www.newspapers.com/image/332305111/

927 "Smokers-Tarpons in Deciding Game of Series Today," *Tampa Daily Times,* (Tampa, FL), June 25, 1927, https://www.newspapers.com/image/333503748/

928 "Obituaries," *Tampa Tribune,* (Tampa, FL), September 26, 1987, https://www.newspapers.com/image/337135408/

929 "Faustino Casares still on move at 83," *Tampa Tribune,* (Tampa, FL), May 14, 1987, https://www.newspapers.com/image/337177183/

930 "Fifty Players Seeking Berths in Miami Team," *Miami Daily News and Metropolis,* (Miami, FL), April 13, 1927, https://www.newspapers.com/image/301944370/

931 "Casares to Pelicans, Miami Men Announce," *Herald,* (Miami, FL), September 18, 1927, https://www.newspapers.com/image/616517691/

932 "Faustino Casares still on move at 83," *Tampa Tribune,* (Tampa, FL), May 14, 1987, https://www.newspapers.com/image/337177183/

933 "Funeral Notices," *Tampa Tribune,* (Tampa, FL), November 11, 1995, https://www.newspapers.com/image/340343622/

934 "Casares, Faustino," *St. Petersburg Times,* (St. Petersburg, FL), November 11, 1995, https://www.newspapers.com/image/326222632/

935 "Palms take Opening Game from Orlando," *Fort Myers Tropical News,* (Fort Myers, FL), May 4, 1926, https://newspapers.uflib.ufl.edu/AA00088916/00210/images/4

936 Sports Reference, Baseball Reference, "Cy Williams," *Baseball Reference*, Accessed April 29, 2023, https://www.baseball-reference.com/register/player.fcgi?id=willia001cy-

937 "Palms Assume League Lead as Moore Humbles Orlando," *Fort Myers Press,* (Fort Myers, FL), August 6, 1926, https://www.newspapers.com/image/212860503/

938 Tilden, Allen, "Pebs are Banking on Hurling Staff," *Birmingham News,* (Birmingham, AL), March 27, 1927, https://www.newspapers.com/image/572930629/

939 "Muskogee Chooses Ed Stauffer," *Springfield Daily News,* (Springfield, MO), April 28, 1927, https://www.newspapers.com/image/671671899/

940 Harry, "Hits and Errors," *Muskogee Daily Phoenix,* (Muskogee, MO), June 24, 1927, https://www.newspapers.com/image/901036035/

941 "From the Press Box," *Muskogee Times-Democrat*, (Muskogee, MO), August 22, 1927, https://www.newspapers.com/image/904811187/

942 "Ray Caldwell Sold to Milwaukee Club," *St. Louis Post-Dispatch,* (St. Louis, MO), September 2, 1927, https://www.newspapers.com/image/140410416/

943 "Travelers Blank Nashville 9-5," *Johnson City Staff-News,* (Johnson City, TN), September 15, 1927, https://www.newspapers.com/image/585441031/

944 "1927 Season in Southern League Ends," *Constitution,* (Atlanta, GA), September 19, 1927, https://www.newspapers.com/image/398183941/

945 Tilden, Allen, "Travelers will Report Monday," *Chattanooga News,* (Chattanooga, TN), March 3, 1928, https://www.newspapers.com/image/603485641/

946 Tilden, Allen, "Rodgers Worries Over Mound Staff," *Birmingham News,* (Birmingham, AL) March 25, 1928, https://www.newspapers.com/image/573483018/

947 "Southern League," *Constitution,* (Atlanta, GA), September 14, 1928, https://www.newspapers.com/image/397716134/

948 Keller, John B., "Tilts with Chisox May Settle Fight," *Evening Star,* (Washington D.C.), September 22, 1928, https://www.newspapers.com/image/864674886/

949 "About Goose Goslin," *National Baseball Hall of Fame,* Accessed April 23, 2023, https://baseballhall.org/hall-of-famers/goslin-goose

950 "Al Bool, Washington Rookie Catcher, is a Base Ball Rover," *Evening Star,* (Washington D.C.), September 23, 1928, https://www.newspapers.com/image/618596209/

951 Sports Reference, Baseball Reference, "Jim Moore," *Baseball Reference,* Accessed April 23, 2023, https://www.baseball-reference.com/register/player.fcgi?id=moore-016jam

952 "Tribe Batters White Sox for 8 Safeties in Turn; Seeds Clouts Home Run," *Register,* (Sandusky, OH), September 5, 1930, https://www.newspapers.com/image/4670874/

953 "Grace Church Extends Congratulations," *Oklahoma City Star,* (Oklahoma City, OK), July 16, 1943, https://www.newspapers.com/image/603656457/

954 "James Stanford Moore," *Find A Grave,* Accessed April 23, 2023, https://www.findagrave.com/memorial/14804185/james-stanford-moore

955 "Palms and Sarasota Open Series at Terry Park Today," *Fort Myers Press,* (Fort Myers, FL), August 2, 1926, https://www.newspapers.com/image/212860275/

956 "Smokers Blank Palms in Final," *Fort Myers Press,* (Fort Myers, FL), September 16, 1926, https://www.newspapers.com/image/212862115/

957 O. L. Milan, "Observations from The Bleachers," *Key West Citizen,* (Key West, FL), April 27, 1939, https://www.newspapers.com/image/842142932/

958 O. L. Milan, "Observations from The Bleachers," *Key West Citizen,* (Key West, FL), May 3, 1939. https://www.newspapers.com/image/842143537/

959 O.L. Milan, "Deciding Game of Championship Series to Be Played Tomorrow," *Key West Citizen,* (Key West, FL), May 20, 1939. https://www.newspapers.com/image/842145176/

960 "Deaths in the Tampa and the Bay Area," *Tampa Tribune,* (Tampa, FL) April 8, 1968, https://www.newspapers.com/image/332013186/

961 "Funeral Notices," *Tampa Times,* (Tampa, FL) April 8, 1968, https://www.newspapers.com/image/328964374/

962 "Smokers Off to Orlando Today," *Tampa Tribune,* (Tampa, FL), July 7, 1919, https://www.newspapers.com/image/325530365/

963 "Hernandez Leads Caps to Killing," *Tampa Tribune,* (Tampa, FL), July 9, 1919, https://www.newspapers.com/image/325531627/

964 "Burt's Bunk," *Tampa Tribune,* (Tampa, FL) September 5, 1919, https://www.newspapers.com/image/325382430/

[965] "Winter Team Wins 2-1 from Cubans," *Tampa Bay Times,* (Tampa, FL) November 2, 1919, https://www.newspapers.com/image/314843483/

[966] Utellum, "Baseball Chat," *Tampa Bay Times* (Tampa, FL) November 4, 1919. https://www.newspapers.com/image/314843636/

[967] "Cubans Meet A.B.C.s Today," *Indianapolis Star,* (Indianapolis, IN) May 9, 1920. https://www.newspapers.com/image/6530562/

[968] "Overtime Victory Goes to Cubans," *Detroit Free Press,* (Detroit, MI) July 22, 1920. https://www.newspapers.com/image/118861886/

[969] "Hernandez Pitches Palms to Victory," *Fort Myers Tropical News*, (Fort Myers, FL), April 23, 1926. https://newspapers.uflib.ufl.edu/AA00088916/00201/images/6

[970] Gates, James L., "Negro Leagues Became Major League with the Help of Groundbreaking Research," *National Baseball Hall of Fame,* accessed April 16, 2023. https://baseballhall.org/discover/groundbreaking-negro-league-stats-research-changed-the-game

[971] "Hustlers To Try to Clinch Flag Today," *Miami Herald,* (Miami, FL), September 4, 1927. https://www.newspapers.com/image/616548190/

[972] Castleberry, F. M., "Palms Make Fine Showing During First Three Weeks of Season; Now Out of First Place for First Time," *Fort Myers Press,* (Fort Myers, FL), May 11, 1926, https://www.newspapers.com/image/212771006/